Growth and Finance

Growth and Finance

Essays in Honour of C. Rangarajan

Editor

SAMEER KOCHHAR

ACADEMIC FOUNDATION

NEW DELHI

ACADEMIC FOUNDATION

First published in 2011
by

ACADEMIC FOUNDATION
4772-73 / 23 Bharat Ram Road, (23 Ansari Road),
Darya Ganj, New Delhi - 110 002 (India).
Phones : 23245001 / 02 / 03 / 04.
Fax : +91-11-23245005.
E-mail : books@academicfoundation.com
www. academicfoundation.com

in association with

SKOCH

Skoch Consultancy Services
www.skoch.in

SKOCH
DEVELOPMENT FOUNDATION

Skoch Development Foundation
www.skoch.org

Cataloging in Publication Data--DK
Courtesy: D.K. Agencies (P) Ltd. <docinfo@dkagencies.com>

Growth and finance : essays in honour of C. Rangarajan / editor, Sameer Kochhar.
p. cm.

ISBN 13: 9788171888665

1. India--Economic policy--1980-1991. 2. India--Economic policy--1991- 3. Finance--India. 4. Banks and banking--India. 5. Bank marketing--India. 6. Reserve Bank of India. I. Rangarajan, C. II. Kochhar, Sameer.

DDC 338.954 22

Typeset and cover design: Italics India, New Delhi.
Printed and bound in India.

Contents

About the Editor/ Contributors

Editor

Sameer Kochhar is President of Skoch Development Foundation, which is a leading think tank on digital, social and financial inclusion issues in India. He has been passionately working towards promoting participatory democracy, empowerment, and bringing improvements in delivery systems. He is CEO, Skoch Consultancy Services, and is an industry veteran with a multifaceted career spanning over two and a half decades. He is India strategy and management consultant to several Fortune 500 as well as large Indian companies for over a decade. He is also Chief Editor of *Inclusion*—a quarterly publication focused on development economics issues. He is considered to be one of the most respected independent voices on inclusive development and citizenship issues in India. He is a member of several expert groups and committees and his research opinion and writings have shaped many a public policy dialogue. He is also a Member of the Expert Group constituted by the Ministry of Panchayati Raj, Government of India advocating a case for strengthening of panchayati raj institutions (village councils) through use of technology. He has written extensively on areas of emerging management practices, infrastructure, governance, technology, finance, economics, e-governance, *panchayati raj* and ICT for development. He has published several widely acclaimed books, namely *Infrastructure and Governance* (2008); *Financial Inclusion* (2009); *Urban Renewal: Policy and Response* (2009); *Speeding Financial Inclusion* (2009); *India on the Growth Turnpike: Essays in Honour of Vijay L. Kelkar* (2010); and *Building from the Bottom: Infrastructure and Poverty Alleviation* (2010).

Contributors

K.C. Chakrabarty, a seasoned banker with an accomplished banking career spanning over three decades donned the role of a central banker on June 15, 2009 after he assumed charge of the office of Deputy Governor in Reserve Bank of India (RBI). His current assignments at RBI include guiding and overseeing the areas pertaining to rural and urban cooperative banks, information technology, payment and settlement systems, customer services, human resource and personnel management. Before taking over as the Deputy Governor, Dr. Chakrabarty graced the seat of Chairman & Managing Director (CMD), Punjab National Bank for over two years and before that, the CMD, Indian Bank for two years. He was also the Chairman of the Indian Banks' Association (IBA) for a brief period. He has recently published a widely acclaimed book with Sameer Kochhar, R. Chandrashekhar and Deepak B. Phatak entitled *Financial Inclusion* (2009).

Udaibir S. Das is an Assistant Director in the Monetary and Capital Markets Department of the IMF. He heads the Sovereign Asset and Liability Management Division and leads a team that covers policy and operational issues relating to sovereign risk, debt, reserves and other sovereign assets, debt capital markets, and related financial stability issues. He is also closely associated with country-specific vulnerability assessments, financial stability surveillance, and actively associated with several international and regional initiatives in financial sector, debt, and capital market areas. Das is a Fulbright-Humphrey scholar with graduate degrees in Economics and Management (US). He was a lecturer in finance at Boston University (US) during 1989-1991. He joined the IMF in 1996. Prior to joining the IMF, he was with the Reserve Bank of India for 18 years. He has published in several professional journals and holds a research interest in central banking, financial stability, debt restructuring, and different aspects of debt and fixed-income markets.

Kartikeya Desai is Vice President at Lok Capital, an innovative platform delivering equity capital combined with technical and strategic support for Indian microfinance institutions and social enterprises serving the bottom of pyramid segment. He is a frequent commentator on policy issues relating to development finance and has contributed substantially to the public dialogue on microfinance and social enterprise. Prior to joining Lok Capital in early 2009, he worked for DSP Merrill Lynch, first in the investment banking group and then in the private equity team. Earlier he worked in the BTS Group in the USA as a management consultant after graduating from the School of International and Public Affairs, Columbia University and the Wharton School at the University of Pennsylvania.

Nitin Desai, a graduate of London School of Economics (LSE), taught economics at two UK Universities, worked briefly in the private sector, had a long stint as a government official in India and then joined the UN in 1990. In India, he joined the Planning Commission in 1973, and worked there till 1988. Later he joined the Ministry of Finance as the Chief Economic Adviser (1988-1990). In the UN, he was Under-Secretary General for Economic and Social Affairs. After his retirement he has been involved in a variety of public policy activities nationally and internationally. He is a member of the National Security Advisory Board (NSAB) and the Prime Minister's Council on Climate Change. He is a Distinguished Fellow of TERI and is an Honorary Fellow of the LSE. He writes a monthly column in the *Business Standard*.

Shyamala Gopinath is Deputy Governor, Reserve Bank of India (RBI). She is also a member representing the RBI on the Financial Stability Board. She is a career central banker, having joined the RBI in 1972 and except for a brief stint with International Monetary Fund (IMF) during 2001-2003, she has since been with the RBI. At IMF she was associated with areas relating to foreign exchange reserves management, safeguard assessment and foreign exchange markets and was part of IMF missions for financial sector assessment programmes to many countries. She has vast experience across the financial policy spectrum spanning banking and non-banking regulation, financial market regulation, public debt management, foreign exchange reserves management, foreign exchange management and payment & settlement systems.

Ashima Goyal is a professor at the Indira Gandhi Institute of Development Research (IGIDR), Mumbai, India. She has been a faculty member in the Delhi School of Economics (DSE) and Gokhale Institute of Politics and Economics (GIPE), India, a visiting fellow at the Economic Growth Centre, Yale University, USA, and a Fulbright Senior Research Fellow at Claremont Graduate University, USA. Her research interests are in institutional macroeconomics, the open economy, international finance, development and governance. She is the author of numerous international and national publications, a book on *Developing Economy Macroeconomics: Fresh Perspectives* (1999), and has participated in research projects with World Bank, Global Development Network (GDN), Reserve Bank of India (RBI), Asian Development Bank (ADB), and United Nations Economic and Social Commission for Asia and the Pacific (ESCAP). Her research has received national and international awards. She is co-editor of a new Routledge journal on macroeconomics and finance. She is also active in the Indian policy debate, and is a member of several government committees, boards of educational and financial institutions. She contributes a monthly column to the *Hindu Business Line*.

Raghbendra Jha, PhD (Columbia), Elected Fellow of the World Innovation Foundation (FWIF), is professor of Economics and Executive Director Australia South Asia Research Centre, Australian National University. He has previously taught at Columbia University and Williams College in the US, Queen's University (Canada), University of Warwick (UK) and Delhi School of Economics, IIM (Bangalore), and Indira Gandhi Institute of Development Research in India (IGIDR). He has authored/edited 23 books. He has more than one hundred papers in leading refereed international scientific journals such as *Journal of Development Economics, Journal of Economic Behavior and Organization, Energy Economics, Southern Economic Journal,*

Applied Economics, Public Finance, Public Finance Review, Public Choice, Journal of Comparative Economics, Empirical Economics, Journal of Asian Economics, World Development, World Economy, and *International Review of Applied Economics,* and in chapters in refereed books by publishers such as Oxford University Press. He has consulted for, among others, the World Bank, the UN, UNDP, the ADB, International Fund for Agricultural Development (IFAD), and Department for International Development (DFID), UK. His research has been funded by major organizations such as the MacArthur Foundation (Chicago), DFID (UK), the Australian Research Council, the AusAID, and IDRC (Canada). His research and teaching interest are in public economics, macroeconomics, development economics and environmental economics.

K. Kanagasabapathy, since May 2009 heads as Director, the EPW Research Foundation, a sister unit of Economic & Political Weekly under the Sameeksha Trust. Educated from Annamalai University, Indian Statistical Institute and University of Surrey (UK), he has a career spanning over more than 40 years in teaching, training and research. Between 2006 and 2009, he served as Consultant and Secretary to the Committee on Fuller Capital Account Convertibility and to the Committee on Financial Sector Assessment. Between 2001 and 2005, he served as Senior Advisor to Executive Director, Indian Chair at the International Monetary Fund (IMF). He retired from the Reserve Bank of India in February 2006, as Adviser in-Charge of Monetary Policy Department, after serving the institution in different capacities for more than 30 years since 1977. His other positions included Director/Chief General Manager, Internal Debt Management Department and Member of Faculty at the Bankers Training College. He was very closely associated with the reforms in money and government securities markets during the 1990s. Starting his career as Assistant Professor of Economics in the Tamil Nadu Education Service in 1968, he also served in the State Government's Finance Department for about nine years till 1977. His professional interests are money, banking and financial markets.

Madhu Kannan is the MD & CEO, Bombay Stock Exchange Ltd. since May 2009. Previously, he was the Managing Director in the Corporate Strategy Group of Bank of America-Merrill Lynch. He joined Merrill Lynch in March 2008 as a Managing Director (Strategy and Business Development). In this role he focused on the development and execution of key strategic initiatives for Merrill Lynch in the emerging markets of Asia and Middle-East & North Africa (MENA) and the Global Sovereign Wealth Funds Group. Prior to the Bank of America-Merrill Lynch, Kannan was Senior Vice President at NYSE Euronext. During his stint at NYSE Euronext, he served in various senior roles across a range of businesses including Vice President, Corporate Client Group, Head of International Listings (Asia Pacific Region), and Managing Director, International Strategy and Business Development of the Exchange. He earned his undergraduate degree B.E. (Hons.) in Electrical and Electronics, M.Sc (Hons.), in Economics from BITS, Pilani, India and MBA in Finance from Vanderbilt University, USA. He was nominated as a Young Global Leader in 2007 by the World Economic Forum (WEF), based in Geneva, Switzerland.

K.G. Karmakar, Managing Director, National Bank for Agriculture and Rural Development (NABARD), born in April 1952, holds a PhD in Management (1996) from the Jamnalal Bajaj Institute of Management Studies, Mumbai and a postgraduate degree in Financial Management (1982). Karmakar has penned over 100 articles on rural credit, financial inclusion, microfinance and development banking. He has also authored six pioneering books including: (i) *Agricultural Project Management for Banks*, (ii) *Rural Credit, Micro Finance and SHGs*, and (iii) *The Silenced Drums on Tribal Development*. For over 35 years, he has served with various banking and financial institutions including the State Bank of India (1975-76), Reserve Bank of India (1976-1983) and NABARD since 1983, and is an authority in agricultural credit, microfinance project management, rural infrastructure development, rural banking and supervision development and planning. His seventh book *Towards Financial Inclusion in India* is being published in February 2011. He has also prepared three major reports for GoI/

RBI relating to High Powered Committee for Financial Restructuring of Handloom Weaving Industry, Working Group on Outreach of Institutional Finance and Cooperative Reforms under Eleventh Five-Year Plan (2007-2012), December 2006 and Task Force on Empowering Board of Directors of RRBs, January 2007, and is a Member of the Committee 'To formulate concrete bankable schemes for rural housing'. He is on the boards of 28 reputed institutions like IIM-Ahmedabad, NIRD-Hyderabad, KVIC-Mumbai , CAPART-New Delhi, etc.

Joseph Massey is the MD & CEO of MCX Stock Exchange (MCX-SX). He is instrumental in formulating and implementing policies, procedures and best practices at MCX-SX, besides overseeing strategic operations and overall functioning of the exchange. Prior to MCX-SX, he was heading the operations of Multi-Commodity Exchange of India. Massey has over 20 years of diverse corporate experience and had stints at leading financial organisations such as Life Insurance Corporation of India, the Reserve Bank of India, Stock Holding Corporation of India, and the Vadodara Stock Exchange. Before joining MCX, he was the head of Interconnected Stock Exchange of India—a collaboration of 15 regional stock exchanges. Massey has widely travelled and gains his rich experience from his visits to the world's top exchanges such as NYMEX, LME, CBOT, CME, NYBOT, CCX, EURONEXT-LIFFE, IPE, NYSE, NASDAQ, PHLX, SEC, CFTC, LSE, SGX and DTC. He has also been a part of various committees of FMC, SEBI and the Government of India on various policy issues pertaining to commodities and securities market. He is also currently the chairman of South Asian Federation of Exchanges (SAFE), a regional forum of exchanges and regulated entities.

Swayam Prava Mishra is a PhD scholar in Economics at University of Hyderabad. Her research area is corporate credit risk assessment. She did her postgraduation in Economics also from University of Hyderabad. She specialises in econometrics, time series econometrics and financial economics. Mishra has presented a paper in an international conference in the area of corporate credit risk assessment. She has select publications on credit scoring models/performance of Indian banks in international and professional journals.

Ravi Narain is currently the MD and CEO of the National Stock Exchange of India Limited. He is the Chairman of the National Securities Clearing Corporation Ltd. and NSE.IT Ltd. He also serves as a Director of the National Securities Depository Ltd. and the National Commodity & Derivatives Exchange Ltd. and several other companies. He is also associated with various committees of the Securities & Exchange Board of India (SEBI) and the Reserve Bank of India (RBI). Narain has degrees in Economics from St. Stephen's College, Delhi University and Cambridge University, UK and a degree in business administration from Wharton School, University of Pennsylvania, USA.

Kirit S. Parikh, Former Member, Planning Commission, Government of India, is Chairman, Integrated Research and Action for Development (IRADe), New Delhi. He is also former (Founder) Director (Vice Chancellor), Indira Gandhi Institute of Development Research (IGIDR), Mumbai. He was honoured with Padma Bushan by the President of India in March 2009. He is a Fellow of the National Academy of Sciences, India. He has a D.Sc. in Civil Engineering and a master's degree in Economics from MIT, US. He has been a professor of Economics since 1967. He was the Chairman of the Integrated Energy Policy Committee, Planning Commission. He was a Member of the Economic Advisory Council (EAC) of the Prime Ministers of India, Atal Behari Vajpayee, P.V. Narasimha Rao, Chandra Shekhar, V.P. Singh and Rajiv Gandhi. In 1978 he was given the Vikram Sarabhai Award for Systems Analysis and Management. In 1999, he was given the Visveswaraya Award by the Engineers' Foundation in Kolhapur. He is also a recipient of Nayudamma Award for contribution to the welfare of mankind through developments in the fields of Economics and Energy in February 2005. He was honoured as the most distinguished and illustrious alumni of the decade from India by the Massachusetts Institute of Technology (MIT), US in September 2007. He was conferred the Distinguished

Alumnus Award by Indian Institute of Technology (IIT), Kharagpur in September 2007. He has authored, co-authored and edited 29 books in the areas of planning, engineering, water resource management, trade policies and so on.

Ravi Parthasarathy, Chairman, Infrastructure Leasing & Financial Services Limited (IL&FS), has had an illustrious career. He started off as a management trainee with Citibank Bombay in 1974 and rose to be its Manager. The stint gave him exposure to merchant banking and corporate banking functions. From Citibank, he moved on to 20th Century Finance Corporation Limited, as Executive Director. By 1987, when he left the organisation, it had grown to be the largest private sector company in the financial services sector in the country. In 1988, Parthasarathy joined the IL&FS, a company, which promotes developing and financing diverse projects in surface transport, power, telecommunications, ports, SEZs, water supply and area development and works closely with Central government agencies, different state governments and local authorities in PPP format, and is responsible for all the operations of the group. Since the IL&FS also specialises in structured finance, broking and private equity, he has his hands full. A science graduate and MBA, Parthasarathy has also been on board of several reputed institutions including Indian Institute of Management (IIM), Bangalore.

Balamurali Radhakrishnan is a freelancer based in Hyderabad undertaking economic and financial research. Prior to this, Radhakrishnan served as a non-paid guest contributor for Europe Arab Bank (EAB), London. As a guest contributor, he worked on various key global economic and financial issues in association with the bank's Head of Treasury, Prof. Moorad Choudhry. Radhakrishnan has co-authored with the professor four articles that were published by EAB's treasury department, and their article on global imbalances was published by the *Business Standard*, India. Prior to commencing his assignment for EAB, Radhakrishnan worked as a Junior Analyst at Dun & Bradstreet India Pvt. Ltd., Mumbai. As a Junior Analyst, he tracked Indian cement and chemical industry, and published quarterly reports on these industries. Prior to joining

Dun & Bradstreet, Radhakrishnan worked as a Research Associate for Brigade Corporation, Hyderabad.

Yaga Venugopal Reddy was Governor, Reserve Bank of India, from 2003 to 2008. Subsequently, he was Member of the UN Commission of Experts to the President of the UN General Assembly on Reforms of International Monetary and Financial System. He is currently Professor Emeritus, University of Hyderabad. He is also Honorary Fellow of the London School of Economics and Political Science. He is a Member of an informal international group of prominent persons on International Monetary Reforms, and is also on the Advisory Group of eminent persons to advise the Finance Minister of India on G20 issues. Prior to being the Governor, he was Executive Director for India, Sri Lanka, Bangladesh and Bhutan at the International Monetary Fund since August 2002. Prior to this, he was Deputy Governor, Reserve Bank of India, for six years. Formerly, he was Secretary, Ministry of Finance, and Additional Secretary, Ministry of Commerce in the Government of India. He served Government of Andhra Pradesh, India in several capacities including Principal Secretary and Secretary (Finance and Planning), Collector and District Magistrate etc. He was also advisor in World Bank. Dr. Reddy was honoured with the Padma Vibhushan Award in 2010. His book *India and the Global Financial Crisis : Managing Money and Finance* was among the best sellers in India (2009). His most recent publication is titled *Global Crisis, Recession and Uneven Recovery* (2011).

Duvvuri Subbarao assumed office as the Governor of the Reserve Bank of India (RBI) on 5 September 2008. Prior to this appointment, Dr. Subbarao served as Finance Secretary to the Government of India from April 2007 to September 2008 and as Secretary to the Prime Minister's Economic Advisory Council (PMEAC) from March 2005 to March 2007. As a member of the Indian Administrative Service (IAS), Subbarao has been a career civil servant. Over the years of 1988-1998, he worked in various positions in State government of Andhra Pradesh and Government of India. Subbarao was a Lead Economist in the World Bank (1999-2004), where he also task managed a flagship study on decentralisation across major East Asian countries which was acknowledged as innovative policy work. He received BSc. (Hons) in Physics from the IIT, Kharagpur and MSc. in Physics from the IIT, Kanpur. Subsequent to joining the civil service, he received an MS in Economics from Ohio State University (1978) and was a Humphrey Fellow studying public finance at MIT during 1982-83. He earned his PhD in Economics from Andhra University (1998). Subbarao maintains a strong commitment to academic pursuits, and has written and lectured extensively on issues in public finance, decentralisation and political economy of reforms.

S.S. Tarapore, Distinguished Fellow, Skoch Development Foundation, has a BA (Economics) from Sheffield University (1958) and MSc. (Economics) from London University (1960). He was awarded the degree of Doctor of Laws (honoris causa) from Sheffield University (1996). He joined the Reserve Bank of India in 1961 as Research Officer and retired in 1996 as Deputy Governor. He was on deputation from 1971-1979, first in the IMF Research Department and subsequently under the IMF Central Banking Service with the Bank of Mauritius as Advisor to the Governor. He has chaired a number of official committees including the Committee on Capital Account Convertibility (1997), the Unit Trust of India Inquiry (2001), the Committee on Procedures and Performance Audit of Public Services (2004-05) and the Committee on Fuller Capital Account Convertibility (2006). He was a member of the Committee on Banking Sector Reforms (1998) and the Advisory Group on Transparency of Monetary Policy (2000).

सत्यमेव जयते

प्रधान मंत्री

Prime Minister

Foreword

It is a pleasure to write this foreword to the festschrift being published in honour of Dr. C. Rangarajan, a distinguished economist and a very close friend. I have had the privilege of knowing Dr. Rangarajan for 40 years now and I can say without hesitation that there would be very few economists as capable of so easily straddling the two worlds of academia and government as he is. Indeed, Dr. Rangarajan has excelled himself in many of the public positions he has held by tempering his economic convictions with a very sound discrimination between what is practically feasible and what is not. Dr. Rangarajan's achievements are immense both in academia and in government. He has taught at Wharton School of Finance and Commerce, Graduate School of Business Administration of New York University and Indian Institute of Management, Ahmedabad. In his public career, he has been Member of the Planning Commission, Governor of Reserve Bank of India, Governor of Andhra Pradesh and Chairman of Twelfth Finance Commission (2005-2010). And currently it is my good fortune to have the benefit of his wisdom, knowledge and experience in his capacity as Chairman of my Economic Advisory Council. If one looks at Dr. Rangarajan's public career, what stand out are his humility and simplicity. Even while making long-term contributions and bringing about major transformations, he has always risen above controversy. As Governor, Reserve Bank of India, Dr. Rangarajan was a part of team of those men and women who ushered in economic reforms in India. Another of his lasting contributions in the same position was giving a new direction to the country's monetary policy and making it an integral part of our economic management. As Chairman of the Twelfth Finance Commission

Dr. Rangarajan brought about a paradigm shift in India's fiscal federalism. I do not wish to mention here his numerous other accomplishments but would only say that we are fortunate to have in our government a person of the calibre and stature of Dr. Rangarajan. The numerous awards he has received in his career bear testimony to his amazing abilities.

This festschrift *Growth and Finance—Essays in Honour of C. Rangarajan* is a fitting tribute to Dr. Rangarajan. It brings together the papers of some very distinguished economists. I have no doubt that it will be of great value to all those who are interested in the Indian economy. I wish the festschrift all success. I also wish my friend, the distinguished scholar and outstanding public servant, Dr. C. Rangarajan all the very best and a very long time in the service of our country.

(Manmohan Singh)

New Delhi

3 February, 2011

Preface

Dr. C. Rangarajan has completed 79 fulfilling years that started in a small town called Ariyalur in what is now Perambalur district. The journey from Ariyalur has taken him all over the world and to the peaks of the financial and economic world in India. Today, there is no one I know of who is more sought after, more often consulted, more dependable, more impartial, more neutral, and more valuable in the advice he gives as far as economic policy matters are concerned than Dr. Rangarajan, and the government is deeply grateful to him for the advice that he gives to the government from time to time.

I wish to pay my personal tribute to Dr. Rangarajan. When we decided to open a bank branch in Ariyalur—and that was because of repeated demands from the people of that district—and one of the nationalised banks agreed to open the branch, I chanced to mention to Dr. Rangarajan at one of the meetings that I was going down to open some bank branches including a bank branch in Ariyalur. That was when he told me that Ariyalur was his hometown. In fact, he had been so scrupulous, some would say scrupulous to a fault, that although he was Governor of the Reserve Bank for many years, no one was allowed to approach him to open a bank branch in Ariyalur, nor did he favour his hometown. When I went to Ariyalur, of course I spoke about Dr. Rangarajan. The town is very proud of its native son. That is how I came to know that Dr. Rangarajan was born in Ariyalur.

I first began to work with him in 1996 when I became the finance minister. I had some exposure to trade policy issues and commerce and the WTO, but not directly to finance. In many ways, I was anti-establishment and he represented the quintessential establishment of India, the Reserve Bank of India. I believe nothing much has changed as far as the Reserve Bank is concerned in presenting establishmentarian views. And in the period of little over a year that I worked with him, I am proud to confess that he was virtually a teacher and a guru. In law, there is a famous maxim, 'once a mortgage, always a mortgage'. I believe that applies to academia: 'once a teacher always a teacher'. I do not think Dr. Rangarajan ever gave up the qualities and attitudes of a teacher. He would patiently and persuasively explain his point of view and try to win over every one else to his point of view. I think I was the first finance minister to share the entire draft budget speech with the Reserve Bank Governor. In the years that I was finance minister, two years then and again five years thereafter, I always shared the draft of the budget speech with the Governor, because I think the Reserve Bank has a very important role to play in framing the budget. We worked together for a little over a year and I enjoyed my many meetings with Dr. Rangarajan.

The second agreement on abolishing automatic monetisation and the abolition of the treasury bills was signed at that time between the Reserve Bank and Montek Singh Ahluwalia as the Finance Secretary, and that I think that was a landmark and a very important change that we brought about. This book, of course, contains a number of essays by people who had worked with Dr. Rangarajan in many capacities, people who were his deputies, people who were his colleagues, people who saw him in different avatars. And while I have not read every essay, the few that I have read converge on one point, namely, there is no one so well qualified, so well trained, with such a fine mind in economics yet so humble, and so modest. The essays are about his contributions at different points of time. I have never seen Dr. Rangarajan chide anyone, I have never seen a frown on his face, I have never heard him raise his voice, I have never seen him walk out in a huff, I have never seen him overrule anyone. If, after years in so many capacities, one can still maintain these fine qualities and yet put one's stamp on policymaking, I think it is a remarkable tribute not only to a very fine intellectual but also a very fine human being. I think who we honour today is not only one of the most celebrated economists of this country but a very fine human being of our times.

No finance minister present or past can afford to disagree publicly with the Reserve Bank of India, but no finance minister present or past can also completely agree with the Reserve Bank of India. The government and the Reserve Bank—while they may have some common objectives—are driven by different *dharmas*. Government has to promote growth and sometimes the price of that growth is inflation, sometimes the price of that growth is high borrowing. The Reserve Bank's *dharma* is to maintain monetary stability and price stability and therefore it necessarily has to be conservative. In a recent interview, when I reflected on the crisis of 2008, I made a bold suggestion that while the Reserve Bank must be autonomous and independent in pursuing monetary policy, at a time of crisis, ultimately, the decision of the government should prevail. I think we managed the 2008 crisis well because, ultimately, the decision of the government prevailed. The stimulus packages were announced, we did borrow heavily, and that is now proven by the fact that the year ended with 6.7 per cent growth and the subsequent years showed a smart recovery. That is not to say that the government should constantly be at loggerheads with the Reserve Bank. I believe that price stability is extremely important, especially in a poor country. There is no tax worse than inflation. All that you gain in the swings is lost in the roundabouts if people have higher incomes but it is eroded by inflation. Especially in a country where still many prices are administered prices, there is a duty to maintain price stability. Today, inflation is high, food inflation is very high, yet some administered prices have to be corrected. There is a very vigorous debate within the government whether the administered prices should be corrected when inflation is high. One could even raise the moral argument, is the government—which means all institutions put together which are responsible for maintaining price stability—entitled or justified in raising administered prices when it has found it difficult to contain inflation? This debate will never end, but this debate is a debate in which the Reserve Bank of India often finds itself at odds with the government or government finds itself at odds with the Reserve Bank of India. But this debate is very vital to the people of India, for the people of any country, especially a poor country.

I am not sure whether we understand all the factors that contribute to price rise, nor am I sure we have at our hand all the tools to control inflation. Some say we do, some say we do not, at least in the case of food inflation I have not heard anyone argue convincingly that we have all the tools to control food inflation. But as long as we are served by dedicated, devoted, distinguished people like Dr. Rangarajan, I think we will be able to weather any crisis, weather any storm. While sometimes the ship of the state will be buffeted by storms, I think men like Dr. Rangarajan at the helm of affairs, especially in places like the Reserve Bank of India or the Planning Commission or the Economic Advisory Council, bring to those in government a sense of reassurance, a sense of comfort that there is someone who will courageously point out your errors, speaks his/her mind, present alternative options and approaches, present cogently argued papers on policy options, and help you and guide you in taking the correct decisions. No government, however well meaning the ministers are, however popular they may be with the people, can manage the economics of a country without solid philosophers and economists like Dr. Rangarajan. He has been a tower of strength, he has been a pillar of India's economic community, he has anchored India's policies as they evolved, and I am sure for many more years he will continue to give us the benefit of his wisdom and advice. I congratulate the Skoch Consultancy Services and Skoch Development Foundation for bringing out this compilation of essays which I think the authors have written as a labour of love, affection and admiration for Dr. Rangarajan.

—P. Chidambaram
Minister of Home Affairs,
Government of India

Introduction

Sameer Kochhar

I

24x7 ATMs, credit cards and loans that allow instant or near-immediate gratification and the freedom to get decent amount of foreign exchange for foreign trips are all taken for granted by many of us today. This was not always so. If you turn the clock back before 1991, when India's economic liberalisation began, all of these were absent and so were the multitude of financial innovations that have now become an inseparable part of our lives. For all this we need to thank a handful of people who supervised the financial reforms process. Leading the list of such policymakers is Dr. C. Rangarajan, the former governor of the Reserve Bank of India (RBI), member of Rajya Sabha, and now chairman of the Prime Minister's Economic Advisory Council. A lot of what we take for granted today can be attributed to the financial reforms that Rangarajan brought about during his stint as the RBI governor in the first half of the 1990s even as he worked as an important member of the reforms team led by the then finance minister and the current Prime Minister, Dr. Manmohan Singh.

Before Rangarajan took over as the RBI governor, he was the deputy governor of India's central bank for nine years. He had sufficient experience to lead the financial reforms charge of a country that was badly bruised by the serious economic crisis of 1991. At the helm of the RBI, Rangarajan helped the country adapt to a new world where market forces played a major role in all walks of economic life.

My first association with Dr. Rangarajan was when I was making a biographical film on him entitled *The Philosopher King*. The film enabled me to see his contributions to India from many different perspectives. This left a profound impression on me—most of all his passion for poverty alleviation and promoting women in earning livelihood. His explanation of the fruits that financial inclusion would bring about in the country's hinterland led me to examine several pilot projects and evaluate other FI initiatives in Skoch Development Foundation. The highpoint of that journey for me is this edited volume.

Rangarajan was born in 1932 in Ariyalur, Tamil Nadu. His father was a judge in the judicial services of the Madras Presidency as it was known during those days. The family moved from place to place. He says he must have studied in more than six schools before he finally took the school leaving certificate examination. He had a reasonably satisfactory childhood, despite the fact that he was attacked by infantile paralysis as a result of which his right hand was somewhat affected. This was when he was just 2-3 years old. But he managed and learnt to write with his left hand. In his house, academics had always been an important factor and on the whole he was brought up in highly academically charged atmosphere.

After completing his honours there were many possibilities, one of which was to take up law. But his father felt at that time that though he had been a judge for a number of years, he was not practising as a lawyer and would not be able to provide him with the kind of support needed to start him off. Economics as a subject had always attracted him even when he was a student. He says that even within the honours programme he took, he was more interested in economics than in another subjects. And he had also decided quite early in life to be a teacher. As soon as he passed out of college, he took up a teaching job. He was employed in Loyola College itself, from where he had done his honours degree. After a few years, he felt he needed to get a higher degree and decided to go in for research. So he went to the University of Pennsylvania to do his PhD. Even while finishing his PhD, he taught for a year at the Wharton School of Finance and Commerce, University of Pennsylvania. He returned to India to teach at University of Rajasthan and also at the Planning Unit of Indian Statistical Institute in Delhi. Thereafter, he went back again and taught a two-year stint at the Graduate School of Business Administration at the New York University. The next flight to India brought him straight to IIM-Ahmedabad in 1968.

For a few years he did shuttle between the United States and India. He again went to US in 1970 to teach at the New York University and returned in 1972. Thereafter, he took a personal decision and made IIM-Ahmedabad (IIM-A) his permanent base. He felt that if one has to be useful, especially in the field of economics, one has to be at home. 'IIM-A offered a congenial environment for people to do work, to teach, research. The students were really a bright lot. And in some sense even superior to the students one taught in the US. Therefore there was a personal great satisfaction,' he recalls.

He reminisces: 'I used to get what they call best teacher award, year after year. That is because, as I mentioned earlier, of my great interest towards teaching as a profession. Once you have the ability to communicate, one can become a good teacher if you make sufficient preparation. I think to be a good teacher, one has to have the natural talent to be able to communicate. One has to prepare oneself: To go to a class without adequate preparation is not a good thing. Once can certainly spend an hour and hour and half in the classroom but to be very effective, one needs to prepare for two hours before going to a class that is going to last for an hour. The main thing is that one should have an interest in teaching. Even when I was a student, I used to be a good debater and won many prizes in that way. This skill runs in the family. My brother was also a very good speaker and orator during his own school and college days. And it was a great satisfaction when I was a student in honours, I got the same prize which my brother had won several years ago. Teaching was a passion, and interacting with young minds was an exciting experience.'

It is not surprising that Rangarajan was rated as the best teacher year after year. One of his students from the last batch he taught, Jayanth Varma, now faculty member of IIM-A told me that his, i.e., Rangarajan's, classes had the pure technical mastery of the subject, he gave them insight and a sort of analytical toolkit, a mode of analysis that told them something about the real world. It was not a set of formulas on the black board, but included something about the dynamic economy... 'that was the true value of his classes.'

Then the big change happened, Rangarajan says that he had never thought in terms of moving away from academics. But when the offer was made, he felt it was worth accepting. 'When an opportunity came like this I felt it is best to take it. And implement what one has been teaching all along. So it was a challenge to move from what one was preaching to acting.' The appointment of a RBI deputy governor from academia was almost a first instance in the history of the RBI. Normally people who were appointed as deputy governors came from the government, with the single exception of Dr. Hazari who was brought in as deputy governor directly.

The shift from academia to a structured organisation did call for some changes. He recalls that in the early days of his being in the RBI, there was a file that came to him on which ED (Directorate of Enforcement) had made a note with which he differed. Rangarajan called the ED, and like a professor tried to persuade him as to why what he had written was not appropriate. The ED just listened to him and in the end said, 'Sir, it is your prerogative to overrule me.' But in essence, the work in the RBI was very similar to what he was doing earlier. The only real difference was that now everything was in real time—your arguments had to be well marshalled, your positions clear and the decisions taken affected a lot of things down the line. One had to do things responsibly and learn to take responsibility for one's actions. Rangarajan rose to the task admirably.

Apart from the main core of monetary policy, Rangarajan was also responsible for computerisation of the banking system and RBI. Today as banks across the country implement core banking solutions (CBS), and you and I can withdraw cash at the drop of a hat, it is Rangarajan's perseverance and conviction of the need for computerisation that made it happen. He says:

> It was an idea whose time had come. In fact, it had come even earlier—the banking system was expanding, transactions were increasing at a rapid pace and use of mechanical devices was not adequate. I felt that unless the banking system became more computerised it will not be able to cope up. For instance, cheque clearance was one area in which RBI took the lead. Otherwise, given the increase in the cheque habit, the pace in the clearing house would have been too slow. In every aspect of banking, improvement in customer service, depended very much on use of computers. Unfortunately, the atmosphere in the beginning was not very favourable. There was a fear that computerisation would lead to displacement of labour and reduce the number of people that have been recruited and so on. And that is why, in some sense, the first committee, very often called the Rangarajan Committee No I, did not even use the word 'computer', it was called mechanisation of the

banking system. We did introduce computers but we camouflaged it by calling it advanced ledger posting machines (ALPM). Because there was an agreement with the unions not to introduce computerisation we had to find an alternative way of doing it. A full scale computerisation of the branches was not possible at that time. Therefore, we limited ourselves to capturing the data in computers in the first instance and then transferring them.

The Rangarajan Committee II moved further and focused on computerisation of all the operations of the branches. It was felt that if a customer goes to the counter, he should be able to do any operations at that particular counter. At that time, there used to be separate counters for every activity. Once the computerisation of the branches was done, it would lead to the customers getting services at a quicker pace. This was indeed an important building block in computerising the entire operations of the banking system.

He remembers, 'At a later stage when I was Governor and was not sitting on any committee, I set up another committee to look into how to use satellite communications in transferring data from one place to another and so on. Formal things happened during my period as Governor which took computerisation to a much higher level. I was surprised the kind of opposition we had to computerisation in those days. Today it has become commonplace. Now, of course, we are moving away from the paper-based payments system.'

As RBI Governor D. Subbarao writes: 'Dr. Rangarajan, like several other distinguished economists, straddled both academia and the government. What makes him unique though is the way he constructively blended what are two disparate worlds. He brought deep scholarship over a range of academic disciplines to bear on public policy. In the reverse direction, through his writings and speeches, he disseminated practical policy dilemmas to the academia. Throughout, he remained deeply sensitive to real life concerns. It is this unique trait that has set him apart as one of today's most credible thinkers and advisors. Fittingly, a critic labelled him as "philosopher king", and not surprisingly, the Government turns to him for advice whenever it is confronted with any intricate economic issue.'

Undoubtedly, Rangarajan had many serious challenges to grapple with. The financial sector had to be reformed so that there could be freer play of market forces that would, in turn, offer more choice to the consumers through enhanced competition. The system of interest rates or the cost of money, which was being determined by the government, had to be reformed so that money was determined more by the market forces, namely supply and demand. A similar fundamental reform was needed in the exchange rate regime where market forces had to be gradually allowed to play the role of determining how many rupees would be available for one unit of the currency of another country.

Rangarajan went about supervising these changes through a slew of steps that changed the financial landscape of the country. The reforms were anything but easy as there were powerful opponents and vested interests to contend with—in political parties, bureaucracy, intelligentsia and industry. Possibly the most traumatic change was for the public sector banks, who after having to adhere to stricter capital adequacy norms that required the government to inject more capital in them, had to report losses for the first time.

'We had to convince people that this was not due to their actions but due to the reforms,' says Rangarajan. Though it caused short-term pain, enhanced capital adequacy norms brought Indian banks in the league of international banks by conforming to international norms. The other major change that the Rangarajan regime brought about was to get PSU banks listed without the government offloading its shares. The strategy was to ensure that the government was the majority shareholder. But with private owners coming up, the management became more transparent and the returns to shareholders came into their radar in a big way. By allowing private players to set up banks, latest technology and developments such as new products—credit cards, car, home, personal and other loans—got ushered in. Existing banks had little option but to follow suit.

Former RBI Governor Y.V. Reddy recalls: 'One thing I found was he is very cool, very pragmatic, you can not see a frown on his face whatever the tensions, he goes into detail, never leaves anything to chance and in any discussion he will keep on discussing, no question of over-ruling anybody. That is what is called the ability to get the best of decisions, especially in crisis situations.'

His focus on the linkage between finance, infrastructure and growth was also evident during his tenure as Member of the Planning Commission, from August 1991 to December 1992. During this period, he played an important role in the formulation of the Eighth Five-Year Plan (1992-1997) which had to acquire a new orientation in the context of the changes in economic policy.

He was governor of the State of Andhra Pradesh between 1997 and 2002. During this period, he held additional charge of Orissa for nearly two years and Tamil Nadu for six months. He was also president of the Indian Economic Association in 1988 and president of the Indian Econometric Society in 1994. He was the chairman of the National Statistical Commission which was set up to reform the Indian Statistical System. It comes as no surprise that he was awarded the 'Padma Vibhushan' in 2002.

The Report of the Twelfth Finance Commission (2005-2010) brought out under his chairmanship was well received both by the Centre and the states. It broke new ground in enabling states to achieve fiscal consolidation.The most interesting part of the Twelfth Finance Commission is fiscal restructuring plans of states. To tread a middle path and trying to give maximum consensus is a tremendous job that Twelfth Finance Commission attempted to do.

When I asked Dr. Rangarajan, what is the way ahead for the country, he replied: 'I personally think growth and inclusion are not opposed to each other. In fact, equity and efficiency should not be posed as opposing considerations. They must be weaved together to produce a cohesion pattern of growth. In some ways growth enables also to bring about greater inclusion. Growth automatically does not bring inclusion. Growth at least generates additional resources, that can be utilised to meet the socio-economic goals and in that sense it will facilitate greater inclusion. A greater inclusion also stimulates higher growth. I see inclusion and growth as being part of a virtuous cycle, one leading to the other and the one stimulating the other. It is true that growth by itself does not carry all segments of the society, but growth has this advantage that if you are going strongly then it can generate the surpluses that are needed to meet the socio-economic goals. In that sense, we are able to implement NREGA scheme much more smoothly now because we are growing at a faster pace and revenues are rising and we can set aside resources for the purpose of meeting this particular goal, but as the growth process becomes more and more inclusive it will itself stimulate the growth process. Therefore I see it as not two opposing ideas. But I see it as more complimentary.'

The man behind such dramatic change in the lives of an average Indian is not surprised with the magnitude and direction of change in the financial landscape. 'The technological possibilities in financial services need to be extended,' he says, when we ask him on what needs to be done so that the fruit of financial liberalisation becomes accessible to all Indians. 'It is clear that offering complicated financial products is not good for the society. New products will have to be launched with caution. Here the regulators' role is important,' says Rangarajan, who attributes the present global financial crisis to complicated financial products with hidden underlying risks.

'Busy official life does make heavy inroads into personal life, but it is still possible to relax,' says Rangarajan, who unwinds listening to vocal and instrumental classical music. I asked him if he ever thought of retiring. 'At the end of every assignment, when I thought so, a new opportunity opened up. Every new assignment required the use of an analytical mind.' The proponents of the India reform and growth story will hope that this reformer's mind will just keep ticking the way it has for so long.

It was a moment of truth when in recognition of his illustrious career and far reaching contribution to the economic reform process, that he was conferred, Skoch Challenger Lifetime Achievement Award, in 2007. Accepting the Award humbly, he stated, 'Skoch Challenger Lifetime Achievement is the most moving of the awards that I have received; this because of the elegance and the affection with which it has been conferred. I accept the Award in all humility.' His words are truly inspiring that continue to guide us in our endeavour to promoting participatory democracy, inclusive economics and inclusive growth in India.

II

This section briefly introduces the essays in this book. This festschrift is enriched by the wealth of experience and analysis that all the contributors have brought to bear on issues close to Dr. Rangarajan's heart and to well-being of the Indian economy and the country's growth prospects.

A watershed reform introduced during Rangarajan's tenure as RBI governor related to the determination of interest rates of government securities, an important determinant of overall interest rates. From being determined by the government in the past, a transition was made to a system where market auctions determined the rate. The new system helped borrowers and lenders take financial decisions based on the right price of funds, and ensured their more productive use. There were other far-reaching impacts as well. One of them was that interest rates now became a more effective tool to send out signals to the rest of the economy and moderate major adverse impacts such as that of the current global financial crisis. An anecdotal history of those tumultuous times is presented by S.S. Tarapore, providing one with critical insight into the moods and swings of the times.

The paper by K. Kanagasabapathy and Balamurali Radhakrishnan addresses transparency and autonomy, the two core areas of debate centring on monetary policy in the last two decades. Both areas are where Dr. Rangarajan's contribution has been enormous. They write that the central bank's authority over monetary policy is derived from the government, and does not exist in isolation completely outside the government. But, subject to this caveat, it is generally established that central banks need to enjoy operational independence in carrying out their tasks, given the overall policy objectives, which may be set by the government independently or in coordination with the central bank. Transparency in monetary policy flows from the operational independence of the central bank. Accordingly, they have developed a new framework for understanding the communication processes, assessing the level and the scope for enhancing policy transparency in the form of an adapted 'Johari Window'.

Among other things, Rangarajan pioneered the concept of inflation threshold, a concept which is visiting us again today. He had anticipated problems and issues way back in the 1970s and the 1980s, which are still relevant today.

Raghbendra Jha's paper goes back to the early theme of curbing inflation. Although the case for price stability as a macroeconomic goal was always strong, no one in India has done more to move this to centre stage than Rangarajan. As RBI governor and in a number of publications, he forcefully laid out the case for price stability. Jha goes on to review the recent economic growth performance of the Indian economy and recounts the sluggish response of poverty to high economic growth. He notes that hunger (calorie deficiency) has actually increased during the post-reform period. Using household level National Sample Survey (NSS) data for 1993-1994 and 2004-05, he shows that calorie intakes in both rural and urban areas are sensitive to commodity (in particular, food grain) prices. Hence, reducing consumer price inflation is likely to yield a rich dividend in the form of lower incidence of hunger. Indeed rising per capita incomes are not likely to be sufficient to reduce hunger.

Among the major reforms introduced during Rangarajan's tenure at RBI that faced stiff opposition was making the value of the rupee market determined. There were many influential people who were certain that a move to reform exchange rates would spell doom for India's currency. However, backed by research and analysis, Rangarajan was quietly confident that reform was the way forward. 'The reforms needed careful planning, boldness of vision and action and required people to be carried along. The success of economic reforms is there for all to see and can be attributed to all three things,' he says.

His contribution in designing the reforms of the external sector as chairman of the High Level Committee on Balance of Payments is considered by many to be unique. He designed how to liberalise the current account and sustain current account deficit, insisted on hierarchical capital flows and in particular how to keep short-term debt in control and external control. This was one of the most original contributions well before the Asian crisis. And only after the crisis everyone started saying that one must contain debt. Also the transformation from a highly regulated external sector into a sort of dual exchange rate and very quickly to unified exchange rate and even more quickly to current account liberalisation in a span of about 3 to 4 years took even the IMF by surprise.

The evolution of the exchange rate regime is the subject of Ashima Goyal's paper. She examines how the exchange rate contributed to three possible policy objectives—maintaining a real competitive exchange rate, neutralising inflationary oil shocks, deepening foreign exchange markets and encouraging hedging. Depreciation allowed just before oil prices crashed compromised the second objective. Inadequate commitment to two-way movement, prior to the crisis, induced firms to take large currency exposures based on expected appreciation. After the crisis capital flows were allowed to drive the exchange rate, aggravating inflation and acting against macro stabilisation. Clearly, she concludes, markets need some guidance to achieve policy objectives.

Rangarajan is not a *laissez faire* man when it comes to functioning of market forces. 'Liberalisation doesn't mean unbridled play of market forces, but only a redefined role of the government,' he says. There would be few who would dispute that view in the backdrop of the current global financial turmoil.

It was Rangarajan who foresaw the importance of independent and effective supervision that witnessed the creation of a unique mechanism—independent supervisory board for banks within RBI. He foresaw the dangers of shadow banking and brought about legislation giving some regulatory jurisdiction for RBI over non-bank finance companies (NBFc). His vision helped build a robust money market and a government securities market. It is, therefore, appropriate that an essay in his honour evaluates how the banking system in India performed during the crisis, as compared to previous year and how it seems to have emerged from the crisis period, in terms of indicators of efficiency, productivity and soundness as per the standard classification by the RBI.

Y.V. Reddy and Swayam Prava Mishra's paper assesses the limitations of such standard indicators to facilitate a realistic assessment and further evaluation, especially for cross-country comparisons. It concludes, subject to the certain limitations, that the Indian banking system was only marginally impacted by the crisis and that different components—public, private and foreign banks—lent remarkable diversity to the system.

Shyamala Gopinath recalls that she 'benefitted immensely from his guidance in negotiating tricky issues during Uruguay Round negotiations on trade in services, in particular, in financial services which finally culminated into GATS. We in the Reserve Bank fondly remember The Philosopher King with utmost respect for his leadership in steering the country out of the crisis in early 1990s, and laying down the foundation of the subsequent policy framework, which has put the economy on a robust and resilient growth path.' Her paper on a macroprudential approach to regulation captures many ideas the foundations of which were laid by Rangarajan himself.

Banks have been at the heart of the global financial crisis and bankers are widely seen as being responsible for the crisis. Quite understandably, there is a deluge of ideas and suggestions on reforming banks, banking and bankers. Subbarao examines these in his paper and writes that regulation and supervision at the institution level is necessary, but not sufficient. Even if each institution is healthy and safe on a stand-alone basis, systemic risk can build up because of procyclical, herd behaviour—what economists call the fallacy of composition. It is therefore necessary to supplement micro-prudential regulation with macroprudential oversight. He concludes by referring to four challenges that the banking sector has to meet head on—deepening financial inclusion, financing infrastructure, strengthening risk management and improving efficiency.

Kirit S. Parikh focuses on how well the Indian economy is integrated with the global economy. He examines the projection he had made in March 2009 as to how the Indian economy would function in 2009-10 and compares it with the actual experience.

Taking the discussion further is Udaibir Das, who looks at an integrated approach for managing sovereign assets and liabilities. The experience of the global financial crisis of 2007-2010, he says has highlighted the need for sovereigns to find more effective ways to manage their financial resources to combat crisis and minimise the financial cost of their expanded role in maintaining financial stability alongside macroeconomic stability. His paper presents some thoughts on the notion of sovereign risk and the salient features of a Sovereign Asset and Liability Management (SALM) framework that could play its part in ensuring more sound and resilient financial health of a sovereign balance sheet. It also draws some stylised lessons based on country lessons, and brings out how a SALM approach could help promote financial stability apart from its benefits for macroeconomic management.

Ravi Narain contends a need to view every initiative to make the financial system more diverse and sophisticated with some degree of scepticism in the wake of the global financial crisis. This may not be the most appropriate lesson from the crisis for India, but we must recognise that there is need for caution in developing financial markets. The global financial crisis was a result of multiple factors, and one of these was a regulatory environment that trusted the market to 'take care of itself'. Financial market innovations and a permissive, even lax, regulatory culture speeded up and gave potency to what was set in motion by global savings imbalances and fiscal and monetary policies followed by major economies, he writes. His paper examines the concept of financial inclusion in the context of the securities market, the extent to which the securities market has delivered and the focus of the recent reforms.

The trade in capital markets of liberalised India has successfully extended from equities and commodities to currencies. A technological revolution has been heralded in the country and it has brought about improvements in areas ranging from agricultural practices to trade practices Ventures in technology interventions and convergence have connected the national economy and the financial system with those of the developed and the developing world and the policymakers are now striving to improve connectivity across the length and breadth of the country.

Joseph Massey points out that financial services are the lifeline of a developed economy which in turn supports growth, employment generation, capital allocation, savings, wealth distribution and risk management. 'Once 100% financial inclusion is achieved, it will not be difficult to imagine capital markets services alone creating employment opportunities for millions of youth through exchange services ecosystem. Further, one can expect India to be the centre stage of business in Asia post convertibility as we emerge as a global financial centre provides full range of financial services for various maturities, risk and markets across the region.'

Dr. Rangarajan has chaired numerous committees which have made far reaching recommendations but there are a few committees under his chairmanship without discussing which, any festschrift remains incomplete. K.C. Chakrabarty recaps some of the recommendations of

Committees chaired by him on technology and financial inclusion. He writes, 'It is his passion to achieve universal financial inclusion and there can be no greater tribute to the master than to transform his vision into a reality through relentless effort. Financial Inclusion indeed needs to be taken up in a mission mode with the involvement of all the stakeholders.'

The RBI has since taken several steps over the last few years to further financial inclusion—encouraging 'no frills' accounts to allow access to basic financial services, initiating and then expanding the Business Correspondent (BC) model and the use of mobile phones for extending banking outreach. More recently, it has expanded the categories of entities that can be appointed as BCs and also allowed banks to charge a commission for services rendered by BCs. There are, of course, formidable challenges to the BC model that we need to address—high maintenance costs, small size of transactions, expanding awareness, improving communication skills and techniques for dealing with semi-literate people in local languages, enlisting the cooperation of the village administrations and overcoming the constraints posed by lack of electricity and sometimes telecommunication access.

Financial inclusion could mean many things but one feature that is always present in any definition is the widening of access to organised credit to households and enterprises who otherwise have to rely on informal sources like moneylenders. Kartikeya Desai and Nitin Desai, in their paper, argue that interventions to promote credit delivery to underprivileged households must be looked at as interventions to correct market failure. It means that the operating philosophy and the structure of the schemes to promote financial inclusion must be based on a good understanding of how credit markets operate and the precise market failures that need to be corrected. Here, they say the strengths of microfinance model need to be harnessed but 'MFIs themselves need to recognise and be reminded by regulators that they are doing a social business and thus profit optimisation, rather than maximisation, ought to be their objective.'

Even when Dr. Rangarajan was looking to develop the foreign exchange rate markets, money markets, debt markets and the securities markets, he was actually looking at the role of RBI in the area of credit. Another dynamic decision that was taken at that time, when everyone in their own wisdom said, 'do not do it', he did allow banks to allow the SHGs to open bank accounts. SHGs were amorphous, not registered having system of their own and it was not accounts in the name of these individual women, it was in the name of the SHG. This was not noticed much, but it was a really dynamic decision taken during this time. He really perceived the SHG movement to go a long way and our repeated experience shows that last mile effort is being done by these women SHGs.

Access to finance by the poor and vulnerable groups is also a prerequisite for poverty reduction and social cohesion. This has to become an integral part of our efforts to promote inclusive growth. In fact, providing access to finance is a form of empowerment of the vulnerable groups. Financial inclusion denotes delivery of financial services at an affordable cost to the vast sections of the disadvantaged and low-income groups. The various financial services include credit, savings, insurance and payments and remittance facilities. The objective of financial inclusion is to extend the scope of activities of the organised financial system to include within its ambit people with low incomes. As Madhu Kannan notes, through graduated credit, the attempt must be to lift the poor from one level to another so that they come out of poverty. The country has moved on to a higher growth trajectory. To sustain and accelerate the growth momentum, we have to ensure increased participation of the economically weak segments of population in the process of economic growth. Financial inclusion of hitherto excluded segments of population is a critical part of this process of inclusion.

Not only banking but integrated rural development is also close to Rangarajan's heart. No other agency has worked more in the field as has NABARD. Since 1982, NABARD has been reinventing its role and enriching the same in tune with the changing environment as necessary for any financial institution to remain relevant. As K.G. Karmakar explains, NABARD's role today ranges from food security and agricultural credit to environmental issues, skills development and rural livelihoods to microfinance and regulatory issues.

The quality of infrastructure is widely regarded as an essential determinant of growth and infrastructure and in this context it is clearly multi-dimensional. Ravi Parthasarathy argues for the use of composite infrastructure indices to catalyse infrastructure development. He says, whilst there may be a difference of opinion on whether infrastructure should be created in response to demand or in anticipation of demand, there is no denying that the availability of quality infrastructure will act as a significant boost to the productive capacities of the Indian economy as a whole. However, the starting point for such a blue print will need to be the statistics relating to various types of infrastructure as well as its geographic distribution for policy and planning purposes as well as in guiding investment decisions. Data relating to infrastructure should be complete, accurate and up to date.

India's management of the triple crises—fiscal, balance of payments, and financial—experienced sequentially between the late 80s and the mid-90s, much of it under Dr. Rangarajan's stewardship set the stage for New Delhi's response to the Asian and, more recently, the trans-Atlantic financial crises. In fact, after the external payments crisis in 1991, India undertook transformative changes in the country's trade, tariffs, and foreign investment policies. These helped improve India's external economic profile, including a reduction in external debt-to-GDP ratios and an increase in trade-GDP and foreign investment-GDP ratios. Most importantly, the changes have enabled India to accumulate foreign currency reserves. The strategy of gradual economic liberalisation combined with risk-averse prudential regulation in the banking and financial sector helped limit India's exposure to the recent financial crises and the subsequent global economic slowdown. An important feature of the reform of the Indian financial system has been the intent of the authorities to align the regulatory framework with international best practices keeping in view the developmental needs of the country and domestic factors.

The improved economic performance in recent years had encouraged the country to become more globally and regionally integrated. This process is unlikely to be reversed by the current global economic slowdown, given the economic and strategic benefits India has derived so far. As the year 2010 draws to a close, the economic growth for the third quarter is an impressive 8.9 per cent, exports have expanded by over 25 per cent, foreign funds have invested $28.6 billion in equity markets, public issue market has revived and foreign exchange reserves swelled by $11 billion to nearly $300 billion. The growth is also broad-based, with recovery in all three sectors—agriculture, industry and services—and in consumption and investment. While the benefits have been significant in terms of numbers as well as structural shifts that have taken place in the economy in the last decade and a half, there are some areas of concern. The financial inclusion drive pioneered by Dr. Rangarajan stems out of such concern.

The RBI's Annual Policy statement for 2010 year reiterates the concern for common person, while enunciating a medium-term framework, for development of money, forex and government securities markets; for enhancing credit flow to agriculture and small industry; for action points in technology and payments systems; for institutional reform in cooperative banking, non-banking financial companies (NBFCs) and regional rural banks (RRBs); and, for ensuring availability of quality services to all sections of the population. The most distinguishing feature of the policy statement relates to the availability of banking services to the common person, especially depositors. Operationally, it has been made clear that RBI will implement policies to encourage banks which provide extensive services while disincentivising those which are not responsive to the banking needs of the community, including the underprivileged.

Access to finance at the grassroots level, particularly to the disadvantaged sections of society, continues to remain a mirage despite being on top of government's agenda for equitable growth. This is even as growth in financial intermediation appears to have outstripped economic growth for several years now, reflecting increased financial deepening. Reforms that trigger growth must be inclusive in the sense of broad-basing growth and mainstreaming deprived and backward segments.

Talking about inclusive growth, Prof. Jagdish Bhagwati's in his recent article says: 'India's economy again exceeded expectations, growing by 8.9 per cent in the second quarter. Those outside India often show exuberance at such high and rising growth, following the nation's economic reforms in the early 1990s. At home, however, you are just as likely to hear condemnation from those worried about the underprivileged this prosperity has bypassed. Such voices present India with a double challenge: they misrepresent the successful way growth has cut India's poverty, but more importantly their critiques stand in the way of a much needed new wave of reforms, which would further benefit India's poorest...Earlier rounds of reforms have generated revenues which can now be spent on targeted health and education programmes for the poor. This is what Indian planners wanted from the 1950s, but could never afford when revenues were as stagnant as the nation's growth rate. Now the current generation can finally deliver.'[1]

The hope is palpable. This is India's decade. The authors in this festschrift share a critical—but overall positive—view of the country's future and outline several areas and recommendations for bettering the lives of citizens. Empirically rich and topically diverse, the book is broad in scope and full of deep analytic insights. Consolidation, competition and risk management are no doubt critical to the future of banking, but I believe that governance and financial inclusion would also emerge as the key issues for a country like India, at this stage of socioeconomic development.

1. Bhagwati, Jagdish (2010). "India's Reform and Growth have Lifted all Boats", *Financial Times (London)*, November 30.

1

Episodes from Monetary and other Financial Policies (1982-1997)

An Anecdotal Presentation

S.S. Tarapore

Dr. C. Rangarajan had a long stint in the Reserve Bank of India (RBI) from 1982-1997, which I would call the Rangarajan era. Although there was a break (August 1991-November 1992), when he was Member Planning Commission, for reasons explained later, in this paper, the period February 1982-November 1997 is treated as a continuum. The official history of the RBI necessarily would be based on the official records which are cold and do not reflect the behind the scenes conflicts and struggles and the eventual execution of policies. It is unfortunate, that in India, anecdotal history is generally neglected as senior officials other than a very few exceptions, do not maintain personal diaries, unlike in some countries such as the UK and the US where the historian has access to the personal diaries of the key players. As a result a lot of anecdotal history is lost to posterity. While this paper is a very limited attempt to undertake an anecdotal presentation, one is conscious of the fact that any such attempt carries with it the predilections of the writer.

The Turbulence of the Early Months (February-November 1982)

Rangarajan's appointment as Deputy Governor in February 1982 raised many eyebrows and explicit doubts were expressed by, the then Governor Dr. I.G. Patel, while recommending Rangarajan's name for the post of Deputy Governor, said that his impeccable academic credentials as an economist were beyond doubt but wondered whether the emollient Professor would be able to handle the strong anti-establishment streak in the RBI. Rangarajan's initial portfolio was extremely restricted, as compared with his predecessor K.S. Krishnaswamy (there was a gap of almost a year between the two appointments), as key portfolios of monetary policy and exchange rate management were not allocated to Rangarajan.

While critics could, with off-hand laconicism and not without justification, dismiss my presentation as merely that of a Rangarajan clone or vassal, it is not known that our initial interactions were rather bumpy! The approach steeply ingrained in the then RBI theology was one of directly allocating credit—akin to a Kaldorian approach—and the money supply projection was a mere derivative of the credit expansion deemed appropriate. In the 1970s, the term 'reserve money' was virtually taboo in the RBI. Before Rangarajan joined the RBI, I had, rather naively, raised the issue of the need to monitor reserve money and the then head of the Credit Planning Cell, Ms. Nalini Ambegaokar, formally reprimanded me for wasting time on such irrelevant concepts! Shortly after joining the RBI, Rangarajan asked V.B. Kadam, the then Principal Adviser, as to whom he could discuss matters relating to reserve money. Kadam suggested that he could discuss the matter with Tarapore. Being the disciplined early riser, Rangarajan called me up at my residence at 6.00 a.m. Being a late night worker and a late riser, my response on being woken up found me at my worst and I abruptly told him that I knew nothing about the subject and why was he discussing the matter with me. When Rangarajan told Kadam about our conversation, Kadam said that one does not talk to Tarapore before 10.00 in the morning. Being a true academic, Rangarajan took no offence but for the next 15 years he always talked to me after 10.00 a.m.

Shortly thereafter, a Working Group on Bank Deposits was set up under Rangarajan's chairmanship and I was appointed as a member. His underlying theme was to advocate an elongation of the maturity structure of deposits from 3-5 years. The view I took in the Working Group, in a formal note, was that the maturity structure should be reduced to one year as it would then better enable banks to adjust to deposit rate changes by the RBI. With true academic spirit he told the Working Group that the case put forth by me was well structured and suggested that rather than a Note of Dissent he would incorporate my entire note in the body of the Report as a minority viewpoint. I am belabouring the point merely to emphasise his unique ability to adopt a Socratic approach of debate and dissent to achieve progress. It is no surprise that despite the fact that he was not in charge of monetary policy his viewpoint prevailed and a new five-year deposit maturity was introduced in October 1982. A notable feature of his thinking was to take note of the evolving changes in the situation and in later years he not only advocated a return to a three-year maturity but a one-year maturity at which the maximum rate prescribed by the RBI would be applicable.

The then prevailing theology was difficult to break through and, more in despair than in anger, Rangarajan said, 'How do I deal with my Principal Adviser (N.A. Mujumdar) who argues that money supply is what it is and that money supply does not matter'. Despite Mujumdar constantly taking a contrary view Rangarajan openly said that no one in the RBI can write as cogently as Mujumdar. Furthermore, Rangarajan was instrumental in fostering the advancement of Mujumdar's career in international central banking circles.

Rangarajan's approach was not to use the vantage point of his position to impose a certain way of thinking but he fostered the building of an analytical framework to underpin the conduct of RBI's policies.

The initial months in the RBI must have been heartbreaking for Rangarajan. Within days of his taking charge as Deputy Governor, in February 1982, the RBI announced that Foreign Currency Non-Resident Accounts (FCNRA) would carry a rate of interest two percentage points above the local currency deposits for the same maturity. Being well-versed in international monetary economics, and having a clear perception that the inflation rate differentials should be reflected in interest rate differentials, offering interest rates in the strong currencies at rates above Indian deposit rates would be a violation of the fundamentals of exchange rate policy formulation. Rangarajan wrote a cogent note to Governor Patel. Patel unequivocally told Rangarajan to forget Gujarat-IIM economics and to concentrate on practical issues of central banking policies. Being unable to break through the then prevailing RBI thinking, Rangarajan was in great despair and the feeling of suffocation was unbearable. It is not known that Rangarajan had seriously considered resigning from the post of Deputy Governor. Fortunately, his inherent patience and tolerance restrained him from taking any drastic action which would have altered the history of the RBI and his own career. It is important to clarify that the Patels and Rangarajan were family friends and the Patels had great personal affection for Rangarajan. The stand-off was more an issue of an academic adjusting to a bureaucracy.

A few months before Rangarajan joined the RBI there was a savage credit crunch, of an intensity not experienced earlier or subsequently. The money market was tight, the bill rediscounting facility was withdrawn and all other refinance facilities were drastically curtailed. In such a milieu, the cash reserve ratio (CRR) and the statutory liquidity ratio (SLR) were raised sharply. This was against the backdrop of the International Monetary Fund's extended fund facility (EFF) which had exacting credit ceilings. There were endemic defaults in CRR (all public sector banks, other than the Punjab National Bank experienced defaults). Rangarajan pondered on the implications of systemic defaults in the CRR and the implications for the efficacy of monetary policy. In some ways, the monetary tightening was thwarted by the large defaults. He, therefore, undertook an analysis of adjusted reserve money which is the reserve money adjusted for changes in the CRR and the defaults. This pathbreaking work, undertaken jointly with Anoop Singh, brought to the fore the need for contemporaneous monitoring of CRR maintenance and timely imposition of penalties on defaults. The practice till then was a rather laid-back approach on imposing penalties and quite often these penalties were waived. In the event, the large systemic defaults in 1981-82 were not condoned but a system of graduated penalties was introduced. For the 1981-82 defaults, the banking system had to pay penalties of the order of Rs. 40 crore which was large relative to the profits of banks.

Again, there was virtually no monitoring of the statutory liquidity ratio (SLR) on a daily basis till the Banking Regulation Act (Amendment) was enforced in 1985 and it was only thereafter that daily maintenance of the SLR was made effective and penalties imposed for defaults.

The first major ordeal by fire faced by Rangarajan was in piloting the draft of the RBI Annual Report for June 1982. The crucial chapter on 'Assessment and Prospects' was entirely written by him and, *inter alia*, he clearly brought out that the way the regulatory framework had been framed, the banks had no discretion on 80 per cent of their lending and hence an overhauling of the regulatory system was necessary. When the draft Annual Report was discussed in the RBI Board it was considered as an assault on the received doctrine of the time. The priority sector allocation had been raised from 33 per cent to 40 per cent in 1980 and over and above the Credit Authorisation Scheme (CAS) there were direct credit allocations by the RBI for food procurement and distribution, petroleum, fertilisers, steel, sugar, etc. It must have been painful to Rangarajan to virtually scrap the draft and a sanitised and deodorised version was eventually published. The official history of the RBI for that period is presently under preparation and it is important that the draft Annual Report for June 1982 is unearthed. It was only in the June 1984 Annual Report that Rangarajan was able to bring back some of the vital issues discussed in the draft Report for June 1982.

September 1982-January 1985

Shortly after Governor Manmohan Singh took over the reins of the RBI, Rangarajan's portfolio was made more meaningful as he was given charge of monetary policy and exchange rate management. In the aftermath of the savage credit squeeze in 1981, during the period January-November 1982, there was a significant easing of monetary and credit policy. The CRR was reduced, refinance for food and exports was raised to an incremental 100 per cent, and the clogged credit lines were significantly opened up by sector-specific refinance facilities for lending by financial institutions.

Manmohan Singh and Rangarajan were conscious of the fact that while political economy considerations seemed to work towards easing lending rates, they had great concern that excess liquidity could fuel inflation. The policy announcements reflected anxiety about the adverse effects of excessive primary money creation and hence there were rapid increases in the CRR in April 1983, August 1983 and in November 1983 a 10 per cent incremental CRR was reintroduced (the earlier incremental CRR had been discontinued in 1980). Following this the CRR was once again raised in January 1984. It was recognised that policy tensions run high each time the CRR was raised and as such the incremental CRR ensured that the effective increase of the CRR was put on auto pilot and hence recourse to increasing the CRR was not necessary till February 1987.

Prior to Rangarajan taking up the key portfolios of monetary policy and exchange rate policy, along with macroeconomic analysis, the approach of the RBI on overall policies was fragmented. In December-January the Secretary's Department, which handled internal debt of the government would ask the Credit Planning Cell (CPC) which handled monetary policy for an estimate of commercial bank deposit growth. The CPC would give a perfunctory note on the deposit growth for the forthcoming year with the proviso that comprehensive work on this would be taken up only at the time of the monetary policy announcement in April. Rangarajan was quick to recognise that such a procedure prempted the RBI from taking a view on the sustainable level of the budget deficit and the borrowing programme, consistent with the monetary policy. Rangarajan then brought about a major change by synchronising all this work in the RBI. Earlier the work on the borrowing programme was a perfunctory exercise in both the RBI and the government at a rather low level. Accordingly, all this work was handled by top management with a comprehensive letter from the Governor to the Finance Minister which was then discussed by top management of RBI with the Finance Minister and top officials in the Ministry of Finance.

Manmohan Singh left the RBI suddenly in January 1985 to take over as Deputy Chairman of Planning Commission. Days before Manmohan Singh left RBI he addressed a letter to the Finance Ministry which was to be followed by a high level meeting between RBI and the government. The Finance Ministry called for a meeting before Governor Malhotra took charge. From the RBI side there were Rangarajan and the present writer while from the government side there were the Finance Secretary P.K. Kaul, Bimal Jalan and Montek Singh Ahluwalia. Manmohan Singh's letter had indicated that for 1985-86, the RBI could agree to a higher borrowing programme provided the government securities rate for the longest maturity was raised from 10.5 per cent to 12.0 per cent. The Ministry's view was that they wanted the higher borrowing programme but with no increase in the interest rate on securities. The meeting ended with an impasse as there could be no agreement. Manmohan Singh having moved to the Planning Commission needed a larger borrowing programme and was concerned about any increase in cost of borrowing—the changed role necessitated a change in Manmohan Singh's view on this matter!

February 1985-December 1990

On Governor R.N. Malhotra taking charge in early February 1985, Rangarajan briefed Malhotra on the impasse on the borrowing programme. It was clear early on that Malhotra and Finance Minister V.P. Singh had a close rapport. Within days the Ministry of Finance agreed to raise the maximum securities rate from 10.5 per cent to 11.5 per cent. During the Malhotra era a significant part of crucial correspondence was between Malhotra and V.P. Singh. Oral communication between Malhotra and the top Finance Ministry officials was laconic and at times abrupt. Hence, much of the persuasive discussions were left to be settled between Rangarajan and the Finance Ministry officials. When the key elements of the monetary policy would be discussed by the Governor with the Finance Minister the top officials of the Ministry would be present but the notable absence was that of Rangarajan. Yet, it was Rangarajan who had to liase closely with the Ministry officials. In fact on a number of issues the Ministry would communicate to the Governor that Rangarajan should be deputed for discussions with the Ministry.

The Sad Saga of Short-Term Deposit Rates

From 1980 onwards, there had been significant efforts towards rationalising lending rates and discretion was given to banks to determine lending rates within a given range. Till 1985, there was no attempt to rationalise deposit rates. For deposit maturities between 15 days and up to less than one year there were prescribed rates for five maturities. To give banks some discretion in setting deposit rates as part of the April 1985 policy Malhotra announced that within a ceiling of 8 per cent banks could fix their own deposit rates for maturities between 15 days and less than one year but this generated a big storm. Initially, the major banks offered rates which were one percentage point higher than the then prevailing rate. The purpose of this discretion was that banks could alter their deposit maturity structure by offering some incentive to increase a particular maturity. The Bank of Madurai chairman, S. Kumarasundaram, was a former officer of the RBI, offered 8 per cent for 15 days maturity with a view to augmenting the bank's deposit at the short end. In response all banks, like sheep jumping off a cliff, offered 8 per cent for 15 days without giving attention to their profits. The RBI's expectation that banks would use their discretion with some finesse to maximise their profits was totally belied. Hence, the RBI had no option but to revert back towards the end of May 1985 to fixing the rates for all maturities.

There is a behind the scenes saga of policy tensions. When Malhotra went over the proposed measures with the Finance Minister, the then Finance Secretary S. Venkitaramanan was present but the Chief Economic Adviser and Secretary Banking Bimal Jalan was held up in another meeting. By the time Bimal Jalan walked into the meeting, the deposit rate change had been already discussed. It appears that neither Malhotra nor Venkitaramanan briefed Jalan about the measure relating to the freedom given to banks to fix deposit rates for the maturities below one year within a ceiling of 8 per cent and hence he heard about this measure only when the policy was announced. The public sector banks approached Bimal Jalan with the plea that unless the *status quo ante* was restored the banks would present the government with losses of Rs. 100 crore which was very sizable as compared with the then profits of these banks.

The setback to deposit rate rationalisation did scald Malhotra, Rangarajan and the present writer. Within days of these developments there was the Golden Jubilee Celebrations of the RBI. At that function the former Governor M. Narasimham and former Deputy Governor R.K. Hazari chided me and said that as a career central banker I had not offered the right advice to the top management.

Malhotra felt intensely about this episode and on his last day in the RBI he said that the April 1985 measure on a limited deregulation of deposit rates was the right measure and had this measure succeeded it would have been possible to move faster in the area of deposit rate deregulation. Malhotra and Rangarajan reflected sterling qualities when they persevered with cautious deregulation. Although Malhotra and Rangarajan bore the cross of this episode, when viewed at this distance of time, they will be considered as the pioneers of interest rate deregulation. The more difficult lending rates deregulation was undertaken without a blip in the second half of the 1980s. On the deposit side, however, banks could be given discretion to fix deposit rates for different maturities, within a prescribed ceiling, only in 1992. In retrospect, it would appear that banks, after serving out life imprisonment, just did not want freedom!

Rationalisation of Selective Credit Controls

The selective credit controls were an intricate maze and even officials directly in charge of this area could not correctly interpret the regulatory framework. It is paradoxical that this most difficult and sensitive area of regulation could be successfully rationalised in April 1985 without a ripple. With this rationalisation, the lengthy dossier on selective credit controls was substituted by a single simple table.

The Chakravarty Committee Report on the Monetary System

The Chakravarty Committee Report (1985) bears the unmistakable stamp of Rangarajan. The Report provides a comprehensive framework for the formulation of monetary policy with feedback. The Report outlined how the monetary-fiscal system could be strengthened and in many ways it was a precursor to the 1991 financial sector liberalisation. The Report set out how the complex interest rate structure could be made more efficient by providing for a single free lending rate while providing for only two concessional rates. One of the significant measures recommended by the Committee was to bring about consistency between the monetary and fiscal accounts. Till the mid-1980s, the budget deficit was defined as creation of ad hoc Treasury bills and changes in cash balances. Rangarajan was instrumental in incorporating the concept of 'net RBI credit to government' into the budget exercise. The way the government implemented this measure was unfortunate as it was stated that the 'net RBI credit to government' was not independently estimated.

Need for RBI-Government Accord

Despite his heavy duties in the RBI, Rangarajan personally undertook a prodigious amount of fundamental research on policy-related issues—this is unequaled, certainly unsurpassed in the annals of the RBI. His Presidential Address at the Indian Economic Association on 'Issues in Monetary Management' (1988) is a fundamental contribution. All along the monetary economist P.R. Brahmananda alleged that the RBI did not have an analytical framework for monetary policy. On hearing the Presidential Address he told me that he would totally withdraw his allegation. In this Address, Rangarajan called for an Accord between government and RBI on the extent of recourse to RBI financing. This was followed by his Kutty Memorial Lecture (1993) on 'Autonomy of Central Banks' where he called for a cessation of automatic monetisation and the phasing out of ad hoc Treasury bills. This eventually resulted in the RBI-Government First Supplemental Agreement (1994) and the Second Supplemental Agreement (1997).

Activation of the Money Market and Auctions of Government Securities

As far back as 1986, Rangarajan initiated work on development of the money market. The 182-day Treasury Bills Auctions were introduced in 1986 and thereafter he took keen interest in implementing the Vaghul Working Group Report on Development of the Money Market (1987). He realised that institutional reform was a basic prerequisite for an active money market. Accordingly, he took on parentage for setting up the Discount and Finance House of India (1988) and only after it was established did he move to implementing the Vaghul Working Group Report. In March 1989, the money market interest rates were freed and new instruments of certificates of deposits (CDs) and Commercial Paper were introduced. It is not known that the introduction of these measures ran into stiff resistance in RBI Top Management. There were a series of internal meetings and Malhotra told Rangarajan that the *sotto voce* was against money market reform. Rangarajan was not dismayed and he used his persuasive skills to bring round RBI Top Management. Vaghul, who had earlier said that if money market reform did not take off, he would blame Rangarajan and Tarapore, retracted and said that he was amazed at Rangarajan's skills in implementing the entire Vaghul Report with consummate skills.

Discretionay Power

Discretionary power was anathema to Rangarajan and hence he was averse to holding the power to decide how much refinance each bank could get. When he advocated the removal of discretion, Malhotra reminded him that discretion was the source of power and he found it incomprehensible that the wielder of discretionay power was advocating its removal. Finally, after much debate, in August 1987, Rangarajan communicated to banks that the Discretionary Refinance facility would be rule based and transparent.

Rationalisation of Lending Rates

Despite the fiasco on very limited deregulation of deposit rates, Rangarajan, following the Chakravarty Report, recognised that other than concessional rates there should be one commercial lending rate which should be free. Accordingly, in October 1988, the maximum lending rate of 16.5 per cent was altered to 16 per cent (minimum). This was a very significant change as it gave banks the discretion for the first time to decide on this lending rate. Some critics, looking at this change in a historical perspective raise the fractious issue as to whether the lending rate of 16 per cent (minimum) was a figure out of a hat. This is an insensate assessment of the process of interest rate fixation at that point of time. Whenever there was a change in deposit/lending rates, Rangarajan would commission an elaborate exercise of the impact on banks, based on the distribution of credit and deposits. It was felt that if the minimum rate was lower than 16 per cent banks would, *ab initio*, raise sharply their actual lending rates to a large number of borrowers. The more important point that critics should take note of was the fact that the discretion given to banks was used by banks with maturity and judgement and the April 1985 deposit rate episode was not repeated.

Rangarajan recognised that the proliferation of lending rates based on the size of the advance and the priority accorded to a sector was cumbersome and he personally took charge of a number of simulation exercises to implement a rationalisation of lending rates. September 1990 is a watershed in that the complex lending rate structure was rationalised into six lending rates. Initially Jalan was rather sceptical that such a major rationalisation of lending rates would not be practical. Over time, however, Rangarajan used his persuasive skills to allay the concerns of the Ministry of Finance that the rationalisation of lending rates was viable. This was a major achievement as lending rates had to be raised, across the board, during the crisis of 1990-91 and it would have been difficult to do so if there was a proliferation of interest rates on lending.

December 1990-December 1992

In December 1990 there were cataclysmic changes in the top management in the RBI. Malhotra suddenly resigned and S. Venkitaramanan was appointed Governor. Malhotra's sudden exit was indeed sad but Venkitaramanan was clearly the saviour for dealing with the balance of payments crisis.

Handling of the Balance of Payments Crisis of 1990-91

It is well known that India's foreign currency assets (other than gold) were at a rock bottom of around US $1 billion. What is not known is that the actual available reserves were lower as they were locked up in assistance to branches of Indian banks overseas, which were not in a position to immediately repay the RBI. Rangarajan had, time and again, warned the government about the impending apocalypse but in the absence of effective governance there was a paralysis in government's policies which put considerable strain on monetary policy. The duo of Venkitaramanan and Rangarajan immediately went on a tour of the major international financial capitals and convinced the authorities in these countries that India would take effective measures and they were instrumental in saving India from a certain international default. Hitherto, the RBI policy on its gold reserves was a strictly passive policy and the RBI neither bought nor sold gold in the international markets; any accrual to the gold reserves was essentially by way of transfer of government confiscated gold to the RBI. The passive policy was so extreme that the confiscated gold was kept in the form in which it was received i.e., as trinklets. The key to the turnaround of the balance of payments crisis was the transfer of gold to the Bank of England, the Bank of Japan and the Union Bank of Switzerland. Although the RBI was a Depository under the IMF, the concerns about India were such that the lending institutions insisted on a physical transfer of the gold. This involved a major operation which was handled by Venkitaramanan and Rangarajan. The transfer of gold was a major risk to the RBI because of the emotive view of the public that such a step would be a slur on India and the risks involved in the physical transfer of gold. The transfer was handled with great finesse and the success of the transfer significantly changed international opinion and lines of credit opened up. This is a major achievement and Rangarajan can rightly claim credit for the successful completion of this operation.

Differences in Perceptions on the Formulation of Monetary Policy

While Venkitaramanan and Rangarajan worked in perfect harmony on balance of payments matters, there was considerable soul searching on the conduct of monetary policy. Venkitaramanan threw a teaser at Rangarajan, in the Committee of the RBI Central Board, and expressed that he had grave misgivings about the analytical underpinnings of the monetary policy often outlined by Rangarajan. Venkitaramanan expressed doubts about the money-income-prices inter-relationship set out by Rangarajan and he commissioned the anti-establishment economists brigade in the RBI to formally set out an alternative monetary policy and he ordered that these studies, which were an indictment of the RBI policies, should be published without any amendment. What embarrassed Rangarajan was that Venkitaramanan categorically assured the RBI Board that he could not ignore Rangarajan's view on how monetary policy should be conducted as Rangarajan was his teacher at Carnegie Mellon University, US and that he always considered Rangarajan as his Guru. Rangarajan expressed great anxiety to his policy team that the package of measures worked out for the April 1991 monetary policy may not be approved by Venkitaramanan. In the event, to our utter surprise, Venkitaramanan approved the entire slew of measures. The measures included: (i) increase in lending/deposit rates, (ii) withdrawal of the large discretionary refinance and reduction in export refinance, and (iii) imposition of a non-food credit-deposit ratio with punitive penalties for violation of the ceiling. Venkitaramanan followed a didactic approach of raising questions, debate and dissent, and then taking the appropriate decisions on policy.

This was quickly followed by a second slew of measures in May 1991: (i) a 10 per cent incremental CRR was introduced, (ii) the imposition of an interest rate surcharge on import finance, and (iii) restrictions on drawals against large limits.

Devaluation of the Rupee in July 1991 and Further Tightening of Monetary Policy

In a two-step operation on July 1 and 3, 1991, the rupee was devalued *vis-à-vis* the US dollar by about 20 per cent—what was called two haircuts in three days. There have all along been apprehensions in government whenever there has to be a formal devaluation of the rupee. When the first step of the devaluation was being put through on July 1, 1991, there was some last minute hesitation in government circles but by then the first step of the devaluation had already been announced. The second step of the devaluation was announced on the morning of July 3, 1991, the day before the RBI Board meeting in Chennai. As the RBI Top Management was flying out to Chennai on July 3, 1991 for the Board meeting it was felt that this would be the end of the measures, at least for that day.

On reaching Chennai, Rangarajan crafted a handwritten order raising the Bank rate, which would need to be authenticated and signed by the Governor—the Governor has the powers of the Board. This gave the go-ahead to announce a slew of measures: (i) the Bank Rate was raised from 10 per cent to 11 per cent, (ii) the maximum deposit rate was raised from 12 per cent to 13 per cent, (iii) the lending rate for Rs. 2 lakh and over was raised from 17 per cent (minimum) to 18.5 per cent (minimum), and (iv) refinance rates were raised sharply. Shortly thereafter, Rangarajan left the RBI to become Member Planning Commission

Role of Rangarajan: August 1991-December 1992

While there was a formal break between August 1991 and December 1992 in Rangarajan's association with the RBI when he was appointed as Member Planning Commission, as mentioned earlier, this period is treated as a continuum of his association with the RBI as the Finance Minister Manmohan Singh advised Venkitaramanan and the present writer that we should consult Rangarajan on all important policy issues. On a personal note I should state that it was a great strain to succeed Rangarajan as Deputy Governor. Rangarajan was generous with his time whenever Venkitaramanan and I needed to consult him. Venkitaramanan would insist that he and I should seek separate appointments with Rangarajan. On one occasion when we had to meet the Finance Minister in the early part of the day, Rangarajan rescheduled his commitments to give us time separately. I cannot adequately express my deep sense of gratitude for his generous and unstinted help.

In October 1991 we met Rangarajan before the announcement of the monetary policy and mentioned that we proposed to: (i) raise the lending rate for advances over Rs. 2 lakh from 18.5 per cent (minimum) to 20.0 per cent (minimum, (ii) raise the Bank rate from 11 per cent to 12 per cent, and (iii) totally withdraw the refinance facilities for food credit, 182-day Treasury Bills and Discretionary Refinance. Rangarajan said that he was fully supportive of the RBI up to this juncture and his view was that no further tightening would be necessary. He cautioned us that if the RBI went in for further tightening we would not have his support.

In the event the RBI did not go in for any further monetary tightening and in fact in February 1992 reduced the lending rate for over Rs. 2 lakh from 20 per cent (minimum) to 19 per cent (minimum). There was a phased reduction in the effective SLR as on all incremental liabilities the SLR was reduced to 30 per cent while the SLR on the base liabilities remained frozen at 38.5 per cent. Another measure was the introduction of a new Non-Resident (Ordinary Non-Repatriable) Rupee Deposit scheme (NRNR) which Rangarajan had strongly advocated when he was in the RBI.

The easing of the overall economic situation, as envisaged by Rangarajan, did materialise and in April 1992 there were further relaxations. The incremental CRR was discontinued. A significant measure was that in the case of term deposits a single rate of 'not exceeding 13 per cent' was prescribed for all maturities from 46 days and over and banks were given discretion to fix their own rates for different maturities. This measure was implemented by banks in an orderly manner and there was no problem as had arisen at the April 1985 measure when banks were given some discretion to set deposit rates. This would have given Rangarajan great satisfaction.

In the April 1992 policy there were two measures which did not have the agreement of Rangarajan. These measures were not part of the package presented to bankers at the meeting. In the course of the meeting, Venkitaramanan in response to the discussions made two impromptu amendments to the policy which had been announced. First, he raised the Savings Bank deposit rate from 5 per cent to 6 per cent. Secondly, in the case of certificates of deposit, any increase in CDs above 5 per cent of their aggregate deposits was exempted from CRR. In fairness, Venkitaramanan said that he was announcing these measures against the specific advice proffered by his Deputy Governor.

The Joint Parliamentary Committee on the Irregularities in Securities Transactions

The sad saga of the RBI and the 1992 irregularities in securities transactions is too vast a subject to be dealt with in this paper. Suffice it to say that Rangarajan had cautioned on this problem in the incipient stages and proposed certain measures. In the event these suggestions were diluted. When the Joint Parliamentary Committee was set up the Committee called Rangarajan to brief the Committee on the matter. Rangarajan's briefing to the Committee is a clear statement on the issues involved and while such irregularities could not be condoned he explained that these irregularities occurred in the context of very large preemptions of banks resources through the CRR and SLR and regulations on interest rates. There were no doubt failures in the monitoring system and market information collecting system. When the securities irregularities are taken up while writing the history of that period I hope that the historians will have access to Rangarajan's briefing to the Committee. It should be recorded that when the issue of penalties on these irregularities came up during Governor Rangarajan's term in the RBI notwithstanding fears about prolonged litigation Rangarajan commissioned detailed work on the extent of the irregularities and he personally undertook to oversee the entire exercise to ensure that there was no error in the exercise by the RBI. In the event he went ahead with imposing penalties which all banks paid up without demur and there was no recourse to any litigation. This will go down in history as one of his major achievements.

December 1992-November 1997

Achievements during Governor Rangarajan's Tenure

It is virtually impossible to set out all Governor Rangarajan's achievements in this paper—a fair and comprehensive presentation would need a series of papers. As such it is conceivable that many of his achievements would not be covered in this paper.

Early on after taking over as Governor, Dr. Rangarajan, introduced special refinance facilities to facilitate increased flow of credit to agriculture and industry and he reduced interest rates and reserve requirements. It is important to take note of these measures as shortly thereafter he was unfairly dubbed as a mindless monetarist.

It is remarkable that despite his onerous duties as Governor, Rangarajan continued with his prodigious analytical output. It is not known outside the RBI that during his tenure as Governor the vital Chapter on Assessment and Prospects was entirely written by him. Even his arch critics have admitted that the series of Annual Reports carried an authentic analysis on the future course of reform and how the monetary transmission process could be improved. It is here that one finds a clear delineation of the exchange rate policy and the rationale for tracking the real effective exchange rate (REER). Control of inflation was of paramount importance to him and according to him this should be the primary objective of monetary policy. He believed that controlling inflation and maximising growth, in the medium term, were not antithetical and he believed that each segment of economic policy should follow the assignment rule i.e., attain the objective to which it is best suited. He unequivocally cautioned on the need to contain the government debt and although he had a strong preference to move to market-related rates of interest on government debt he ensured that there would not be chaos in the government securities market. To ensure that real rates of interest were reasonable, he recognised the need to keep the inflation rate low so that nominal rates of interest were reasonable. Thus, a strong, unequivocal and timely monetary policy was central to his approach. Nonetheless, his actions showed that his policies on interest rates and reserve requirements had an essence of upward and downward movements in accord with the evolving situation. Illustratively, from January 1993 to mid-1994, he eased monetary policy and as inflation picked up he had no hesitation in tightening monetary policy as the rupee came under pressure. Thereafter, from November 1995 he once again eased monetary policy. When an assault on the exchange rate again started in early 1996, he had no hesitation in taking measures which would, once and for all, singe the speculative attack on the rupee—he withdrew the foreign currency denominated export refinance facility which was subject to misuse and he took bold measures to introduce close monitoring of the cancellation of forward contracts as also intra-day trading transactions of authorised dealers. This completely killed the speculative attack on the rupee. These appropriately timed and decisive measures showed how the efficacy of policy could be improved.

It would not be possible, in this paper, to do justice to his achievements as Governor, but it would be even more unjust not to record a few select highlights. Notable among them are the cessation of automatic monetisation of the budget deficit and the two Supplemental Agreements between government and the RBI to phase out ad hoc Treasury Bills and to limit the ways and means advances of the Central government. These measures will go down in monetary history as major reforms after 40 years of permissive financing of the budget deficit. The deregulation of interest rates, the reduction of reserve requirements without of loss of monetary control, reining in inflation to a 11-year low, strengthening the banking system by a tightening of prudential norms, the setting up of new private sector banks, allowing public sector banks to access the capital market the strengthening of the forex reserves and a clear enunciation of the exchange rate policy. There was the unification of the exchange rates in March 1993 and the smooth move over to current account convertibility. Given my association with work on capital account convertibility after I left the RBI, it is incumbent on me to categorically state that the outline of the work on capital account convertibility was conceptualised by Rangarajan as far back as 1995-96.

FCNRA Losses

Early on during his term as Governor, Rangarajan had to face the problem of huge losses to be borne by the RBI because of the exchange rate guarantees on the Foreign Currency Non-Resident (Accounts) (FCNRA) deposits resulting from exchange rate guarantees provided to banks. The RBI's accounting is on an accrual basis and hence the entire loss would have to be provided for in the RBI balance sheet for June 1993 and as such there would be no profit transfer to government and yet there would be a gaping hole in the RBI balance sheet. Again, there would be a reputational risk of the RBI having gone bust. The matter was being handled very competently by Deputy Governor R. Janakiraman and Additional Secretary

Budget Janaki Kathpalia. The correspondence between the two was getting high pitched and there was a total impasse. The matter was discussed at a pre-dinner meeting at the house of Montek Singh Ahluwalia where Rangarajan, Shankar Acharya and the present writer were present. The approach to this meeting was to collectively resolve the problem. What ultimately got agreed was that as the government operated on a cash basis, the entire liability could be taken off the RBI balance sheet and taken over by the government. The RBI, in turn, would undertake transfer additional profits each year equivalent to the loss being borne on a cash basis by the government during each year. Here is an illustration of Rangarajan at his best, reconciling different viewpoints. He defied the old dictum that, 'for every winner there is a loser' and he converted this into a win-win solution.

Handling of Capital Flows and Coordination of Monetary and Exchange Rate Policies

With the large inflows and consequent monetary expansion and rising inflation, the RBI had to reverse monetary policy gears from mid-1994. When the outflows started in mid-1995, the RBI had to handle a speculative attack on the Indian rupee, squelch inflation while continuing with financial liberalisation, freeing interest rates and reducing reserve requirements. The rapid alternative tightening and easing of monetary policy was heavily criticised but by deft handling Rangarajan ensured external and internal stability. In the second half of 1995-96 the rupee came under severe strain and the RBI undertook large sales of forex which resulted in a liquidity bind. Initially, the RBI eased the liquidity pressures by injecting large funds into the money market. This encouraged market players to borrow in the money market at relatively low rates and remit the funds abroad. To tackle this problem the RBI withdrew its entire money market support at one stroke and call money rates rose to stratospheric levels; the capital outflows stopped and pressure on the rupee eased. This enabled the RBI to quickly restore normalcy in the money market.

After a brief respite there was once again a speculative attack on the rupee. As a measure of confidence building, Rangarajan favoured a very gradual easing of reserve requirements while I advocated the tightening of reserve requirements. In retrospect it would appear that I was using the right analytical framework to derive faulty practical policies while Rangarajan dispensed with textbook solutions to work out correct practical policies.

Unfair Criticism of RBI Policies

It is indeed very unfortunate that Rangarajan was criticised for measures he used to stabilise the rupee and also curb inflation. The RBI was unfairly blamed for its tight monetary policy and the slowdown in output in 1997-98 was erroneously attributed to the RBI's monetary policy. Despite the Annual Report of June 1996 prominently showing the month-to-month liquidity movements in the very first Chapter of the Report which conclusively showed that the tightening was very temporary and over the year there was an injection and not a withdrawal of liquidity. Yet, analysts even today point to wrong RBI monetary policies as having contributed to the slowdown in activity in 1997-98. What was most hurtful was that when there was a change in the government, the new government formally attacked the RBI for an inappropriate monetary policy. Given the absence of any real autonomy for the RBI it is not fair for a new government to attack the RBI for policies the earlier government was four square behind the RBI. If one were to want to know how a government should stand by its central bank, there is the history of the then Finance Minister, Pranab Mukherjee's brilliant defence of the RBI in a Calling-Attention Motion in the Rajya Sabha in 1982. This should be mandatory reading for the critics of the RBI. I hope when the history of this period is written up it will record, in detail, Pranab Mukherjee's handling of the attack on the RBI. I think it is necessary to clarify certain personal issues.

Unfounded Rumours of Dissension in RBI Top Management

There were wild rumours in the RBI that I was contemplating resigning during 1995-96 as Rangarajan and I had different perceptions on reserve requirements. This is far from the truth. There were many occasions when we had different perceptions and in fact different views were encouraged. The problem was entirely different as the matter was one on which we had identical views!

When the call money rates reached extremely high levels the Ministry of Finance and the RBI had close consultations. Lenders, particularly financial institutions, were charging usurious rates of interest in the call money market. It was agreed that moral suasion should be used to persuade financial institutions, who were after all guests in the money market, to moderate their demands for high interest rates in the call money market. If the financial institutions were not amenable to moral suasion, action could be taken to debar them from the money market—at least for some time. I had been charged with the task of communicating our stand to the Top Management of all the financial institutions that they should not charge more than 25 per cent which was the rate charged on CRR defaults. Other than the Life Insurance Corporation (LIC), all financial institutions continued with their Shylockian tendencies and put their thumbs in the RBI's eyes. It has all along been known that financial institutions were the favourite sons of the government and we were unable to take any action. I had then formally submitted to the Governor that since I was the one who had persuaded the LIC not to charge high rates of interest that it would be incumbent on me to give the LIC a Japanese style public apology with due consequences. It was not any conflict with the Governor—in fact he had indicated that some penalty would be necessary if the financial institutions did not behave. It was a sense of our helplessness that I had offered to apologise to the LIC. Governor Rangarajan felt that he was fully committed to the line of action taken by us and hence it was for me to decide what sort of action both of us should take. Suffice it to say that I closed the matter.

RBI's Reservations on PPP Agreements

There is yet another incident which needs to be mentioned. While the public private partnership (PPP) agreements for the power sector were being signed, a foreign party insisted that if the State Electricity Boards defaulted on payments, the state governments would make the payment and if the state governments failed to make the payment the Central government would make the payment. Furthermore the requirement was that if the Central government failed to make the payment the RBI would make the payment. We had indicated that RBI was not in the game of giving guarantees and moreover, it would be inappropriate for RBI to sign a document which would refer to a Central government default on a payment and our considered advice was that the Central government should also refuse to sign such a clause. The matter should end with the Central government agreeing to make up any shortfall in payment. The upshot of all this was the highest authorities in the country indicated that these clauses should be signed as demanded and that we should make up our mind. Sad to say, RBI was made to sign a document which put the Central government in very poor light, especially as the Central government was also signing this document. Such conflicts were the exception and on many occasions when the RBI took a stand contrary to the government, the government was so enlightened that it would accept the judgement of the RBI.

Concluding Observations

I would submit that all the achievements of Governor Rangarajan pale into insignificance when we consider the quintessential Rangarajan, the true scholar, who would encourage those working under him to articulate their views even if they were diametrically opposed to his own view. How many Governors would tell the Finance Minister why his Deputy disagrees with him and would encourage his Deputy to articulate his viewpoint before the Finance Minister? For the benefit of history it should be made known that during the Rangarajan era there was unprecedented symbiosis between RBI and the top officials of the Ministry of Finance and debates on various issues would be truly in academic spirit. Illustratively, Governor Rangarajan and the Chief Economic Adviser Shankar Acharya would be in agreement on a certain issue while the Finance Secretary Montek Singh Ahluwalia and the present writer would take a different line.

In the final analysis, what would take precedence—Rangarajan's achievements in the RBI which got him recognition as one of the best central bankers in the world or his academic achievements or his unusual human trait of helping those who hurt him? Generations to come will scarce believe that Plato's 'Philosopher King' walked the corridors of the Reserve Bank of India in flesh and blood.

2 Transparency and Autonomy Issues in Monetary Policy

K. Kanagasabapathy and
Balamurali Radhakrishnan

Introduction

Secrecy was the hallmark of central banking particularly with regard to monetary policy during the period of financial repression, swaying over most countries till about mid-1970s. This was followed by the opening up and liberalisation of the economies, and integration of financial markets. Efficient financial markets are characterised by less uncertainty or greater stability. That can best be achieved by greater transparency in public policies, such as monetary policy. As central banks also operate through market-based instruments, transparency has gained in importance during the past two decades.

Transparency has two dimensions: first is the transparent policy and institutional framework which are emphasised in the IMF's 'Code of Good Practices on Transparency in Monetary Policy'; and second is the transparent communication policy and practices which help in steering market expectations and enable achieving policy objectives more effectively.

Independence or autonomy of the central bank at least at the operational level emerged as a prerequisite for transparency as also for ensuring accountability of the central bank. Furthermore, transparency in public policy is an important defining feature of any democracy, where the governance structure is ultimately accountable to the public. But, applying these principles to monetary policy, an important arm of public policy, assumes a different dimension. The relationship between the government and the central bank in these matters is subtle in an emerging market country like India with multiple public policy objectives. However, if a central bank is not provided with enough space for its independent operations, it cannot be transparent as well.

In the above backdrop, this paper focuses upon the mainstream views on transparency and autonomy in the formulation and conduct of monetary policy, including those emanating out of the IMF Code. It develops a novel framework for understanding the communication processes behind transparency and the scope for improving transparency in the form of an adapted 'Johari Window (JW)', which is essentially now used as a management concept of analysing interpersonal and intergroup dynamics. It also undertakes a broad interpretation of the Indian case, and makes an assessment and brings out the scope for further strengthening operational independence of the central bank and improving transparency practices. The paper concludes with a brief comment on post-financial crisis scenario.

Mainstream Views on Transparency and Autonomy

Most of the ideas pertaining to both transparency and autonomy of central banks emerged since mid-1970s. Governments' concern about growth and unemployment hindered the central banks to choose inflation controlling monetary policies in the 1970s. As it was highly unlikely for growth and unemployment to surpass its natural rate without having any harmful impact on the economy in terms of increased inflation rate, such influence by the governments in monetary policy decision-making ultimately resulted in deteriorating price levels in those countries. Therefore, separating the monetary policy decision-making authorities from the government and giving them more incentives to control inflation were considered as major steps to restore the higher inflation prevailing in those days to the normal level (Crowe and Meade, 2007). However, giving independence to the central banks held them more accountable for their policy actions than before, and this higher accountability requirement led to improvement in transparency practices.

The central bank is said to have greater independence when its legal mandate specifies a clearly defined objective for monetary policy, and it should have a complete freedom to set polices that cannot be overridden by the government. Following a widespread inflation in 1970s, largely driven by time inconsistency problem, central banks were given the responsibility to frame inflation-fighting policies, although those policies were perceived unpopular. With the operational independence, central banks were enabled to create policies that were not vulnerable to short-term political gains, and have the responsibility to devise policies that are consistent with its mandated objectives. It was also obliged to communicate its policy stance and its strategies to achieve the mandated objectives to the government or public.

The more transparent rule-based policy frameworks such as monetary targeting and later inflation targeting necessitated clear communication from the central bank in a market oriented environment. These changes in policy frameworks in a way strengthened transparency practices of central banks. Overall, among other things, central banks' reputation for controlling inflation, coupled with their frequent communication practices with the general public about their long-term policy objective, played a vital role in helping them curb inflationary expectations (Mishkin, 2000).

With financial innovations making monetary targeting approach ineffective, most central banks shifted to adoption of the inflation-targeting approach. As central banks were subject to institutional commitment under this framework, there have been tremendous improvements in the operational independence, which ultimately led to increased transparency. Generally, it was believed that inflation-targeting and money growth targeting central banks are more transparent than exchange rate targeting central banks (Geraats, 2005).

While central banks in the advanced economies showed a plausible upward progress in the transparency practices, those in emerging and developing economies also attained greater transparency. Interestingly, rise in transparency is not only pertained to inflation-targeting framework but also to other monetary frameworks. Geraats conceived five aspects of monetary policy transparency: (i) political transparency, (ii) economic transparency, (iii) procedural transparency, (iv) policy transparency, and (v) operational transparency. Each aspect of the monetary transparency has seen a varying degree of improvement over a period of time (Geraats, 2005).

Political transparency concerns openness about policy objectives and institutional arrangements that clarify the motives of monetary policymakers. Economic transparency concerns economic information used by central banks to make monetary policy decisions. Procedural transparency refers to the manner in which prevailing economic scenario is translated into the monetary policy actions. Policy transparency describes how quickly the central bank communicates its policy decision to the general public, and clarification about the monetary policy decisions. Operational transparency refers to the openness about the unanticipated shocks to the monetary transmission process. Depending upon the institutional structure and framework, the extent of these transparencies could vary from country to country.

The IMF Code

Since late 1990s, the IMF's Code has emerged as an important benchmark for assessing transparency in monetary policy. These codes incidentally cover aspects relating to autonomy as well, implicitly bringing out the fact that these two are intertwined. These codes essentially focus upon the policy and institutional framework.

The Code has four broad sets of principles. The first requirement is clarity on roles, responsibilities and objectives of the central bank. This broadly covers legal clarity on objectives, institutional framework for monetary policy and disclosure of the institutional relationship between monetary policy and fiscal operations.

The second is openness in the process of formulating and reporting policy decisions. This covers disclosure of the framework, the instruments and targets used by the central bank, periodic reporting of macroeconomic situations, timely explanation of changes in monetary policy settings, public consultation over the proposed changes and disclosure of regulations on data reporting by financial institutions. The third relates to public availability of information on monetary policy. And the fourth is accountability and assurances of integrity by the central bank.

Johari Window as a Framework for understanding Policy Transparency

Transparency can be viewed as the absence of information asymmetry between the central bank and other economic agents. Improved communication policy and practices help in reducing this asymmetry. Generally, central banks communicate policy objectives and strategies to achieve them, assessments of economic conditions, and rationale of its policy decisions. Communicating policy objectives and being transparent on policy strategy and assessment of economic outlook reduces uncertainty and thereby enhance policy effectiveness.

Central banks are either explicitly or implicitly, accountable to the outcome of their policy actions, and therefore, responsible to provide information on the progress of monetary policymaking. Also, when the actual inflation is deviated from the target value, the central bank is accountable to clarify the government or public on why it had happened. Further, it should be transparent on the intended policy strategies to converge the deviated value with the target. To provide clarity on its decision-making, central banks should also publish information on their current assessment of the economic conditions and outlook.

Transparency is thus closely linked to communication between the central bank and market participants and also with the government if policies are framed jointly in consultation with the government. There is a general perception that the central bank knows everything and they should share the information. But, communication in this regard should be viewed as a two-way process. Thus, apart from communication from the central bank to market participants, the process should encompass also the consultation with and feedback from the latter in a collaborative fashion. The fact is that in most of the circumstances, the central bank is as much wise or ignorant as others on matters of understanding economic relationships, emerging scenarios and the impact of policy instruments on target variables. Therefore, overall transparency gains can be improved by expanding the area of openness by sharing information and expanding the scope of communication channels between the central bank and outside stakeholders.

The authors feel that there is a need to explore the possibility of extending the management concept of 'Johari Window (JW)' to transparency in public policies with particular reference to monetary policy. The JW is named from its creators, Joseph Luft and Harry Ingham who presented the window as a device for building self-awareness in relationship at Western Training Laboratories in 1955. This concept talks about the openness of a person in a two-way matrix of from/to 'self' and 'others' consisting of four quadrants.

The JW's commonly used four quadrants from the point of view of self and others are:

A: Open area: What is known by the person about him/herself and is also known to others.

B: Blind area: What is unknown by the person about him/herself but which others are aware.

C: Hidden area: What the person know about him/herself but not disclosed to others.

D: Dark/mystery area: What is unknown by the person about him/himself and is also not known to others.

To improve the group dynamics and strengthen the performance as a group, the open area needs to be enlarged by sharing and disclosing information about self to others, and getting feedback and collaborating with others thereby reducing both hidden and blind areas and to the extent possible even the unknown area by exploring and learning through experience and research. The idea behind this is that each person having a strong mutual understanding with the team is far more effective than a team whose members have large hidden, blind and/or dark areas.

After going through some of the references relating to both the changes in communication policies of central banks and the JW, the authors are convinced that the JW framework will be a useful framework in assessing transparency practices in respect of monetary policy. Adapting the JW to the central bank as the 'self' and market participants and other stakeholders as 'others', the framework for monetary policy transparency can be depicted as in Figure 2.1.

Figure 2.1

Framework for Monetary Policy Transparency: Data, Information & Processes

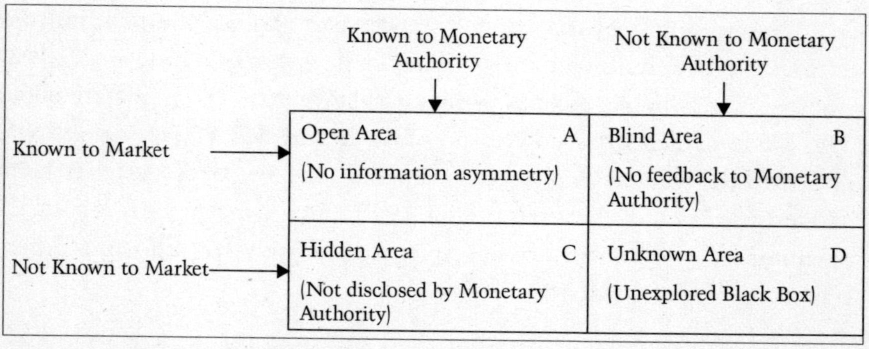

Source: Adapted from Johari Window.

The manner in which communication process can improve the area of openness can be depicted as in Figure 2.2

Figure 2.2

Enhancing Transparency through Collaboration/Feedback, Disclosure/ Communication and Learning from Shocks/Research

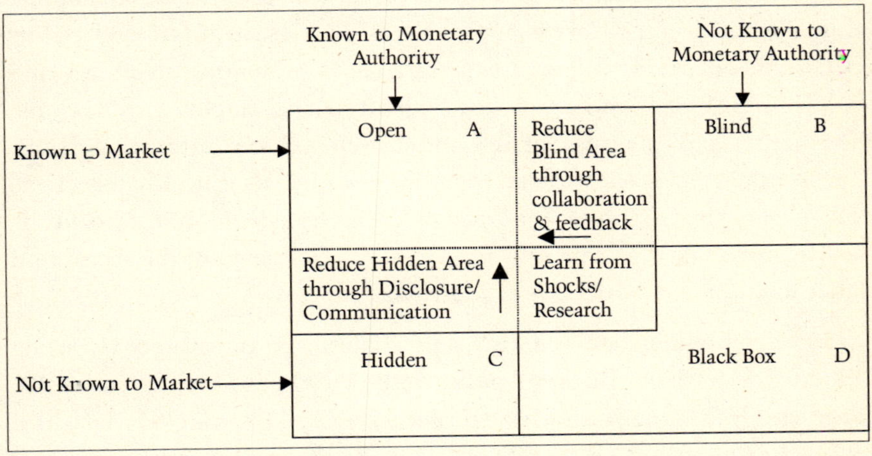

Source: Adapted from Johari Window.

The beauty of this concept is that performance enhancement comes from all as a group. For instance, in the case of monetary policy, the objectives such as price stability and growth are of interest to everyone, except that players like the central bank and the government have a larger say between the two, because of their institutional status and responsibilities. As they are accountable to achievement of policy objectives, it is in their best interest to extend the area of openness in the JW. This way of strengthening group dynamics can be extended to any area of public policy and to any number of stakeholders with a common goal to be achieved. The Right to Information Act goes a step further by making disclosure compulsory under most circumstances from public authorities, even as the public authorities have the right as regulators to obtain private information in public interest. In the area of inter-regulatory coordination also, this concept can provide an elegant framework within which openness in communication can be established and overall regulatory system can be made more effective.

A Broad Interpretation of the Indian Case

The policy and procedures of the Reserve Bank of India (RBI) evolved in the post-reform period since 1991 have ensured gradual expansion of the open area of JW. RBI has, over time, developed a communications policy suited to its objectives, the important principles of which are: articulating the hierarchy of objectives in a given context in a transparent manner, emphasising a consultative approach as well as autonomy in policy operations; anchoring inflation expectations by promoting credibility and understanding of monetary policy; explaining its stance with reasons, information and analysis but refraining from explicit forward guidance. The speeches, press releases and interviews of officials generally reflect the principles of the communication policy. Whatever is communicated to the media can be taken to represent the views or statements of the institution rather than the personal views of individuals.

The communication and disclosure policies and transparent operating procedures within the bank have reduced the hidden area in JW considerably. The consultative process at every stage introduced since 1990s has resulted in constant feedback on policy measures and instruments reducing the blind area to a great extent. On the impact of RBI's communication on financial markets, the most notable contribution has been in generating a better understanding, debates and sensitivities among the market participants and analysts, of the issues involved in money, finance and macro-stability. This process has been critical for India partly because the legacy of a planned economy required unlearning as well as relearning and partly because the financial sector reform process as well as the context has been somewhat more unique to India than in many other emerging market economies (Reddy, 2008). And, strengthening of data/information base combined with research and survey activities help throw more light at least on some parts of the dark area enhancing the understanding of the transmission mechanism of monetary policy in a better manner. An illustrative list is provided in Table 2.1

Table 2.1

Improvements in Transparency Practices Enlarging the Open Area of JW

A. Communication and Disclosure

- Publication of more information on central bank's operations and also money and financial markets (the RBI weekly statistical supplement now runs into eight pages from only four earlier).
- More detailed pronouncement of policy with clear statement of stance, after careful assessment of macroeconomic and monetary developments. A detailed supplement to policy statement assessing macroeconomic and monetary developments.
- More frequent interventions in the market.
- Speeches of top management and press statements.
- Assessment of downside as also upside biases to projections.

B. Operating Procedures

- Financial Markets Committee to monitor and review day-to-day market developments.
- Resource management discussion with select banks.
- Consultation with Economists/Media.
- Consultation with industry/trade/other associations representing various stakeholders.
- Internal working groups on major policy issues and sharing of reports with the public.

C. Consultative Process

- Technical Advisory Committee on financial markets.
- Technical Advisory Committee on monetary policy.
- Inter-institutional coordination with other regulators.
- Coordination committees with the government, such as on debt and cash management.
- Regulatory changes through consultative process accommodating comments from market players and public.
- Extensive interactions with multilateral institutions and other central banks.

D. Strengthening of Information/Database

- Business confidence and expectations surveys.
- Inflation expectations survey.
- Survey of forecasters.
- Surveys on lead indicators.

Transparency with Regard to Objectives and Targets

In the formulation and conduct of monetary policy, the two major building blocks are the objectives of monetary policy and the intermediate targets chosen for attainment of those objectives. For ensuring transparency, these objectives must be clearly stated and preferably laid down in the central banking legislation. There was strictly speaking no monetary policy in India, as is conventionally known, but only a kind of monetary regulation styled as 'controlled expansion' with a plethora of credit controls and directions till mid-1980s. There were bi-seasonal credit policies and the credit flow was regulated according to plan priorities. Credit to government was ensured through statutory liquidity requirements for banks and portfolio restrictions on investment and insurance institutions.

In a broad sense, the objectives of monetary policy can be no different from the overall objectives of economic policy. The broad objectives of monetary policy in India have been: a) to maintain a reasonable degree of price stability; and b) to help accelerate the rate of economic growth. The emphasis as between the two objectives changes depending upon the prevailing economic condition (Rangarajan, 1997).

While the twin objectives of monetary policy in India, *viz.*, price stability and ensuring adequate flow of credit stay put over time, a precise statement of these objectives and a framework for achieving these objectives evolved only since mid-1980s following the Chakravarty Committee's Report (1985). C. Rangarajan who was at the helm of affairs at that time in the RBI had been instrumental in giving a shape to the monetary targeting approach recommended by the committee, by providing a framework designed in terms of interaction and relationships between the three parameters, namely money, output and prices. While this framework was evolved when India remained mostly a closed economy, the design continues to find relevance through the period of multiple indicators approach operative since 1998 is a testimony to the robustness of the design. The instruments used to achieve the objectives including liquidity management practices however have undergone a radical shift from direct to indirect and from administered to market oriented over the post-reform period since early 1990s. These changes were also spearheaded in early 1990s when C. Rangarajan had a second stint as Governor of the RBI.

Of the various objectives, price stability is perhaps the one that can be pursued most effectively by monetary policy. It is the price stability which provides the appropriate environment in which growth can occur and social justice can be ensured. In a society in which a significantly large proportion of the population is in the unorganised sector, with no protection against price rise, inflation militates against social justice.

The policy design evolved by the Chakravarty Committee recognised that money had an impact on both output and prices. The process of money creation is a process of credit creation. The credit given to government and the private sector has a favourable impact on output. But, at the same time the increased money supply raises demand with an upward pressure on prices. The output effect and the price effect must be taken together to judge the overall effect on the economy. The choice of M_3 or broad money as an intermediate target variable had the advantage that in balance sheet terms, it had a direct relationship with the expansion of credit. Even though the year to year variations were not precisely captured by this model, the relationship held reasonably well over a period of time. Even if money supply accommodated to changes in prices, there must be a limit to this accommodation if the spiraling effect is to be avoided.

The monetary policy documents irrespective of the change in approach to multiple indicators continue to provide indicative projections for output growth, desirable level of inflation and the required growth in M_3. The trend in these three parameters with reference to projections and outcomes is presented in Table 2.2 and Figure 2.3. The trend shows that the RBI could rein in inflation in the range of about 5-7 per cent in the post-reform period, except post-financial crisis recently, as against 6 per cent which was conceived by C. Rangarajan (1996) as the threshold level of inflation for India to maximise output in the long run. The inflation objective in the current decade has further been made conservative to 4 per cent which was indicated by the Chakravarty Committee and further to 3 per cent over the long period.

Seeds for Central Bank Autonomy

The issues relating to autonomy were intertwined with transparency. The 1980s posed the significant problem of created money. The five-year plans accorded a role to monetised deficit for plan financing but its quantum was to be limited to the extent it was non-inflationary. The single most important factor that influenced the conduct of monetary policy since 1970s had been the phenomenal increase in the reserve money contributed primarily by the RBI credit to government. The significance and rationale

Table 2.2

Major Monetary Policy Parameters: Projections and Outcomes since 1983-84

Year (April-March)	Annual Increases in Per cent								
	Real GDP			WPI Threshold Inflation			M_3 (Broad Money)		
	P	A	A-P	P	A	A-P	P	A	A-P
1983-84	-	7.9	7.9	-	7.6	-	Lower than 16.6% (i.e., 1982-83)	18.2	-
1984-85	-	4.0	4.0	Curb inflationary expectations	6.0	-	Growth of overall liquidity and primary money creation to be kept below that in 1983-84	19.0	-
1985-86	Same order as in 1984-85	4.2	-	Avoid resurgence of inflation	4.8	-	Lower than 1984-85	16.0	-
1986-87	Somewhat higher than 1985-86	4.3	-	The rate of inflation to be kept under check	5.1	-	M_3 growth to be contained below the high annual average level of the previous four years i.e., 17.5%	18.6	-
1987-88	5.0	3.5	-1.5	Avoid re-emergence of inflationary pressures	10.7	-	M_3 growth will be below expansion in 1986-87 i.e., 18.6%	16.0	-

contd...

...contd...

Year (April-March)	*Annual Increases in Per cent*								
	Real GDP			*WPI Threshold Inflation*			*M_3 (Broad Money)*		
	P	*A*	*A-P*	*P*	*A*	*A-P*	*P*	*A*	*A-P*
1988-89	-	10.2	10.2	-	5.7	-	M_3 growth to be below the average for the previous three years i.e., 16.9%	17.8	-
1989-90	4.5	6.1	1.6	-	9.1	-	M_3 growth to be contained at a level lower than the average of the last four years i.e., 17.1%	19.4	-
1990-91	Around 5.0	5.3	0.3	-	12.1	-	To bring about a sharp reduction of M_3 growth by about 4 percentage points over previous year i.e., 15.4%	15.1	-
1991-92	4.0 (3.0)	1.4	-2.6	7.0 (max 9.0)	13.6	6.6	14.0(13.0) [1]	19.3	5.3
1992-93	3.5[2]	5.4	1.9	8.0	7.0	-1.0	10.4	14.8	4.4
1993-94	5.0	5.7	0.7	- [3]	10.8	-	12.0(14.0)	18.4	6.4
1994-95	N.A.[4] (5.5)	6.4	-	7.2[5](6.8)	10.4	3.2	14-15(16)	22.4	7.9
1995-96	5.5(well above 5.5)	7.3	1.8	8.0	4.5	-3.5	15.5	13.6	-1.9
1996-97	6.0	8.0	2.0	6.0	5.4	-0.6	15.5-16.0	16.2	0.5
1997-98	6.0-7.0	4.3	-2.2	6.0	4.3	-1.7	15.0-15.5	18.0	2.8
1998-99	6.5-7.0(6.0)	6.7	-0.1	5.0-6.0	5.4	-0.1	15.0-15.5	19.4	4.2

contd...

...contd...

Year (April-March)	Annual Increases in Per cent								
	Real GDP			WPI Threshold Inflation			M_3 (Broad Money)		
	P	A	A-P	P	A	A-P	P	A	A-P
1999-2000	6.0-7.0	6.4	-0.1	5.0	5.6	0.6	15.5-16.0	14.6	-1.2
2000-01	6.5-7.0(6.0-6.5)	4.4	-2.4	4.5	6.4	1.9	15.0	16.8	1.8
2001-02	6.0-6.5(5.0-6.0)	5.8	-0.5	5.0	1.8	-3.2	14.5	14.1	-0.4
2002-03	6.0-6.5 (5.0-5.5)	3.8	-2.5	4.0	6.0	2.0	14.0	14.7	0.7
2003-04	6.0 (6.5-7.0) with an upward bias	8.5	2.5	5.0-5.5 (4.0-4.5)	4.8	-0.5	14.0	16.7	2.7
2004-05	6.5–7.0(6.00–6.50)	7.5	0.8	5.0(6.5)	5.3	0.3	14.0	12.0	-2.0
2005-06	7.0(7.0–7.5)	9.5	2.5	5.0–5.5	3.9	-1.4	14.5	21.1	6.6
2006-07	7.5–8.0(8.0)	9.7	2.0	5.0–5.5	6.6	1.4	15.0	21.7	6.7
2007-08	8.5	9.0	0.5	5.0 (4.0–4.5)	7.5	2.5	17.0–17.5	21.4	4.2
2008-09	8.0–8.5 (7.5–8.0)	6.7	-1.6	5.5 (7.0)	1.2	-4.3	16.5–17.0	18.6	1.9
2009-10	7.5	7.4	-0.1	8.5	11.0	2.5	16.5	16.7	0.2
2010-11*	8.5	-		5.5	-		17.0	-	-

Notes: The Actual real GDP data has been revised by the CSO; M_3 data has been revised by RBI from the year 1999-2000 onwards.

* - Based on Second Quarter Review of Monetary Policy 2010-11.

P= Projected; A=Actual. Figures given in brackets are as reset in October Statements of Policy. Differences between actual and projected have been calculated with reference to April statement and to the midpoint, where a range is indicated.

1. Reset based on fresh information and acceleration in inflation rate to 8.9 per cent up to 21 September 1991.
2. Projection given in October statement.
3. No projection for inflation given; some further moderation in inflation rate was indicated.
4. No projection for growth rate was indicated in April; in October, an implicit rate was given.
5. A reduction in inflation rate by 4 percentage points was envisaged.

Source: (Data for the period 1985-86 to 1990-91) Mohanty, Deepak (2010). "Monetary Policy Framework in India: Experience with Multiple – Indicators Approach", Speech delivered at the Conference of the Orissa Economic Association, February.

Figure 2.3

Monetary Projections and Outcomes

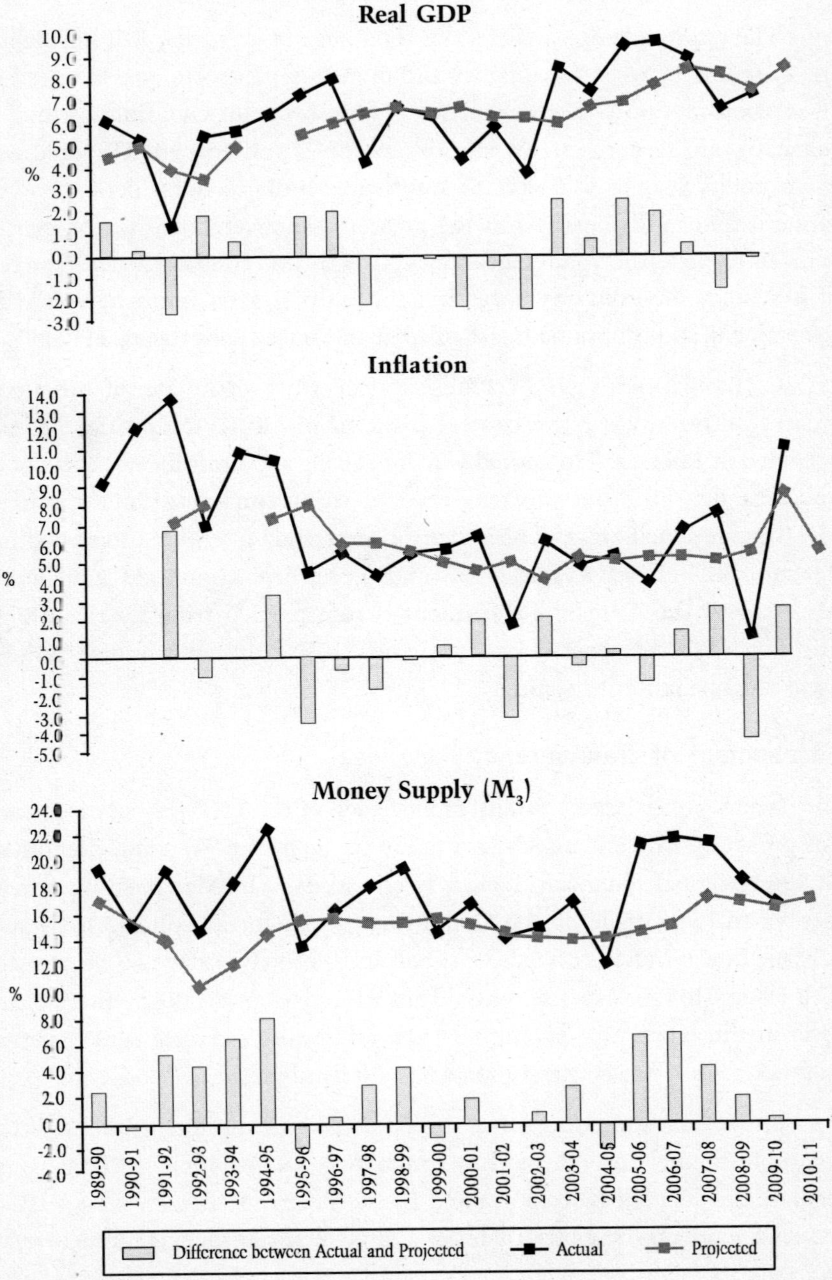

for monetary targeting in the Indian context essentially arose from the unique institutional arrangements that were prevalent for financing the budget deficit.

The growing budget deficits and their absorption by the RBI highlighted the close link between fiscal policy and monetary policy but also the need for close coordination between the two. The essence of coordination lied in reaching an agreement on the extent of expansion in RBI credit to government year to year. That would set a limit to fiscal deficit and its monetisation and thereby provide greater maneuverability to the central bank to regulate the volume of money. It is in this context the introduction of a system of monetary targeting mutually agreed upon between the government and central bank assumed significance (Rangarajan, 1988).

C. Rangarajan (1993) came out forcefully in favour of procuring greater autonomy for the central bank in his Kutty Memorial Lecture delivered at Kolkata. This paved way for setting the limit for net issue of ad hoc treasury bills and putting an end to automatic monetisation of government deficits in 1994-95 that ultimately led to elimination of ad hoc treasury bills effective April 1997 and fixing limits for ways and means advances to the Central government. Later, participation by the RBI in primary issues of government securities was withdrawn under the new fiscal responsibility legislation.

Assessment of Transparency Practices

India's compliance to transparency code of the IMF was assessed early this decade by IMF and an advisory group set up by the 'Standing Committee on International Financial Standards and Codes'. In March 2009, a fresh assessment was made by the Committee on Financial Sector Assessment (CFSA). In the Indian context, legal and institutional clarity can be assessed with respect to four aspects: central bank objectives; overriding powers of the government; powers of appointment and removal of a central bank governor and the relationship between monetary and fiscal policy.

The legislation concerning the objectives of monetary policy is the preamble to the Reserve Bank of India Act, 1934 which reads as: '...to regulate the issue of Bank notes and the keeping of reserves with a view to securing monetary stability in India and generally to operate the currency and credit system of the country to its advantage.' The preamble lays down the broad objective for the central bank as a whole, but not the specific objectives of monetary policy.

The multiple objectives—of maintaining price stability, ensuring credit flow to productive sectors, supporting growth, maintaining orderly conditions in financial markets, and creating an environment of financial stability—have evolved over time, thanks to the erudition of RBI governors, the emphasis on each aspect varying according to the situation. While these expanding and varying objectives cannot be considered inconsistent with the preamble, it is doubtful that there is sufficient legal clarity on all of them. For instance, regarding financial stability, there is no accepted definition. It is also unclear as to who should be responsible for financial stability.

The second issue relates to government's ability to issue directions to the central bank. The law is very strong here. The government can issue directions in the public interest in consultation with the RBI governor. While no such recorded direction is evident, the central bank is vulnerable to being overridden by the government.

As a peer-reviewer for the CFSA panel report, Sir Andrew Large considered this issue from several angles. The override can be prompted by a conflict over objectives, targets or a policy decision. In the case of the targets—if such targets were to be introduced—there would need to be a transparent framework. This might well include a situation where the government sets the target itself. If the government overrides actual policy decisions, it would undermine the role of the central bank, and effectively transfer to the government or political arena the setting of policy itself.

Sir Large concludes that transparency of process is the best antidote to 'unwarranted' government override. This would reduce the perceived need for such override; if the government chooses to override through means other than the process laid down by the legislation that would raise questions about its motives.

Reddy (2008) observed that the government happens to be a significant player in many emerging market economies, especially in the financial sector. It is quite possible that there are communications or signals, if not directions, from the Ministry of Finance often on issues relating to monetary policy or banking, a sector predominantly government-owned. If these are consistent with those of the central bank, they reinforce the central bank policies, but if these are divergent, it poses a dilemma for central bank communication and to that extent a central bank may be constrained in freely articulating its policies.

In the interest of strengthening transparency and improving the autonomy of the central bank, it would be appropriate if a legislative review is initiated by the proposed Legislative Reforms Commission announced in the budget for 2010-11. The review should cover the four dimensions that form the crux of the autonomy and transparency debate: clarity on objectives, overriding powers of the government, appointment and removal of governors and institutional relationship between monetary and fiscal operations.

Policy Independence

The RBI is certainly not independent in a *de jure* sense because the government enjoys overriding powers in the statute. It can remove the head of the institution without assigning any reason, it can supersede the governing board, and it can issue directions on policy matters. But, *de facto*, the RBI seemed to have gained a lot more independence in operating monetary policy and choosing the timing and extent of applying its tools and freely articulating and communicating with the public. Since it is legally subordinated to the government, the RBI can however, obviously enjoy independence only to the extent that government chooses to allow it, implicitly or explicitly. The central bank, therefore, seems to be independent within a boundary set by the government; but the problem is that there is no defined or recognisable boundary and, worse, it seems to shift from time to time.

Since government is responsible for the overall economic policy, it may be legitimate for them to talk on any policy matter. But, since the RBI is entrusted with the function of monetary policy, public pronouncements from the government on these matters should be restrained and not make it appear as if the central bank's policies are framed under the directions of the government.

India is an exception in having multiple inflationary indicators and none of them reflecting the commonly accepted representative consumer or retail price index (RPI), nor the producer price index (PPI). Nevertheless, for policy purposes, the wholesale price index (WPI) inflation has been generally used for a variety of reasons such as large coverage of commodities and high frequency release of data despite the index being biased to commodity prices without taking into account any services. In the current scenario of services sector growth, this index is seen less and less representative of inflation in India. Therefore, one priority for the government should be to evolve a representative consumer price index (CPI) as a measure of inflation.

Inflation expectations play an important role in shaping the inflationary consequences of economic activity and it is fully recognised by the central bank if we go by policy statements. The RBI has done a yeomen service by initiating inflation expectation surveys since about 2005. While these surveys are thoroughly analysed by the central bank researchers and transparently published, and contain very useful information, they carry the rider that they in no way reflect the views and forecasts of the RBI. These surveys of inflation expectations however, provide useful directional information on near-term inflationary pressures and also supplement other economic indicators to get a better indication of future inflation. The movement of the inflation expectations in recent surveys shows that the future inflation expectations are usually higher than the current inflation. This is indicative of continued firming up of inflationary expectations. RBI should evolve ways of incorporating the survey results in gauging pressures on inflation expectations.

Overall, one gets an impression that transparency issues of monetary policy may need a review even if the review leads to maintenance of the status quo. As regards the framework, the monetary targeting approach replaced the earlier credit planning in mid-1980s. This approach gave way to the multiple indicators approach since April 1998, which had its sway for more than a decade. The time is perhaps ripe now to take a relook in the context of evolving views in the aftermath of the global financial turmoil.

Concluding Observations: Post-Financial Crisis Scenario

The management of the financial crisis has given rise to apprehensions that it might have compromised central bank autonomy *vis-*

a-vis their respective governments. The governments and central banks acted in unison in laying the road to recovery after the global crisis intensified in mid-September 2008. The US authorities, believing that the Great Depression of the 1930s was accentuated by the inaction of central banks, were not prepared to repeat that mistake and took the reins of the Fed to follow a pump-priming policy. This has given rise to a debate on whether the central banks have lost their independence. Some efforts have arguably been taken by governments, for example in the US, to make inroads into the powers of central banks. There is a sudden realisation that the Fed operations are shrouded in secrecy and should be closely audited by the Congress.

In a recent post-financial crisis paper, Geraats (2010) has argued that information effect of communication is harmful when dealing with the bank's liquidity problems. For instance, when a central bank discloses a weakness in a bank's liquidity position, private sector tends to show abrupt response to this information disclosure, and ultimately undermine that particular bank's stability, leading to its collapse. However, if the problems in the liquidity position of banks are communicated periodically, private sector can analyse the actual problem precisely and likely to show a prudent behaviour.

At the height of the financial crisis, central banks unveiled many unconventional measures primarily to support money market operations, which had been hit hardly by the sub-prime crisis. Geraats finds that central bank communications can be highly effective under such circumstances and that unconventional monetary policy measures need not harm the credibility of the central bank.

When we talk of central bank autonomy or independence, it implies that some delegated space is provided to the central bank implicitly or explicitly by law or otherwise, in the public policy space, so that conflicts of interest are avoided.

A few other factors have also weakened the case for central bank independence, post-crisis. The whole idea of 'independence' gained prominence since late 1970s in the context of the objective of price stability. The pursuit of an explicit inflation-targeting regime required operational independence in the use of policy instruments, particularly in interest rate setting. Along with this came the committee approach to decision-making, and an accountability framework for central bank operations.

This rigid framework delayed central bank response to the crisis. For instance, the initial response of Bank of England was not adequate, when the first symptoms of inter-bank money market failure surfaced in mid-2007. The failure to respond swiftly to the Northern Rock debacle is a case in point. Second, with separation of regulation and supervision of financial institutions, either the information flow across regulators was missing or there was stiff resistance from central banks acting as lenders-of-last-resort (LOLR) and bailing out firms. Third, there were holes in the regulation of financial markets and since these markets operated across countries, with globalisation and free capital flows, the cross-border impact could not be adequately captured by any single central bank and required action in unison. It was against this backdrop that, when Lehman Brothers failed, Europe's major central banks banded together with their counterparts in Japan, the US and Canada to inject more dollars into global money markets in a bid to stave off the growing global financial crisis.

This involved close cooperation between the governments and central banks as also among different regulators, in particular of securities markets. These interventions and the coordinated policy actions that followed were exceptional by any historical standard.

The above experience has resulted in relegation of the goal of price stability, no doubt an important one, in favour of financial stability. But, the definition of the financial stability objective, and the question of where the accountability for it should rest are matters of debate now. The institutional framework for attaining financial stability and the kind of independence to be accorded to all stakeholders in achieving this objective should be examined in the light of the recent global experience.

That the government should make inroads into whatever independence the central banks are left with does not appeal as a desirable solution. In a recent note, the IMF has urged that the independence of central banks should be restored in the interest of achieving price stability as a primary goal. Basically, any regulator should be free of political interference in its day-to-day operations, once its roles are defined. On the other hand, the kind of operational independence accorded to central banks in the context of maintaining a single goal of price stability under a rigid framework also needs to be revisited.

In the recent crisis, treasury took an upper hand in advanced countries, and that was in larger public interest. It is nevertheless clear that treasuries also acted through the central banks. But, this should not set a new phase of treasury dominance or fiscal dominance over monetary policy.

References

Amato, D., S. Morris and H.S. Shin (2002). "Communication and Monetary Policy", *Oxford Review of Economic Policy* 18(4). UK: Oxford University Press.

Bernanke, S. (2010). "Central Bank Independence, Transparency, and Accountability", Speech delivered at the Institute for Monetary and Economic Studies International Conference. Tokyo: Bank of Japan.

Blinder, Alan S. M. Ehrmann, J. De Haan, M. Fratzscher and David-Jan Jansen (2008). "Central Bank Communication and Monetary Policy: A Survey of Theory and Evidence", *NBER Working Paper* 13932. Cambridge: National Bureau of Economic Research.

Crowe, C. and E. Meade (2007). "The Evolution of Central Bank Governance around the World". *The Journal of Economic Perspectives* 21(4): 69-90. Fall.

Cruijsen, van der A.B. (2008). "Optimal Central Bank Transparency", *DNB Working Paper* 178. The Netherlands: De Nederlandsche Bank NV.

Dincer, N. and B. Eichengreen. (2009). "Central Bank Transparency: Causes, Consequences, and Updates", *NBER Working Paper* 14791. Cambridge: National Bureau of Economic Research.

Freedman, C. and D. Laxton (2009). "Inflation Targeting Pillars: Transparency and Accountability". *IMF Working Paper* No.09/262. Washington: International Monetary Fund.

Geraats, M. (2002). *Central Bank Transparency*. Cambridge: University of Cambridge.

———. (2005). *Transparency of Monetary Policy: Theory and Practice*. Cambridge: University of Cambridge.

———. (2009). *Trends in Monetary Policy Transparency*. Europe: The CESifo Group.

———. (2010). "Talking Numbers: Central Bank Communications on Monetary Policy and Financial Stability". Paper prepared for the 5th ECB Statistics Conference on *Central Bank Statistics: What did the Financial Crisis Change?*

Geraats, M. and C.W. Eijffinger (2005). *How Transparent are Central Banks?*. Cambridge: University of Cambridge.

Gai and Shin (2003). "Transparency and Financial Stability", Prepared for the *Financial Stability Review*. London: Bank of England.

Luft, J. (1999). *The Johari Window: A Graphic Model of Awareness and Interpersonal Relations*. Dennard Clendenin. NCORE Conference Workshop. Memphis, Tennessee

Mishkin, S. (2000). "From Monetary Targeting to Inflation Targeting: Lessons from the Industrialised Countries", Prepared for the Bank of Mexico Conference, *Stabilisation and Monetary Policy: The International Experience*. Mexico City. November 14-15.

Papademos, L. (2008). "Monetary Policy Communication and Effectiveness", Speech delivered at the *Annual Meeting of the Allied Social Science Associations*. New Orleans.

Rafferty, M.C. and M. Tomljanovich (2001). "Central Bank Transparency and Market Efficiency: An Econometric Analysis", *Journal of Economics and Finance* 26(2), Summer 2002 .

Raje, Nitisha (2010). *Monitoring Economic Indicators for Monetary Policy: Some Data Gaps*, IGIDR Seminar Paper (*mimeo*).

Rangarajan, C. (1988). "Issues in Monetary Management", *Presidential Address*. Indian Economic Association.

———. (1993) "Autonomy of Central Banks", Tenth Kutty Memorial Lecture, *Perspectives on Central Banking*. Reserve Bank of India.

———. (1996). "Monetary Policy and Price Stability", Address at the Econometric Society's Regional Conference at New Delhi, *Perspectives on Central Banking*. Reserve Bank of India.

———. (1997). "Dimensions of Monetary Policy", *Ananthakrishnan Memorial Lecture*. Chennai.

Reddy, Y.V. (2001a). "Autonomy of the Central Bank, Changing Countours in India", Lectures on *Economic and Financial Sector Reforms in India*. Oxford University Press.

———. (2001b). "Communications Policy of the Reserve Bank of India", 150th Anniversary of the Reuters Group. Mumbai. August 28.

———. (2008). "The Virtues and Vices of Talking About Monetary Policy: Some Comments". Remarks at the 7th BIS Annual Conference at Luzern, Switzerland.

Reeves, R. and M. Sawicki (2005). "Do Financial Markets React to Bank of England Communication"?, *External MPC Unit Discussion Paper* No. 15. London: Bank of England.

Roca, M. (2010). "Transparency and Monetary Policy with Imperfect Common Knowledge", *IMF Working Paper*, No.10/91. April. Washington, DC.

Swanson, T. (2004). "Federal Reserve Transparency and Financial Market Forecasts of Short-Term Interest Rates", *2004 FEDS Papers*. Washington: Federal Reserve System.

Thornton, L. (2002). *Monetary Policy Transparency: Transparent About What?*. St. Louis: Federal Reserve Bank of St. Louis.

URISA Leadership Academy (n.d.). *Johari Window*. Alan Chapman Adaptation, Review and Code 1995-2006, based on Ingham and Luft's Original Johari Window Concept. *www.businessballs.com*

Woolford, M. (2005). *Central-Bank Communication and Policy Effectiveness*. Cambridge: University of Cambridge.

The views are authors' own. The authors express thanks to Shruti J. Pandey for helping in producing figures and tables and graphs. Some of the ideas expressed here appeared earlier in the columns of The *Hindu Business Line* by one of the authors.

3 Inflation, Macroeconomic Policy and Hunger

A Variation on a Theme by C. Rangarajan

Raghbendra Jha

... In just decades, you have achieved progress and development that took other nations centuries. ...

(US President Barack Obama in his address to the Indian Parliament on 8 November 2010)

Introduction

India's recent economic transformation, particularly since the watershed economic reforms of the 1990s, has been remarkable. This is only partially reflected in higher trend GDP per capita growth rates, not to speak of the resilience of the economy to the sharpest downturn in worldwide economic activity and trade since the Great Depression. To adequately capture India's economic transformation one would need several indicators, in particular those that reflect the quantum leap in opportunities available to common citizens. When such sustained economic growth occurs in a country of over a billion people, more than half of them under the age of 25, against the backdrop of a political system of multi-party parliamentary democracy, a federal structure and in the presence of widespread poverty the unique nature of such transformation becomes evident. This is indeed unparalleled in human history.

Dr. C. Rangarajan's work has been central to India's rapid transformation. His credentials as an academic economist are stellar enough. To top this he has been at the centre of almost every aspect of policy formulation and execution since the early 1990s. To mention just a few—he has been India's central banker, headed the Twelfth Finance

Commission (2005-2010) and has been chairman of the Council of Economic Advisors (CEA) to the Prime Minister. His work, advice and economic administration have been pivotal to India's recent economic success. Not only has he formulated and guided successful economic policy but has, no doubt, been instrumental in addressing episodes of economic crises. In addition to all this he has been governor of some states, has served as chairman of key economic committees in the Government of India and the Reserve Bank of India (RBI) and as a nominated member of the Rajya Sabha. This list of accomplishments is no doubt incomplete. Truly it is not possible to imagine India's recent economic success and eminently evident potential for further growth without acknowledging the contribution of C. Rangarajan.

This paper is written as a tribute to Dr. Rangarajan and goes back to an early theme, 'curbing inflation', developed by him in his role as India's central banker. Although the case for price stability as a macroeconomic goal was always strong, no one in India has done more to move this to centre stage than Dr. Rangarajan. As RBI governor and in a number of publications (Rangarajan, 1997 and 2004) he forcefully laid out the case for price stability.

Whereas the case for price stability as a goal of macroeconomic policy has been considered unexceptionable for some time, a strong body of thought has considered some inflation to be conducive for economic growth in the context of an emerging market economy like India. For a good review of this argument and a survey of the literature see Li (2006).

Li (2006) uses data for 90 developing countries (including India) and 28 developed countries for the period 1961 to 2004 and shows that the relationship between inflation and economic growth is non-linear. For developing countries the estimation suggests the presence of two thresholds in the function relating economic growth and inflation. At rates of inflation lower than that of the first threshold, the effects of inflation on growth are insignificant and even positive; at moderate rates of inflation, which are between the two threshold levels, the effects of inflation are significantly and strongly negative; at extremely high rates of inflation, the marginal impact of additional inflation on economic growth diminishes. The first threshold level of inflation is estimated at 14 per cent per year, and the second threshold level at 38 per cent per year. For developed countries there is a unique threshold (24 per cent). The magnitude of the negative effect of inflation on growth declines as the inflation rate increases.

However, the contributions of Li and others have one important drawback from the policy perspective. Nowhere is it shown that the inflation levels being considered are sustainable levels of inflation, in particular they say nothing about the level and direction of movement of expected inflation. It is quite likely that at rates of inflation even below the (lower) threshold level of inflation for developing countries (14 per cent) expected inflation might be going up in which case actual inflation would be accelerating in the subsequent time periods. Hence, to fully understand the relation between inflation and growth we need a measure of non-accelerating inflation. The proper relation to estimate should be between this measure and economic growth. In other words, we need to estimate a Non-Accelerating Inflation Growth relation (NAIG). To the best of my knowledge there is no work in this area.

Pending the availability of robust results on this relation Dr. Rangarajan would be right to consider a rate of inflation of 14 per cent unacceptable.

In this paper, I re-emphasise Rangarajan's view on price stability and make it more specific by considering a typically (unanticipated) advantage of stabilising the consumer price index (CPI). The plan of this paper is as follows. It briefly reviews the recent economic growth performance of the Indian economy and recounts the sluggish response of poverty to high economic growth. The paper also indicates that hunger (calorie deficiency) has actually increased during the post-reform period. Using household level National Sample Survey (NSS) data for 1993-94 and 2004-05, it further shows that calorie intakes in both rural and urban areas are sensitive to commodity (in particular food grain) prices. Hence, reducing consumer price inflation is likely to yield a rich dividend in the form of lower incidence of hunger. Indeed rising per capita incomes are not likely to be sufficient to reduce hunger. Before concluding, the paper briefly reviews some policy challenges to stabilising consumer prices.

Poverty Reduction, Undernutrition and Macroeconomic Performance

As remarked above economic growth has been very robust in India in recent years. Table 3.1 gives a summary of recent growth performance for the aggregate economy and major sectors. It is clear that the economy has come out of the global financial crisis (GFC) relatively unscathed. Real GDP growth in 2010-11 has been forecasted to be 8.5 per cent and to then approach the previously attained 9 per cent.

Table 3.1

Rate of Growth at Factor Cost at 1999-2000 Prices (Per cent)

	2000-01 to 2007-08 Average	*2005-06*	*2006-07*	*2007-08*	*2008-09*	*2009-10*
Agriculture, forestry and fishing	2.9	5.2	3.7	4.7	1.6	-0.2
Mining and quarrying	4.9	1.3	8.7	3.9	1.6	8.7
Manufacturing	7.8	9.6	14.9	10.3	3.2	8.9
Electricity, gas and water supply	4.8	6.6	10.0	8.5	3.9	8.2
Construction	10.6	12.4	10.6	10.0	5.9	6.5
Trade, hotels and restaurants	10.3[a]	12.4	11.2	9.5	5.3	8.3
Transport, storage and communication		11.5	12.6	13.0	11.6	
Financing, insurance, real estate and business services	8.8	12.8	14.5	13.2	10.1	9.9
Community, social and personal services	5.8	7.6	2.6	6.7	13.9	8.2
GDP at factor cost	7.3	9.5	9.7	9.2	6.7	7.2

Note: a = This refers to trade, hotels, restaurants, transport, storage & communication.

Source: *Economic Survey*, Ministry of Finance, Government of India, 2009-10.

Even though India's real GDP growth is impressive[1] the structural composition of this growth is such that its impact on poverty reduction has been sluggish (Jha, 2004). In fact, as Table 3.2 indicates, the poverty elasticity of India's growth is lower than that of Bangladesh, Vietnam and Sri Lanka.

1. Per capita real GDP growth has, in recent years, been in excess of 7 per cent.

As a consequence poverty reduction in India, despite the high growth rate, has been slow. Based on NSS household level data for the 21-year period from 1983 to 2004-05, Table 3.3 demonstrates this point. In the rural sector whereas the severity of poverty (poverty gap and square of poverty gap) has come down quite sharply the headcount ratio has only had a modest decline from 46.5 per cent to 28.7 per cent. Also the pace of decline of poverty has come down after the reforms. Whereas the headcount ratio fell by 6.5 percentage points in the four-year period between 1983 and 1987-88, it fell only by 8.5 percentage points over the 11-year period 1993-94 to 2004-05. Inequality recorded a modest rise.

Table 3.2

Economic Growth and Poverty Reduction in Select Asian Countries (1995-2005)

Country	*Average Annual Growth of Per Capita GDP*	*Annual Rate of Poverty Reduction (PPP $0.75 a day ultra poverty line)*	*Ratio of Annual Rate of Poverty Reduction to Annual Per Capita GDP Growth Rate*
India	4.9%	-2.6%	-0.5
Bangladesh	3.7%	-3.9%	-1.1
Sri Lanka	3.4%	-10.3%	-3.1
Vietnam	6.2%	-13.5%	-2.2

Source: IFPRI (2010).

In the urban sector the severity of poverty had a more modest decline than in the rural sector. The headcount ratio declined 4.9 percentage points in the four-year period 1983 to 1987-88 and only by 6.7 percentage points in the post-reform 1993-94 to 2004-05 (11 years). Inequality in the urban sector increased sharply.[2]

The sense of disappointment at the poverty impact of the reforms pales into insignificance when one considers progress in reducing hunger over this period. In an influential study Deaton and Dreze (2009) have shown that average calorie consumption was about 10 per cent lower in rural areas in 2004-05 than in 1983. The proportionate decline was larger

2. Of course, there are well-known spatial differences in poverty attainments across the country, however in this paper I am concentrating on the aggregate picture.

Table 3.3

Comparable Estimates of Poverty and Inequality: All India

Rural

	Headcount Ratio (per cent HCR) Uniform 30-day Rule (using official poverty lines)				*Poverty Gap using Official Poverty Lines*				*Squared Poverty Gap using Official Poverty Lines*				*Gini Coefficient*			
	1983	1987-88	1993-94	2004-05	1983	1987-88	1993-94	2004-05	1983	1987-88	1993-94	2004-05	1983	1987-88	1993-94	2004-05
All-India	46.5	39.0	37.2	28.7	12.36	9.29	8.5	5.8	4.87	3.23	2.84	1.76	30.4	29.9	28.6	30.5

Urban

	Headcount Ratio (per cent HCR) Uniform 30-day Rule (using official poverty lines)				*Poverty Gap using Official Poverty Lines*				*Squared Poverty Gap using Official Poverty Lines*				*Gini Coefficient*			
	1983	1987-88	1993-94	2004-05	1983	1987-88	1993-94	2004-05	1983	1987-88	1993-94	2004-05	1983	1987-88	1993-94	2004-05
All-India	43.6	38.7	32.6	25.9	11.4	10.2	8.0	6.2	4.4	3.8	2.9	2.0	33.9	35.0	34.4	37.6

Note: The figures in Table 3.3 are computed using calorie-based poverty lines. Recently the Tendulkar Committee Report has argued in favour of augmenting these poverty lines by adding essential expenditures on health and education. As expected poverty rates are higher using these measures.

Source: Adapted from Himanshu (2007).

among the more affluent sections of the population, and smaller for the bottom quartile of monthly per capita expenditure (MPCE). In urban areas, there was only a slight change in average calorie intake over this period. Consumption of proteins and other nutrients declined, but that of fat increased in both rural and urban areas.[3]

Using NSS household level data for 1993-94 and 2004-05 Gaiha *et al.* (2010a) indicate that if we use the higher calorie requirement[4] of 2,400 calories per day, over 71 per cent of the rural households were undernourished in 1993. Using the lower intake of 1,800 calories per day, we find a sharp reduction to well below half the proportion (about 31 per cent), implying a large concentration of households in the calorie daily intake range of 1,800-2,400. The proportion of undernourished rose from 71 per cent to nearly 80 per cent in 2004. Also, the proportion below the lower cut-off rose from about 31 per cent to close to 37 per cent. By any standard, these imply high incidence of calorie deprivation. What is also significant is that, while the mean calorie intake of those below 1,800 rose slightly (from 1,491 to 1,516), the mean intake of the larger concentration of households in the next higher range (1,801-2,400) remained about the same. The decline in calorie intake over this period in urban areas was much less severe.

One reason for the deterioration in calorie intake is that both access to and consumption of food grain have declined in India in recent times. The latest *Economic Survey* of the Government of India indicates that food grain production in India declined from 208 kg per annum per capita in 1996-97 to only 186 kg per annum per capita in 2009-10, i.e., a drop of 11 per cent. In addition India has, until recently, been exporting 7 million

3. Food security and the absence of undernutrition are often used interchangeably in the literature. However, these are distinct concepts, both analytically and operationally. Having enough to eat (food security) is only one facet of having adequate nutrition. The adequacy of nutrition is spelt out in a number of indicators such as the adequate intake of macronutrients (calorie and protein) and micronutrients (carotene, iron, riboflavin, calcium, etc.) and is also expressed in anthropometric terms such as 'right range of BMI' for adults and indicators of stunting and wasting in children. That said, this paper will continue the extant practice of interpreting food insecurity as inadequate intake of nutrition, in particular calories.

4. Gopalan *et al.* (1971) delineate nutritional requirement for different groups of Indians. For adult males doing heavy work in the rural sector the minimum calorie requirement per day is 3,900. Thus 2,400 is a relatively modest average requirement.

tonnes of grain every year. Higher real incomes lead to lower cereal demand for the rich. But, this is certainly not the case for the poor. Lower cereal demand could be an indicator of distress purchases as food demand is curtailed to enable essential non-food purchases, particularly health and education. Thus, Gaiha *et al.* (2010a) indicate that per capita cereal demand in rural India fell by 9.6 per cent between 1993 and 2004. In urban India the decline was 2.6 per cent.

Undernutrition apart from being an unwelcome human development outcome can have serious productivity and labour marker consequences as well. In Jha *et al.* (2009) we test for the existence of a Poverty Nutrition Trap (PNT) in the case of calories and four key micronutrients—carotene, iron, riboflavin, and thiamine—for three categories of wages (sowing, harvesting, and other) and for male and female workers separately for rural India in 1993-94. A PNT is said to exist when undernutrition leads to low productivity, hence low wages which then translates to low nutrition, thus completing a vicious cycle.

We conclude that PNT exists in one third (i.e., 10) of the 30 cases. It exists for female harvest wage and female sowing wage for calories. In the case of carotene, male workers engaged in harvesting are subject to the PNT, whereas both male and female workers engaged in harvesting are subject to PNT in the case of iron. In the case of riboflavin female workers engaged in harvesting and sowing and male workers engaged in harvesting are subject to PNT. Since harvesting is physically more demanding than sowing, there is a higher incidence of PNT in harvesting.

Whereas the PNT holds for calories only in the cases of female sowing and female harvesting wages, it holds for males in the case of male harvesting wages (carotene, iron, and riboflavin). For females PNT holds in respect of harvesting and sowing wages for calories, thiamine, and riboflavin, PNT does not exist for females in the case of carotene, and it exists only for harvesting wages in the case of iron. Hence, an analysis which concentrates exclusively on energy intake may present an incomplete picture of the existence of PNT. This analysis shifts the focus to lack of nutritional adequacy as a facilitator, if not a precondition, for participation in labour market activities. Even if some workers succeed in participating, their wage earnings will not allow them to escape the PNT. Indeed, a mild labour shock (e.g. associated with a crop shortfall) would worsen their plight, as the risk of loss of employment would be considerably higher. In particular, female workers are more prone to PNT than male workers, and there is a persistent gender inequality in rural India. We find that improving nutrient intakes can have significant effects on rural wages and, therefore, on the possibility of breaking PNT as well as reducing poverty. Thus, public policy should concentrate urgently on providing direct nutritional supplements to the nutritionally vulnerable (including infants and children and expectant and lactating mothers) in addition to pursuing direct poverty alleviation policies.

Turning around the Nutrition Shortfall: The Role of Macroeconomic Policy

Deaton and Dreze (2009) argue that the decline in calorie intake is largely the result of people adopting a more sedentary lifestyle as a consequence of economic growth. Hence, their calorie intake requirements may have declined. They claim that this decline is not attributable to changes in relative prices, based on an aggregate measure of the price of food. They argue that there has been a steady downward shift of the calorie Engel curve due to lower calorie 'requirements', mainly with better health and lower activity levels associated with ease of obtaining drinking water, extensive use of bicycles and motor bikes and improved public transportation.

However, this is a proposition to be tested. It may be the case that lower food intake is a result of higher relative prices of food grains, reflecting lower availability (Gaiha *et al.*, 2010b). This also exacerbates the extent of undernourishment. Tables 3.4 and 3.5 report results on estimates of calorie demand functions for rural and urban India using household data for 1993-94 and 2004-05. This analysis uses unit prices as opposed to aggregate prices with the former being calculated as expenditure on a commodity divided by quantity. Both estimates are quite robust and show substantive and significant negative price effects, particularly with respect to cereal prices.

Tables 3.4 and 3.5 therefore provide an alternative explanation (complementary to that of Deaton and Dreze, 2009) of changes in the

Table 3.4

Demand Function for Calories with Interactions in Rural India, Pooled (1993-2004)

	Number of obs =	34371
Robust Regression	F (29,34341) =	390.62
	Prob > F =	0.0000

Log Per Capita Calories Intake	*Coef.*	*Std. Err.*	*t*	*P>t*
Time Dummy (0=1993, 1=2004)	-1.7202030	0.1074764	-16.01	0.0000
Log prices—Rice & Wheat	-0.1643080	0.0122206	-13.45	0.0000
Time Dummy x Log Prices—Rice & Wheat	0.1912146	0.0160706	11.90	0.0000
Log prices—Inferior Cereals	0.0014121	0.0019965	0.71	0.4790
Time Dummy x Log Prices—Inferior Cereals	0.0040812	0.0049966	0.82	0.4140
Log prices—Milk-&-Products/Ghee-Butter	0.0268269	0.0043931	6.11	0.0000
Time Dummy x Log Prices—Milk & Products/Ghee-Butter	-0.0415876	0.0056037	-7.42	0.0000
Log prices—Vanaspati-oil	-0.0974666	0.0199761	-4.88	0.0000
Time Dummy x Log Prices—Vanaspati-oil	0.2853931	0.026419	10.80	0.0000
Log prices—Sugar	0.1345795	0.0148711	9.05	0.0000
Time Dummy x Log Prices—Sugar	-0.0372944	0.0211966	-1.76	0.0790
Log Prices—Eggs	0.0303439	0.0049822	6.09	0.0000
Time Dummy x Log Prices—Eggs	0.0536936	0.0096437	5.57	0.0000
Log Prices—Meat/Fish/Poultry	-0.0068966	0.0050049	-1.38	0.1680
Time Dummy x Log Prices—Meat/Fish/Poultry	0.0145125	0.0073598	1.97	0.0490
Log Prices—Pulses/Nuts-DryFruits/others	0.0129167	0.0022753	5.68	0.0000
Time Dummy x Log Prices—Pulses/Nuts-DryFruits/Others	0.0227518	0.0037374	6.09	0.0000
Log prices—Fruits	0.0027890	0.0035553	0.78	0.4330
Time Dummy x Log Prices—Fruits	-0.0362391	0.0052745	-6.87	0.0000
Log Prices—Vegetables	-0.0854007	0.0068099	-12.54	0.0000
Time Dummy x Log Prices—Vegetables	-0.0413706	0.0100546	-4.11	0.0000
Log Per Capita Expenditure (mpce) predicted	0.3878064	0.008267	46.91	0.0000
Highest Education—Male (1=above middle)	-0.0239072	0.0041859	-5.71	0.0000
Highest Education—Female (1=above middle)	-0.0622271	0.0053098	-11.72	0.0000
Caste—SC	0.0203524	0.004911	4.14	0.0000
Caste—Other	0.0264889	0.0041445	6.39	0.0000
Log Number of Adult Males	0.0652757	0.003479	18.76	0.0000
Log Number of Adult Females	0.0369016	0.0038056	9.70	0.0000
Log Household Size	-0.1251275	0.0054197	-23.09	0.0000
_cons	5.9085940	0.0883373	66.89	0.0000
Omitted Caste: ST				

Source: Gaiha *et al.* (2010 b).

Table 3.5

Demand Function for Calories with Interactions in Urban India, Pooled (1993-2004)

Robust Regression	Number of obs =	24803
	F (29,24773) =	409.12
	Prob > F =	0.0000

Log Per Capita Calories Intake	*Coef.*	*Std. Err.*	*t*	*P>t*
Time Dummy (0=1993, 1=2004)	-0.9195787	0.1190358	-7.73	0.0000
Log Prices—Rice & Wheat	-0.0507352	0.0132674	-3.82	0.0000
Time Dummy x Log Prices—Rice & Wheat	-0.0364669	0.0182183	-2.00	0.0450
Log Prices—Inferior Cereals	-0.0028333	0.0018964	-1.49	0.1350
Time Dummy x Log Prices—Inferior Cereals	-0.0037751	0.0047698	-0.79	0.4290
Log prices—Milk & Products/Ghee-Butter	0.0229197	0.0058593	3.91	0.0000
Time Dummy x Log Prices—Milk & Products/Ghee-Butter	-0.0234831	0.0092065	-2.55	0.0110
Log Prices—Vanaspati-oil	-0.0096175	0.0229671	-0.42	0.6750
Time Dummy x Log Prices—Vanaspati-oil	0.2258828	0.0301314	7.50	0.0000
Log Prices—Sugar	0.1074968	0.018126	5.93	0.0000
Time Dummy x Log Prices—Sugar	-0.0839290	0.02589	-3.24	0.0010
Log Prices—Eggs	0.0338505	0.0073154	4.63	0.0000
Time Dummy x Log Prices—Eggs	0.1050475	0.0150977	6.96	0.0000
Log Prices—Meat/Fish/Poultry	0.0001105	0.005595	0.02	0.9840
Time Dummy x Log Prices—Meat/Fish/Poultry	0.0073838	0.008409	0.88	0.3800
Log prices—Pulses/Nuts-DryFruits/Others	0.0142654	0.00324	4.40	0.0000
Time Dummy x Log Prices—Pulses/Nuts-DryFruits/Others	0.0035167	0.0050589	0.70	0.4870
Log Prices—Fruits	-0.0074601	0.0048532	-1.54	0.1240
Time Dummy x Log Prices—Fruits	-0.0309567	0.007751	-3.99	0.0000
Log Prices—Vegetables	-0.0379003	0.0076518	-4.95	0.0000
Time Dummy x Log Prices—Vegetables	-0.0788958	0.0122692	-6.43	0.0000
Log Per capita Expenditure (mpce) predicted	0.2820716	0.0117622	23.98	0.0000
Highest Education—Male (1=above middle)	-0.0075396	0.0055565	-1.36	0.1750
Highest Education—Female (1=above middle)	-0.0272972	0.0057865	-4.72	0.0000
Caste—SC	-0.0056799	0.0083835	-0.68	0.4980
Caste—Other	-0.0082267	0.0071583	-1.15	0.2500
Log Number of Adult Males	0.0835158	0.0038817	21.52	0.0000
Log Number of Adult Females	0.0420094	0.0041871	10.03	0.0000
Log Household Size	-0.1933290	0.0088469	-21.85	0.0000
_cons	5.9775790	0.1175861	50.84	0.0000
Omitted Caste: ST				

Source: Gaiha *et al.* (2010 b).

consumption of calories over the period, 1993-2004. This explanation is embedded in a standard demand theory framework, with food prices and per capita monthly expenditure (as a proxy for income) cast in a pivotal role. Since expenditure and calories could be mutually endogeneous we instrument the former. Based on different experiments, robust demand functions are estimated. Our results show consistently robust food price and expenditure effects. The elasticity of calorie demand with respect to cereal prices is negative and significant in both the rural and urban sectors, with the urban value being slightly higher. A number of other prices also have significant negative effects. Besides, shifts in food price elasticities over time are significant. Over and above these effects, there are shifts in demands due to factors other than those specified in the demand equations. In the context of calories, for example, it is plausible that part of the reduction in their consumption was due to health improvements and less strenuous activity levels—especially but not necessarily confined to rural areas.

Hence, while Deaton and Dreze's (2009) explanation is not rejected, it is arguable that it is complementary to the demand based explanations.

From the macroeconomic policy point of view the implication is that for poverty reduction merely expanding incomes will not do. It is important to stabilise prices, particularly consumer prices. This conclusion reasserts the case for inflation stabilisation as a key goal of macroeconomic policy in India. It sharpens this case by showing that stabilising the CPI is important for its own sake. Not only does it help control inflation defined more generally but it also yields rich dividends in the sense of reducing the incidence of hunger. Jha *et al.* (2010a) show that the nutritional dividends from such intervention through the public distribution system (PDS) can be quite high even at modest real income transfer per household (roughly equal to one day's wages for one person per household per month).

Some Difficulties in Stabilising the CPI in India

In India price stabilisation measures, such as offloading of stocks of food grains into some retail markets, may not easily and speedily permeate through to the rest of the country. The most important reason for this is the incomplete integration of agricultural markets so that market shocks/

price stabilisation measures have imperfect flowthrough (Jha *et al.*, 2006). For instance, under the Government of India's Ministry of Labour, Labour Bureau estimates that while the average monthly price of rice in the country in October 2009 was recorded as Rs. 20.56 per kg, the price across 78 consumption centres ranged from Rs. 10.34 to Rs. 30.55 per kg. Figure 3.1 traces the mean, standard deviation and coefficient of variation of wholesale monthly rice prices in 70 centres from 1970:1 to 1999:12. Standard deviation and mean are measured on the left vertical axis whereas coefficient of variation is measured on the right vertical axis. Over this time period the (unit free) coefficient of variation doubled, indicating increase in the spatial dispersion in prices over time.

Figure 3.1

Measures of Mean and Dispersion of Monthly Wholesale Rice Prices in 70 Markets in India—1970:1 to 1999:12.

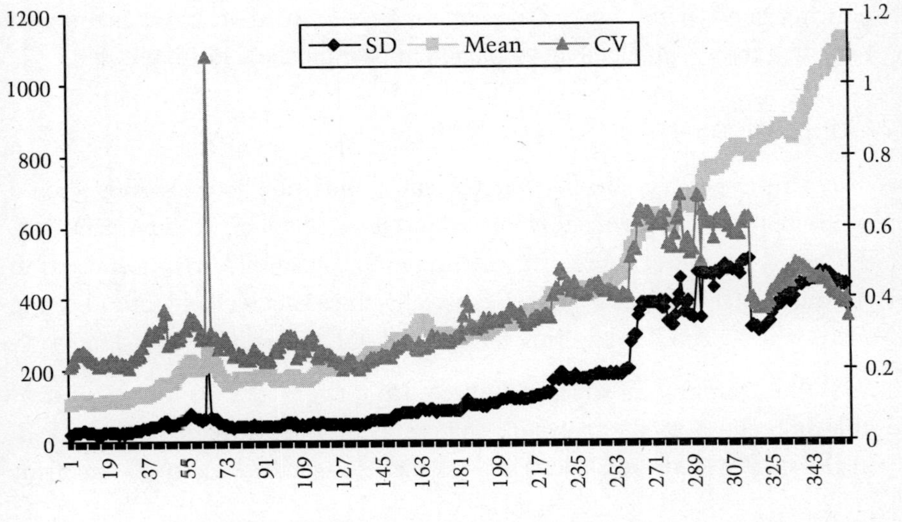

Note: Horizontal axis refers to elapsed months since 1970:1. Mean and Standard Deviation are measured along the left vertical axis and coefficient of variation along the right vertical axis.

Source: Author's computation based on data available in *Agricultural Situation in India.*

India's archaic system of regulations on food grain markets (both wholesale and retail) needs to be urgently reformed to facilitate more effective internal trade (Kumar *et al.*, 2010). Operations such as those of the Food Corporation of India (FCI) are quite inefficient. They report that the marketing costs of private traders is only about 70 per cent of the costs of the FCI. Further there have been issues relating to procurement, storage and distribution of food grain in FCI godowns. In recent times large quantities of grain have decayed in FCI godowns. Jha *et al.* (2010b) show that large-scale leakage from the public distribution system (PDS) implies that real income transfers through the PDS are meagre. This is particularly discomforting because the real income transfers needed to significantly lower the incidence of calorie deprivation are modest to begin with.

An upshot of the argument here is that supply-side policies are an indispensable tool in combating consumer price inflation and over-emphasis of demand-side measures as exercised by monetary policy should be eschewed.[5] In any case the response of CPI to a change in an interest rate measure such as the call money rate impact-effect of an interest measure such as the call money rate on CPI is subject to a wide and rapidly growing band of response. One cannot be certain that a rise in interest rates will have a predictable and stable impact on the CPI (Jha, 2008).

Conclusions

This paper has argued that restricting inflation to low levels should continue to be the cornerstone of macroeconomic policy in India. However, this policy should be more nuanced. In particular, careful attention needs to be paid to stabilising food prices, especially since this is likely to lead to the additional dividend of lowering hunger and enhancing labour productivity.

This paper has also indicated that there are some structural impediments to good supply-side management which need to be removed. In the intermediate run additional policies designed to decisively augment

5. In fact if inflation is initiated by supply-side factors such as a drought, as is the case with the inflation of 2009-10, supply shocks will reverberate through the economy. The inflation following from these supply shocks will lead to a rise in expected inflation which, in itself, affects aggregate supply adversely. The higher the rate of expected inflation, the lower will be the gap between actual and expected inflation and the smaller the resulting (positive) deviation of output from the trend. Merely reducing demand against the background of recurring adverse supply shocks will, other things remaining unchanged, only lower output growth without having a substantial impact on inflation. The bottom line is that without tackling supply-side constraints, there can be no easy victory in the fight against inflation.

investment and productivity in Indian agriculture need to be put into place. Needless to say, Dr. Rangarajan will be at the forefront of such efforts. It is an honour and a privilege to pay tribute to his work.

References

Deaton, A. and J. Dreze (2009). "Food and Nutrition in India: Facts and Interpretation", *Economic and Political Weekly* 44(7): 42–64.

Gaiha, R., R. Jha and V. Kulkarni (2010a). "Prices, Expenditure and Nutrition in India", *Working Paper* 2010/15. Canberra: Australia South Asia Research Centre, Australian National University.

———. (2010b). "Demand for Nutrients in India, 1993-2004", *Working Paper* 2010/16. Canberra: Australia South Asia Research Centre, Australian National University.

Gopalan, C., B. Sastri and S. Balasubramanian (1971). *Nutritive Value of Indian Foods.* Hyderabad: National Institute of Nutrition; Indian Council of Medical Research.

Himanshu (2007). "Recent Trends in Poverty and Inequality: Some preliminary results", *Economic and Political Weekly* 42(6): 497–508, February 10 .

International Food Policy Research Institute (IFPRI) (2010). "Tackling the Agriculture-Nutrition Disconnect in India (TANDI): What do we Know and what do we need to Know". *(mimeo)*.

Jha, R. (2004). "Reducing Poverty and Inequality in India: Has Liberalization Helped", in A. Cornia (ed.), *Inequality, Growth and Poverty in an Era of Liberalization and Globalization*. New York: Oxford University Press.

———. (2008). "Inflation Targeting in India: Issues and Prospects", *International Review of Applied Economics* 22(2): 259–70.

Jha, R., K.V.B. Murthy and A. Sharma (2006). "Market Integration in Wholesale Rice Markets in India", *Economic and Political Weekly* 40(53): 5571–7.

Jha, R., R. Gaiha and A. Sharma (2009). "Calorie and Micronutrient Deprivation and Poverty Nutrition Traps in Rural India", *World Development* 37(5): 982–91.

Jha, R., S. Bhattacharyya and R. Gaiha (2010a). "Social Safety Nets and Nutrient Deprivation: An Analysis of the National Rural Employment Guarantee Program and the Public Distribution System in India", *Working Paper* 2010/4. Canberra: Australia South Asia Research Centre, Australian National University.

Jha, R., R. Gaiha and M. Pandey (2010b). "Food Price Subsidy under Public Distribution System in Andhra Pradesh, Maharashtra and Rajasthan", *Working Paper* 2010/7. Canberra: Australia South Asia Research Centre, Australian National University.

Kumar, G., D. Roy and A. Gulati (2010). "Liberalizing Foodgrains Markets: Experiences, Impact and Lessons from South Asia", *IFPRI Issue Brief* 64, August.

Li, M. (2006). "Inflation and Economic Growth: Threshold Effects and Transmission Mechanisms", Department of Economics, University of Alberta. (*mimeo*).

Rangarajan, C. (1997). "Mr Rangarajan Examines the Objective of Monetary Policy and Price Stability in relation to the Economy of India", *BIS Review* 8. Available at *http://www.bis.org/review/r970203b.pdf* (Accessed 11th November 2010).

———. (2004). *Select Essays on the Indian Economy*. New Delhi: Academic Foundation.

4 From Growth to Inclusive Growth

The Current Challenges

Joseph Massey

In its history of 60 years as an independent nation, India has evolved through several phases of growth and development. The nation has taken it all with an indomitable spirit and fortitude coupled with economic and financial wisdom. This makes the history of economic and financial evolution of India marked by times—both challenging and cheering.

An era of planning started immediately after independence and socialistic pattern of society was adopted along with democratic planning. Later on the policymakers aspired to go beyond the trickle-down approach and the license raj gave way to liberalisation. India witnessed a slowing growth rate by early 1970s. Liberalisation was initiated in 1980s but took its full swing only in 1990. The BoP (balance of payment) crisis hit the nation and it prompted the policymakers to reconsider the economic fundamentals. Globalisation and liberalisation eventually became the mantras of the day and the decade.

Liberalisation: The Beginning of Growth Era

The comprehensive framework of financial liberalisation was designed by the High Level Committee on Balance of Payments appointed in 1991 under the chairmanship by Dr. C. Rangarajan. The Committee suggested that liberalisation need not be adopted in an absolute manner but could also include in its fold an element of gradualism and prudential regulation. It recommended liberalisation of the current account transactions and complete current account convertibility while taking gradual steps towards capital account convertibility. The Committee recognised the need to encourage capital flows that were non-debt creating such as foreign direct investment (FDI) and portfolio investments rather than debt creating flows or loans from the international capital market and stressed the need for strict regulation of external commercial borrowings particularly short-term debt and volatility breeding inflows from NRIS along with gradual liberalisation of outflows. The Committee also suggested introducing a market-determined exchange rate regime, fiscal and monetary measures to promote exports and regulate imports and measures to keep the current account deficit in check.

Post-liberalisation, foreign trade and investment policy underwent drastic changes and a more conducive environment was provided for foreign investment. Export promotion was given a preference over import substitution. Managed floating system gave way to a market-based exchange rate system and the RBI has been given the role to intervene in the forex market with the intention of preventing volatility and the resulting instability. Public sector banks have continued to dominate the financial sector but private sector has been encouraged and licences are being issued to new private sector banks. Above all, since 1990s, monetary policy came up as an independent instrument of economic policy.

Growth Dynamics

Indian economy has taken rapid strides since liberalisation and has kept abreast with global trends. There has been a phenomenal transformation of the economy from the 'License Raj to Liberalisation', from the 'Hindu rate of growth' mainly dictated by low levels of agricultural output to aspiring for a double digit rate of growth with considerable contributions from manufacturing and services sector. The policies have transformed from bank nationalisation to considering allotting banking licences to non-banking financial companies (NBFCs) and large corporates. On the trading front, India has emerged from an importer of food grains to a major exporter of food grains with a record production of over 230 million tonnes and a major exporter of software, gems and jewellery. The trade in capital markets of liberalised India has successfully extended from equities and commodities to currencies. A technological revolution has been heralded in the country and it has brought about improvements in areas ranging from agricultural practices to trade practices. Ventures in technology interventions and convergence have connected the national economy and the financial system with those of the developed and the developing world and the policymakers are now striving to improve connectivity across the length and breadth of the country.

India's growth rate since liberalisation has been impressive though it declined from 9.2 per cent in 2007-08 to a 6.7 per cent in 2008-09. A modest recovery to 7.4 per cent was observed in 2009-10. Policymakers expect to achieve a 9-10 per cent growth rate in the near-term. A look at the GDP growth rates reflects that India enjoys an average growth rate of above 5 per cent since 2001 (Table 4.1).

Table 4.1

India's GDP Growth Rate at Market Prices

Average			*Actual*			
1990-1995	*1996-2000*	*2001-2005*	*Dec-06*	*Dec-07*	*Dec-08*	*Dec-09*
5%	*5%*	*6%*	*9%*	*10%*	*9%*	*6%*

Source: CMIE

India stayed unruffled during South East Asian crisis of 1998 when it managed to keep its fiscal deficit to lower levels in comparison with those of the crisis-hit countries like Malaysia and Thailand. The policymakers have been exercising strict financial control and fiscal prudence and aiming to keeping the fiscal deficits in check. The Eleventh Five-Year Plan (2007-2012) Approach Paper indicates that the Centre has planned to limit the combined fiscal deficit of the Centre and the sates to 6 per cent. It rose to more than 6 per cent of GDP in 2008-09 during the recent financial crisis. As a response to the crisis, the Indian government deviated a bit from fiscal consolidation and introduced the fiscal stimulus packages. As a result, the economy could manage to stay less affected by the crisis. Currently, India's fiscal deficit is 6.7 per cent as against over 10.6 per cent of US and 11.4 per cent of UK. The finance ministry expects fiscal deficit for the year ending March 2011 to stay around the targeted levels of 6.8 per cent of the GDP. It is also being expected that the deficit will decline to 4.8 per cent in 2011-2012 and to 4 1 per cent by 2012-13.

After the South East Asian crisis, India has pursued a policy of maintaining higher levels of forex reserves to take care of current account deficits as well as liquidity risks and to keep up confidence in the markets.

Figure 4.1

Trend in Fiscal Deficit as Per cent of GDP

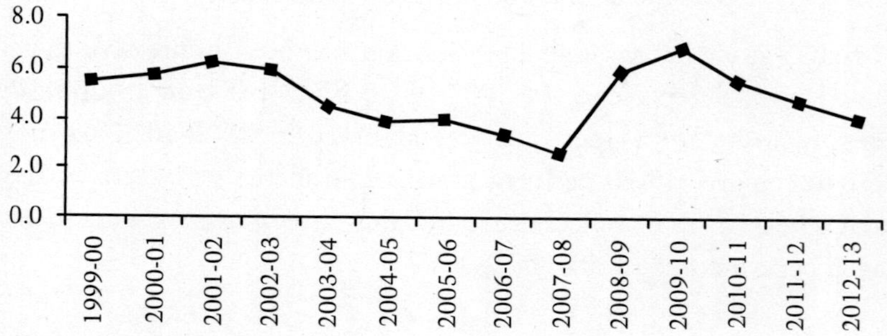

Source: Budget Documents.

Foreign Institutional Investor (FII) net investments in India during April-July 2010 amounted to almost $9 billion while cumulative FII net investment during the period amounted to nearly $100 billion. It is recommendable that as on September 17, 2010 India holds forex reserves worth $260.8 billion against a mere $1.2 billion in December 1990 and $9.2 billion in March 1992.

Equity market is an indicator not only of the state of capital markets but of the economy as a whole. The Sensex has recovered post the recent crisis and has breached the level of 20,000. Investors across the globe have regained confidence in the Indian economy. The market capitalisation of India has witnessed a rise to almost $1.4 trillion on account of strong economic growth and increasing investments in the capital markets.

Post-1990s, Indian economy has witnessed significant economic and financial sector reforms generating robust economic growth which is almost nearing a double digit. However, higher growth rate achieved and rapid strides taken in the fiscal and financial spectra have not resulted in achieving the desired levels of development—human, economic and financial. UNDP sources state that between 1980 and 2007 India's human development index (HDI) has rose from 0.427 to 0.612 today. India lags behind in human development and ranks only 134th among 182 countries in the UN-HDI list which is indicative of dismal levels achieved by the country in life expectancy, literacy and GDP per capita. This suggests that the ideal of inclusive growth is missing from the economic growth achieved so far and is yet to be realised. Social and economic justice has remained the guiding principle behind India's planning strategy. The aim of India's Ninth Five-Year Plan (1997-2002) was achieving 'growth with social justice' while the key objective of the Eleventh Plan has been to achieve inclusive growth and secure all the opportunities of growth and development. Inclusive growth implies a growth pace in which everyone contributes and everyone has a share. Apt and sufficient investments in social sectors have therefore remained an important aspect of the government's efforts to achieve inclusive growth. On the supply side driving inclusive growth, financial intermediaries are expected to take a proactive role in securing access to the formal financial system to the multitudes. This also includes facilitating the funding needs of the investors including young entrepreneurs and the small and medium enterprises (SMEs). On the demand side, the lower income groups and the investing class demand financial conveniences to meet their health, educational and entrepreneurial expenses respectively. The Eleventh Plan document observes that the country has made rapid strides in economic growth since liberalisation but the growth has not been as inclusive as desired particularly after mid-1990s and a vast segment of population has remained excluded from the fruits of growth and improvements in livings standards.

Growth and the Hidden Gaps

Savings

Corporates and policymakers across the globe have come to identify a new model developing in the world trade patterns, a model which reflects that the savings of emerging markets do not drain in the United States, Europe or the developed world, but they find their way to the areas experiencing higher growth rates. Here lies the opportunity for a country like ours that experiences not only one of the highest savings rates in the world but also one of the highest growth rates. India has been experiencing a robust trend in gross domestic savings as a proportion of GDP since 2000. India's gross domestic savings rate is one of the highest in the world and has remarkably rose from 23.6 per cent of GDP in 2001-02 to over 30 per cent currently. RBI estimates indicate that the net financial saving of the household sector in 2008-09 is 10.9 per cent of GDP at current market prices. A comparison with international standards suggests that India's gross household savings rate as percentage of disposable income is substantially higher. Table 4.2 is reflective of the same:

Table 4.2

Household Savings as Per cent to Personal Disposable Income (2007-2009)

United States	*United Kingdom*	*Germany*	*Korea*	*India*
2.9%	3.6%	10.5%	3.1%	32%

Source: OECD Economic Outlook Data.

Since 1990s the household sector preferred diverting their savings towards financial assets (Kapila, 2002). The preference for financial assets against physical assets was attributed to greater financial intermediation and to a bias towards investing in less risky assets like bank deposits, contractual savings and small savings instruments. Still more than 50 per cent of household sector savings are diverted to physical assets (Figure 4.2). This is an alarming trend as over the years the extent of intermediation in India has increased and there is scope for further intermediation.

Figure 4.2

Distribution of Physical and Financial Savings in India (As a Per cent of Household Savings)

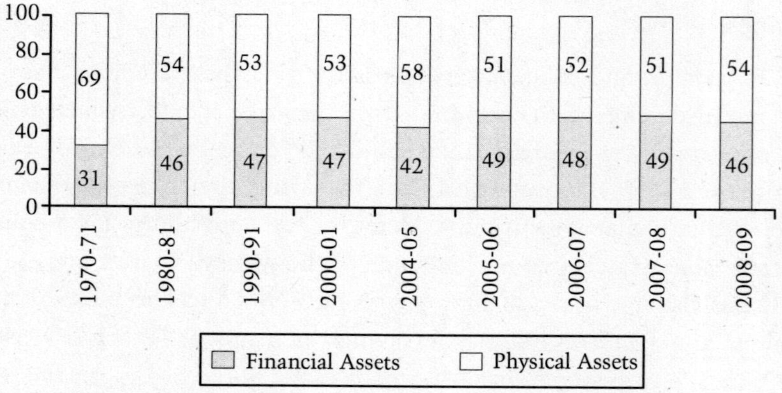

Source: CMIE (2010). *National Income Statistics*. July.

Financial institutions have a more concrete role to play in this front. Currently there are 170 scheduled commerical banks and over 20 insurance companies in the market providing numerous financial products and services to a whopping 400 million customers in India. There is need to efficiently mobilise the household savings and make these available for developmental projects.

Of the financial assets, more than 75 per cent is held in low interest bearing bank deposits, it being the only option to many of the small savers, especially in rural areas. In a developed country like United States, financial assets held by households (as on March 2010) was in the form of currency and deposits (14.2%), bonds (8.9%), investment trusts (12.1%), shares and equities (31.4%), insurance and pension reserves (29.9%) and in others (3.5%) (Federal Reserve, 2010). Table 4.3 shows the savings and investment behaviour of Indian households, witnessed during 2006-09.

Table 4.3

Savings & Investment of Indian Households: 2006-2009

Financial savings as % to gross household savings	63%
Deposits	53.26%
Shares & debentures	8%
Mutual funds	6.4%
Government securities	-3.36%
Insurance funds	18.6%
Pension/Provident	10.16%
Physical assets as to gross household savings	52.3%

Source: DCIS.

Credit

Access to credit is an important requirement to generate growth. Wider a set of financial conveniences that households are able to access, the better are they placed in meeting their expenses towards health, education and other requirements. It also equips them in getting financial capital, building their assets and engaging in some business to earn a living as well as to meet financial shocks, if any. However, credit needs of every household are different and to meet these, it is necessary to have a variety of financial products and services that suit the needs of the rich and the poor. It is challenge for the service providers to innovate financial products that are tailored to suit the households because credit needs across the segments lie unmet on account of problems in suitability.

According to NSSO data (2008), more than 80 per cent of Indian population depends on agriculture but 45.9 million out of a total of 89.3 million farmer households do not have access to credit, institutional or non-institutional. Besides, only 27 per cent of rural households are able to access a financial institution (*Economic Survey*, 2007-08) and only 13 per cent avail loans from the banks in the income bracket of less than Rs. 50,000. Credit disbursement procedures are so cumbersome that only 53 per cent people resort to borrowing from the institutional and non-institutional sources only for emergency purposes.

The Flow of Risk Capital to SME

Financial intermediaries and institutions can be highly instrumental in mobilising savings especially when a vast number of SMEs in India face constraints in raising risk capital. The draft Eleventh Plan has underlined the importance of SME sector and has stressed the need to promote and protect the same. The development of SMEs is vital for the growth of the economy as they contribute greatly to our foreign trade and to employment. A whopping 44 per cent of the total manufactured exports are contributed by the small-scale sector and is the second largest sector contributing in employment generation after the agricultural sector.

This prompts an immediate need for the regulators to give top most priority to the introduction of SME stock exchanges given their capability to help the entrepreneurs and entities in raising the much needed risk capital and reducing their excessive dependence on bank lending or other channels of credit. It must be realised that it is the SMEs that can potentially reactivate investors to come to the capital markets from local area where the companies are located. Arranging risk capital for SME will create scaling up in decentralised basis and generate hubs and infrastructure in such areas. Global business and Indian growth funded by such investment in SME should benefit pan India for which wide low cost distribution is required. Besides, development of an active SME equity market in India could provide alternative source for raising risk capital to the entrepreneurs. Exchanges are long been considered as financial infrastructural institutions. The role of a stock exchange is beyond providing a trading platform, which includes capital formation for industry, wealth creation and distribution across society, low cost distribution network, product innovation and global alignment, building an efficient financial sector infrastructure and eco-system, and enhance credibility of market through better enforcement, regulation and transparency. Some of the prominent exchanges exclusively designed for SMEs are as in Table 4.4.

Table 4.4

Prominent SME Stock Exchanges

Exchange	*Name of the Market*
TSX Group	TSX Venture
Korea Stock Exchange	Kosdaq
Shenzhen Stock Exchange	ChiNext
Tokyo Stock Exchange	Mothers
London Stock Exchange	AIM

Note: TSX Venture - Toronto Stock Exchange; Kosdaq - Korean Securities Dealers Automated Quotations; Mothers - Market of the high-growth and emerging stocks; AIM - Alternative Investment Market.

Lower Penetration of Capital Markets

Indian capital markets suffer from abysmally lower levels of penetration. The following table clearly indicates India's position in the level of direct penetration in the equity markets which is one of the lowest as compared to developed markets as well as to countries like China despite the huge population base.

Table 4.5

Penetration in Equity Markets

Country	*Demat/Custody Accounts (i.e., Direct User Base) in Million*	*Population in Million*	*Individual Holding of Shares as % to Total Population*
India	16	1,173	1.4
Russia	3	139	2.2
South Korea	4	48	7.5
China	125	1,330	9.4
UK	10	61	16.4
US*	55	310	17.7

Note: *approximately based on household participation and size of average household in those countries. In United States, the overall equity and bond ownership rate is around 47 per cent of US households (54.5 million) and about 43 per cent of the US households owned mutual funds as per ICI/SIFMA Survey.

Source: SEC, ECB, Exchange and depository websites.

Rapid and inclusive growth takes place when funds are not only efficiently and effectively mobilised but are also channelised. This requires developed primary and secondary markets. Primary markets are instrumental in raising funds for the corporate sector while secondary market provides an outlet for investors to step in and out at various investment stages and thus promotes capital formation at all levels and at all times.

In India, capital formation takes place in a constrained manner in the secondary market which is marked by low turnover liquidity and low participation. Turnover velocity as a measure of market liquidity shows turnover as a percentage to their market capitalisation. Table 4.6 denotes the turnover liquidity in Indian markets in comparison with other countries.

Table 4.6

Turnover Liquidity

Country	*United States*	*Korea*	*China*	*India*
GDP	14.4	0.9	4.3	1.2
Equity share trading value	47	1.6	7.8	1.0
Equity share traded as a per cent to GDP	326%	170%	181%	87%
Turnover velocity (July 2010)	NYSE: 137.21% NASDAQ: 348.85%	KSE: 173.51%	SSE: 129.9% SHZE: 281.1%	BSE: 17.11% NSE: 53.89%

Source: World Federation of Exchanges (2009).

During the last decade (2000-01 to 2009-10), the turnover in equity cash segment grew at a compounded annual growth rate (CAGR) of just 10 per cent as average daily turnover increased from Rs. 9,321 to Rs. 22,574 crore. However, in the same period, the average daily turnover in the equity derivatives market rose by 150 per cent to Rs. 72,393 crore from Rs. 19 crore in 2000-01. Across the years market capitalisation increased to a great extent but subsequently the capital markets became more concentrated and unbalanced growth was observed in them. The corporate debt market too has remained underdeveloped despite the various policy measures taken.

In India there has been an increase in the contribution from top five cities to total share trading from 78 per cent in 2001-02 to 84 per cent in

2009-10 while the same is just 65 per cent in China. This indicates the high degree of concentration in Indian secondary markets and equity capital culture limited to few cities. Capital formation has stood limited as around 75 per cent of trading is in cash-settled futures and option. Besides, over 75 per cent of cash equities trading in India is intra-day in nature which is also cash-settled. The following figure is indicative of the same.

Figure 4.3

Share of Cash Trading Volume, Mutual Fund Ownership and Income by Cities (FY 2009, Per cent)

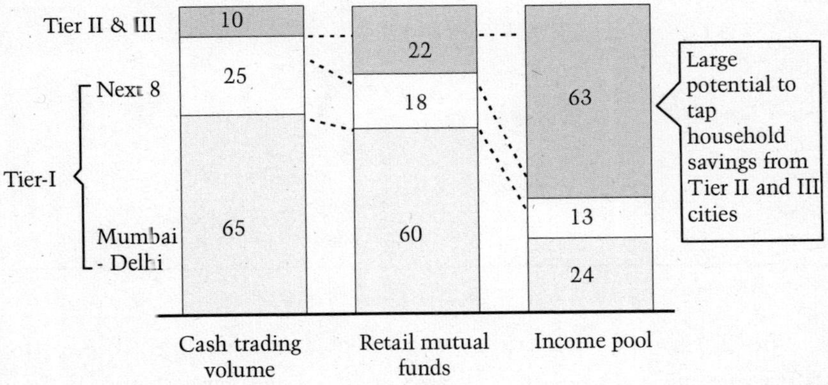

Note: 1. Tier I cities: Top 10 cities by population. 2. Tier II: Next 90 centres by population. 3. Tier III: Next ~320 centres by population. Beyond Tier-III, centres are defined as semi-urban.

Source: Mckinsey.

Not much has been done to introduce financial products tailor-made to meet the investment needs of every class of the population. This is reflected in the extent of financial exclusion in India. Only about 40 per cent of the population across the country has bank accounts and the ratio is much lower in the northeast region of the country. Less than 10 per cent of population avails of any life insurance cover. Above all, less than 2 per cent of population directly participates in the Indian capital markets. Further, the financial instruments too are not developed to the desired extent.

Underdeveloped Corporate Bond Market

The excessive intermediation only adds to the cost to the entrepreneurs in raising capital. A developed corporate bond would have provided alternative source for raising risk capital. While, India is conspicuous with absence of active SME exchange, the underdeveloped corporate bond is posing severe constraints to corporate India in raising capital especially for infrastructure funding. Table 4.7 shows the status of our corporate bonds.

Table 4.7

Status of Corporate Bonds

Equity market capitalisation as % to GDP	110%
Market cap of corporate bond as % to GDP	
India	3%
Malaysia	43%
Singapore	34%
Hong Kong	35%
Corporate bond as % to total bond market	
India	5%
Malaysia	45%
Singapore	41%
Hong Kong	52%

Source: WFE and ADB; (as of December 2009).

The Table 4.8 illustrates extent underdevelopment of other instruments like interest rates futures, currency derivatives, etc., in India in comparison with developed markets. It is absolute necessary for having active markets for various asset classes and instruments for the development of overall financial market in the country.

Table 4.8

India and the World: Trading across Asset Classes (in US $ Trillion), 2009

Asset Groups	*USA*		*Europe*		*Brazil*		*India*	
Equity	47	5.2%	12.4	1.8%	0.6	4.7%	1.2	16%
Equity derivatives	59	6.5%	28.8	4.3%	1.5	11.2%	3.7	51%
Interest rate	724	80.4%	620.9	92.8%	7.9	58.8%	0.0	0%
FX derivatives	21	2.3%	0.0	0.0%	3.4	25.1%	0.8	11%
Commodity	50	5.5%	7.2	1.1%	0.02	0.2%	1.6	22%
Total	901	100%	669.3	100%	13.4	100%	7.3	100%

Source: World Federation of Exchanges and Exchange websites.

Meeting the Gaps...

Financial Inclusion and Deepening

The path to inclusive growth passes through financial inclusion. Indian economy and financial sector has displayed a long-term growth trajectory but the growth is yet to transform into inclusive growth. The extent of exclusion, social and financial, has posed impediments to inclusion. A major chunk of population has not been able to access even the basic opportunities and services emerging in the financial sector.

The goal of financial inclusion has repeatedly been stressed in the policy pronouncements and Reserve Bank of India (RBI) aspires to achieve 100 per cent financial inclusion in the near future. As a part of the policy initiative, in June 2006, the Government of India constituted a 'Committee on Financial Inclusion' under the chairmanship of Dr. C. Rangarajan. The Committee submitted its report in January 2008. It has defined Financial Inclusion as 'the process of ensuring access to financial services and timely and adequate credit where needed by vulnerable groups such as weaker sections and low income groups at an affordable cost.' This is a broader definition of financial inclusion than the one adopted in the UN Blue Book (2006). As per the UN definition, an inclusive financial sector should provide access to credit to all bankable people and firms, insurance to all insurable people and firms, and to savings and payment services for everyone. It is noteworthy that Dr. Rangarajan has identified a greater scope for financial inclusion in India by considering the concept in the wider contexts and peculiarities of an emerging country like India.

One of the major recommendations of Rangarajan Committee included launching of a National Rural Financial Inclusion Plan (NRFIP) to make financial services including credit accessible to at least 50 per cent of the financially excluded rural households by 2012 and to the remaining by 2015. It also recommended constitution of two funds with National Bank for Agriculture and Rural Development (NABARD)—the Financial Inclusion Promotion & Development Fund (and the Financial Inclusion Technology Fund with an initial corpus of Rs. 500 crore each to be contributed by GoI/RBI/NABARD to facilitate inclusion efforts by groups and agents and also to provide low cost technology solutions. This has already been accepted and implemented by the GoI. The Committee also recommended enhancing the outreach of microfinance programmes and institutions and improving their access to credit along with improving access to microfinance to the urban poor.

Thus, financial inclusion promotes growth by catering to the growth needs of every element in the society. However, financial inclusion does not take place on its own. It needs to be fostered by the government and the regulators. Besides, financial intermediaries and institutions and capital market players need to take up additional responsibilities apart from the conventional roles.

I have often expressed my view in various business fora that market players need to cast off the conventional notions of social responsibility or charity with regards to financial inclusion. In fact, business fraternity needs to realise that there lies a profitable business opportunity in financial inclusion. The late management guru, C.K. Prahalad pleaded that fortune lies at the bottom of the pyramid and businesses need to exploit the vast demand base of the consumers. The same holds true in the financial sector too. Such an attitude can enable banks and financial institutions contribute to financial inclusion on a larger scale and at a rapid pace.

Banks can be highly instrumental in fostering financial inclusion given 400 million account holders and 80,500 branches. RBI launched the Lead Bank Scheme back in 1970 which was followed by the establishment of regional rural banks (RRBs) in 1975. Recognising the potential for financial institutions to help achieve greater financial inclusion, the High Level Committee to Review the Lead Bank Scheme (2009) has suggested continuation of the scheme with a decentralised approach. The efforts of the government and the RBI have been to deepen and widen the financial system in the country. They have been making efforts to develop a suitable and sustainable financial institutional setup to promote savings and investment. Now the RBI aspires to provide a bank account to those desirous to have or are potential users but has also widened the definition of financial inclusion to provide a wider scope to make access to financial products and services easier. As a part of its 100 per cent financial inclusion drive, RBI has enabled *kirana* store owners, retired defence personnel and school teachers NGOs/MFIs, trusts, non-profit companies, post offices, cooperative societies to assist as business correspondents (BCs) in reaching the unbanked areas. Now, RBI desires to move-in for profit companies to act as BCs for promoting financial inclusion. Off late it has also recommended using the services of for profit organisations to help as business facilitators. Dr. Rangarajan has suggested that the cost arising from assignment of facilitators be shared by the government, banks and the customers. He believes that microfinance institutions should keep the cost to borrowers at lower levels so that they can repay the same in future and also subsidies could be avoided.

To foster financial inclusion banks need to give higher priority to market segmentation and come up with innovative products and offerings that enhance the reach of financial services to the masses. Rangarajan (2004) cites the opinion of Jan Tinbergen that there should be as many instruments as there are objectives, if all objectives are to be fulfilled. He has rightly pointed that small and medium-sized banks can also effectively compete if appropriate niche strategies are adopted. He suggests that simplification of procedures for granting loans to small borrowers, farmer-friendly rural bank branches and microfinancing can enhance financial inclusion in India. He has underlined the need to bring about improvements within the existing credit delivery system rather than adding new institutions to banks, rural banks, cooperative societies or micro-finance agencies and that the rural bank branches need to extend their roles beyond credit disbursement and help in matters relating to agriculture and rural development.

Financial Education

A survey conducted among retail and institutional investors across 12 Indian cities by MCX-SX in alignment with Nielsen company suggests that Indian equity market is underpenetrated and underdeveloped. It has highlighted that a lack of financial knowledge has been a major barrier to participation in the markets, and the respondents have expressed a strong desire for financial training. They have also suggested introduction of competition as a means to get the best financial services at affordable and competitive rates.

One of the major impediments in spreading financial inclusion is the lack of financial literacy. This is the reason behind more than 50 per cent of savings of the household sector and getting drained in non-financial investments. If banks provide simpler and affordable products, the less financially literate and the lower income groups would be easily attracted the formal financial system.

The Mutual Funds offer schemes called micro-SIP (Systematic Investment Plan) that allows people to invest with just Rs. 50/-. Here, a person is required to invest regularly and is permitted minimum withdrawals. This encourages the people to save regularly and withdraw judiciously. However, a person lacking financial literacy finds constraints in knowing how much returns does he/she earn and is concerned about the safety of money. Such demand constraints can be removed if there is financial literacy among the masses.

In its efforts to increase financial literacy RBI has set up a multilingual website in 13 languages explaining in an entertaining manner subjects like banking, money, importance of saving, RBI's functions, etc. It has also undertaken a project titled 'Project Financial Literacy' to spread information regarding the RBI and general banking concepts to various target segments such as school and college going children, women, rural and urban poor, defence personnel and senior citizens. This also implies that financial education may be included in the curriculum of the formal educational system for bringing awareness among young generation and spreading banking and saving habits among the younger lots. Dissemination of price information by exchanges and other intermediaries in vernacular languages could go a long way in fostering financial education and inculcating investing habits among all the segments of the population.

Financial and education institutions, financial intermediaries and local correspondents have to take up greater responsibility in elevating the levels of financial literacy in the country. RBI has recommended that financial literacy and customer education should be incorporated in the business strategies of banks and they should stay committed to this task. Business networks, technological aids and other resources can be effectively used by the intermediaries to adopt low cost business models. Criteria regarding financial literacy and inclusion could be adopted in the performance evaluation of their field staff by banks and other institutions.

Financial Integration and Cross-Selling

All the segments of the population should invest their savings into financial products that could fetch higher returns than those invested conventionally in savings account and fixed deposits. People also need to avail other financial conveniences such as insurance policies, pension plans in order to manage risks and old age. A World Bank Policy paper on finance observes that a probable reason why the poor might not save in financial assets might be the lack of appropriate products in the respective markets. It is worthwhile to mention here that Rangarajan Report has on financial inclusion underlined the importance of tackling the issues of financial inclusion in a holistic manner and has recommended that efforts be made to look into insurance and remittance needs of lower income groups.

Answer to the above gaps lies in greater integration. Financial integration can be achieved if there is integration between the financial intermediaries. On this front, differences in the business lines and revenue segments of different intermediaries have tapered down. Under financial convergence or integration, all financial services can be made available to customers under one roof. Convergence of financial services at last mile will create low-cost financial services model for all services as against stand-alone vertical for each services end to end. A bank can accept deposits and lend money and can also offer investment banking, credit card services, or sell insurance policies at the same time. Commercial banks have already started marketing and selling the mutual fund schemes on recommendation by the RBI. Further, India Post engages in selling saving schemes, gold coins, etc., apart from its conventional functions relating to postal services. However, further integration is needed between capital market players. Integration of network of banks, exchanges, insurance companies, fund houses and other financial bodies and institutions can facilitate enhanced financial inclusion and the intermediaries also can benefit from cross-selling.

Recently, banks have been performing various functions apart from the conventional banking activities. Banks generate revenues from their various business segments such as retail banking, commercial banking, investment banking, asset management, portfolio management, transaction services, etc. These services cater to different customer bases like retail clients, institutional clients, corporate, firms, etc. Many of the above services of banks charge fees to clients for availing the service. These fee-based services contribute significantly to the revenue of banks globally as well as domestically. Major chunk of the fee-based revenue comes from capital market activities which involves equity markets, debt market, derivatives markets and host of other services to corporate clients *viz.*, merger and acquisition advisory, project advisory, financial engineering, etc.

Table 4.9

Fee-Based Revenues of Indian Banks (2007-2009)

S. No.	*Bank*	*Average Fee-Based Revenues as a % of Total Revenues*
1	Citi Bank India	70
2	HSBC Bank India	55
3	Standard Chartered Bank India	35

Source: Annual reports of respective banks.

Mutual Funds

Mutual funds play an important role in mobilising the household savings for deployment in capital markets. Besides, they are the best possible investment vehicles for risk diversification. The mutual fund sector in India is rapidly becoming a favoured sector for investment given the high volatility experienced in the stock markets in the recent years.

Since 1990s, mutual fund assets have grown steadily in India, and are now estimated at $160 billion. The gross mobilisation of resources by all mutual funds during 2008-09 stood at Rs. 54,26,353 crore. While banks have around 80,500 across the country, fund houses have only 2,500 branches. As a result, only 7.7 per cent of the country's total savings are diverted to mutual funds compared with 18 per cent in insurance and 55 per cent in bank fixed deposits. The penetration of mutual funds is limited to a few cities, mainly top 10 cities. Significantly mutual fund houses promoted by Indian banks accounted for around 300,000 crore of the 750,000 crore of assets under management (AUM) (as on August 2009).

According to Association of Mutual Funds in India (AMFI), there are over 64,000 distributor agents, of which 4,250 are corporate. Mutual fund penetration is still restricted to the top 8 cities. There are around 40 asset management companies (AMCs) offering around 630 schemes giving large scope for investors with diversified risk appetite. In India, where population is over 1.1 billion, there are a total number of only 44.5 million investor accounts or less than 20 per cent households holding mutual funds. In contrast, in the United States, as per ICI/SIFMA survey, the overall equity and bond ownership rate is around 47 per cent of US households (54.5 million), and about 43 per cent of the US households owned mutual funds. This demonstrates that there lies a huge gap in the mutual fund industry's penetration and there is ample scope for the industry to develop in India. The sector's expansion is supported by a growing middle class in India, and backed by Indian overseas workers investing part of their earnings at home. Out of a population of more than 1.1 billion, only 230 million are middle class. That leaves a further untapped chunk of population that will be upgraded to middle class. Once that happens, it throws a lot of potential source of investments.

Exchanges

Exchanges help investors in raising the risk capital through the primary market as well as provide the exit route via the secondary market. The exchange platforms are well equipped to protect participants from financial risks in participation through online risk management and surveillance mechanism.

The primary issues like Coal India's initial public offer (IPO) helps in distribution of wealth and inclusion of population excluded in the capital markets. The IPO has been reported to be the country's largest attracting bids worth more than Rs. 1.81 lakh crore. Data suggests that it has been subscribed 11.64 times, with institutional segment being subscribed approximately 25 times, and the retail and high networth individual (HNIs) portions being subscribed 0.8 times and 1.4 times, respectively. The IPO also triggered a lot of retail participation and a considerable increase in the number of demat accounts in the country. Thus, exchanges and disinvestment has been aiding the cause of financial inclusion and also guiding the retail participants to the market.

Off late Securities and Exchange Board of India (SEBI) has allowed mutual fund transactions through existing stock exchange infrastructure. This is a step towards enhancing penetration of mutual fund products beyond urban regions. Stock exchanges, depositories and clearing corporations function as infrastructure companies in the securities market. The stock exchanges have superior reach with over 200,000 exchange terminals spread over 1,500 towns and cities. Through this, the convenience and ease available to secondary market investors can be availed by mutual fund investors too. Besides, the network of broking companies have spread to semi-urban and are now increasing focus on retail investors. Such cross-selling will create enough products and services for each intermediary to have economies of scale to maintain infrastructure of smallest of the towns.

In the exchanges arena, to keep the regulators more focused and promote efficiency, the government has adopted non-convergence in the securities and commodities markets' regulation in 2003. A whole new industry grew with these policy initiatives. Dr. Rangarajan had been supportive of this initiative as an economist who understood the art of policymaking relevant for the industry striking a perfect balance of focus on practical implementation ability, public good and growth.

Integration venture between India Post and Insurance

There is a robust growth of 30-40 per cent in premiums (2003–2008); the per capita insurance premium is low on account of large population and the vast extent of financial exclusion. Insurance Regulatory and Development Authority (IRDA) had initiated a publicity campaign to foster awareness about insurance products and to enable customers to make more use of the insurance products by taking informed decisions.

Recently, IRDA has allowed India Post to sell policies of multiple insurance companies. This initiative can help financial inclusion significantly given India Post's distribution network that is largest in India. It provides an efficient distribution channel for insurance companies looking out for low cost distributors with a wider network and will also help the postal department with a new revenue segment. According to the revised guidelines by IRDA, India Post can serve as a corporate agent of two non-life insurers, two life insurance companies, one agricultural insurance company and one health insurance company. Further, it is expected that Central and state government employees in the rural areas would volunteer to act as insurance agents for India Post as they are more trusted by the local folks and have a better knowledge about local population. Such an effort at integration can really trigger inclusion on the back of a robust network of 1.55 lakh offices of India Post as against 11,800 offices of 22 insurance companies existing in India.

Competition and Technology: The Catalysts in the Growth Process

Competitive atmosphere if provided and encouraged by the government breeds efficiency in markets and efficient market system is the backbone of the current global economy. Competition aids in realising the potential of markets and facilitates ease, convenience and cost-effectiveness of products. It also helps in expanding the customer base as well as proper targeting and segmentation on the supply side, while attracting the customer groups and increasing the aggregate demand on the demand side. A policy of a broader competitive framework needs to be pursued and while pursuing the same; attention needs to be concentrated on certain crucial areas like technology and automation.

In order to inject an element of efficiency at realistic costs as well as to enhance service and have larger coverage, government has taken relevant step in sectors like banking, insurance, aviation and telecom. As a result, currently there are over 170 banks, over 20 insurance companies, 15 airliners and 14 telecom companies at the service of India's investing population. This has actually worked wonders and has benefited the end-users. For example, telecom tariffs in India have come down to as low as 1 paise a second. The following table reflects the competition existing in the sectors mentioned:

Mutual Funds	Banks	Capital Market
	Number of	
AMCs: 44	Commercial Banks: 170	National Stock Exchange: 2
Branches: 2,500	Branches: 80,500	Brokers: 2100
Agents: 64,000		Trading Terminals: 200,000
	As on December 2009	
AUM: $165 bn	SCBs Agg. deposits: $875 bn	Market Cap: $1120 bn
Users:~47 mn	Users: ~600 mn	Direct Investors:~15mn

Life Insurance Business	2001	2009
Companies:	11	23
Offices:	2,200	11,800
Agents:	0.1 mn	~3 mn
Sum Assured:	$160bn	$600 bn
Subscribers		260mn

Telecom Sector	2002	2009
Service Providers	13	14
	2001	2009
Subscribers:	36 mn	500 mn

Source: IRDA, RBI, SEBI, AMFI and TRAI.

Competition in stock exchanges is necessary for the inclusive development of capital market. The performance of stock exchanges can not only be measured in terms of turnover, but also the level of inclusion and penetration in the country. In United States, there are 14 Securities and Exchange Commission (SEC) registered national securities exchanges and interestingly some of the exchanges got the licences quite recently. Besides new stock exchanges, US has more than 73 Alternative Trading Systems (ATS) and Europe has several Multilateral Trading Facilities (MTFs) providing trade matching and clearing support without listing securities. Therefore, there is a very competitive trading environment. However, such competition is missing in India as single exchange largely dominates the market with over 90 per cent market share in equity and equity futures and options trading.

RBI has considered fostering competition as an important step in promoting financial inclusion. The average population coverage by a commercial bank branch in urban areas has improved from 12,300 in June, 2005 to 9,400 in June 30, 2010 and in rural and semi-urban areas from 17,200 in June 30, 2005 to 15,900 in June 30, 2010. However, a large chunk of underprivileged population is financially excluded. RBI is promptly considering giving some additional banking licences to corporates and also to NBFCs. Similar moves to foster competition in exchanges business could also help in attracting retail participants towards the markets.

United States

National Securities Exchanges	*Avg. Daily Share Traded Value (in US $Bn)(July 2010)*	*Market Share (%)*
NASDAQ OMX*	106.4	47.3
NYSE EURONEXT*	74.1	33.0
BATS	27.5	12.2
EDGE DIRECT	7.5	3.4
Boston EX	6.6	2.9
National SX	1.3	0.6
Chicago SX	1.2	0.5
CBOE	0.4	0.2

Note: *Group total.

Source: Bats trading.

Europe

Trading Platforms (Europe)	*Avg. Daily Share Traded Value (in US $Bn)(April 2010)**	*Market Share (%)*
SLE Group	14.5	23.2
Euronext	9.6	15.5
CHI-X	8.7	14.0
Deutsche Boerse	7.8	12.6
Spanish Exchanges	6.3	10.1
Nasdaq OMX Nordic	4.0	6.4
SIX Swiss	3.9	6.1
BATS Europe	2.7	4.3
Others (24 platforms)	4.8	7.9

Note: *Excluding OTC reported and dark pools.

Source: Thomson Reuters's European Market Share Report.

In early 1980s a High Level Committee chaired by Dr. Rangarajan was appointed to consider the issues and plan for computerisation and mechanisation of the banking industry in India over a timeframe of five years (1985-1989). The Committee aimed to improve the banks' customer services and came up with two models that were later developed and implemented. One of the models aimed for front office mechanisation keeping the back office operations manual while the other model aimed at back office automation (including general ledger) keeping the front office work manual. In 1988, Rangarajan Committee (II) drew a detailed plan for further computerisation of the banking system in the country extending automation to areas like SWIFT, ATM, fund transfers, electronic mails, etc. It recommended computerisation of around 2,500 branches located at high activity centres and regional and zonal offices and installing cash dispensers at locations like airport, railway stations etc.

Technological advances have served as catalyst in the growth process of Indian economy and contributed immensely to promote growth and employment in various sectors along with promoting exports. 'Adhar', the Unique Identification Project by the government stands testimony as to how technology can be harnessed to help financial institutions in their konw-your-customer (KYC) norms. It is also expected to help every individual to establish her/his financial identity in the nation's economy in a country with over 1 billion population.

Technology has the potential to reduce barriers and distances. With strength of 70-80 million Internet users and 5.2 million broadband Internet connections in India, the actual Internet penetration rate in India is only 7 per cent. This extent of coverage is dismally low if compared with 25 per cent in China and Singapore, and 75 per cent in United States. Teleconferencing, communication through Internet and mobile phone are highly beneficial in large countries with rural economies and broadband can prove more beneficial in the developing world than in the developed world. It is welcome step that Government of India and Telecom Regulatory Authority of India (TRAI) have been working out a national broadband plan to connect India's towns and villages.

Conclusion

India has traversed a long path to growth and has reached a stage of development where she aspires for inclusive growth and development to prevent inequality in society. India has the potential to realise the set objectives given a policy environment that supports financial inclusion, promotes financial integration and competition and gives prime importance to competitive market forces including efficient allocation of capital. Once 100 per cent financial inclusion is achieved, it will not be difficult to imagine capital markets services alone creating employment opportunities for millions of youth through exchange services ecosystem. Further, one can expect India to be the centre stage of business in Asia post-convertibility as we emerge as a global financial centre that provides full range of financial services for various maturities, risk and markets across the region. Financial services are the lifeline of a developed economy which in turn supports growth, employment generation, capital allocation, savings, wealth distribution and risk management.

References

Arora, Nikesh (2010). "Time to Fire up Internet Engines in Rural India", *Economic Times*, October 18.

Business Standard (2010). "Coal India IPO Subscribed 12 Times", *Business Standard*, October 21.

CII & IRDA (2010). *Indian Insurance Sector: Stepping into the Next Decade of Growth*. September.

———. (2010). *Communique* 19(3), March.

Federal Reserve (2010). "Flow of Funds Accounts of the United States", *First Quarter*.

IDBI (2008). "The Need for Financial Inclusion with an Indian Perspective", Economic Research, March 03.

Kapila, Uma (2002). *Indian Economy Since Independence*. New Delhi: Academic Foundation.

Kochar, Sameer (ed.) (2010). *India on the Growth Turnpike*. New Delhi: Academic Foundation.

MCX-SX (2010). *Indian Equity Investors Survey 2010*.

Ministry of Finance (2010). "Fiscal Developments and Public Finance" *Economic Survey 2009-10*. New Delhi: Government of India.

Mohan, Rakesh (2006). "Economic Growth, Financial Deepening and Financial Inclusion", *Annual Bankers' Conference 2006*. November.

Office for National Statistics (2010). *Fiscal Deficit Data*. September 30. United Kingdom.

Palkhiwala, Nani A. (2006). *We the Nation: The Lost Decades*.

Rangarajan, C. (2004). *Select Essays on Indian Economy*, Volume I. New Delhi: Academic Foundation.

NABARD (2008). *Report of the Committee on Financial Inclusion*. January.

RBI (various years). *Annual Report*, various issues.

SEBI (various years). *Annual Report*, various issues.

———. (2009). *Handbook of Statistics on the Indian Securities Market*.

Subbarao, Duvvuri (2010a). *Financial Education: Worthy and Worthwhile*. March.

———. (2010b). *Harnessing Technology to Bank the Unbanked*. June.

Thorat, Usha (2008). *Financial Inclusion and Information Technology.* September.

http://www.usgovernmentspending.com/federal_deficit_chart.html. Accessed on October 22, 2010.

The views expressed in this article are personal and do not reflect in whatsoever manner, those of MCX – SX

5 Should Banking be made Boring?

An Indian Perspective

Duvvuri Subbarao

The focus of this book *Growth and Finance* is a fitting tribute to Dr. C. Rangarajan's enormous intellectual contribution to macroeconomic management in India for over three decades. His work and advice—as governor of Reserve Bank of India, as chairman of the Twelfth Finance Commission (2005-2010), as member of the Planning Commission, and for over the last five years, as chairman of the Economic Advisory Council to the Prime Minister (PMEAC) had a profound impact in setting economic policy directives for India.

Dr. Rangarajan, like several other distinguished economists, straddled both academia and the government. What makes him unique though is the way he constructively blended what are two disparate worlds. He brought deep scholarship over a range of academic disciplines to bear on public policy. In the reverse direction, through his writings and speeches, he disseminated practical policy dilemmas to the academia. Throughout, he remained deeply sensitive to real life concerns. It is this unique trait that has set him apart as one of today's most credible thinkers and advisors. Fittingly, a critic labelled him as 'philosopher king', and not surprisingly, the Government turns to him for advice whenever it is confronted with any intricate economic issue.

When Dr. Rangarajan joined the Reserve Bank of India (RBI) in 1982 as Deputy Governor, India's economic philosophy was dirigiste, dominated by deep apprehensions about market forces and a strong faith in government intervention. In the financial sector, this meant an elaborate system of controls and regulation with the RBI even mandating innumerable interest rates for both depositors and borrowers. Such a labyrinth of controls and micro-management must have bewildered a fresh entrant from the academia. Dr. Rangarajan was, of course, fully sensitive to the development considerations that led to this deviation of practical policy from academic prescription. Nevertheless, consistent with the reform ethos, during his tenure first as Deputy Governor and then as Governor of the RBI, Dr. Rangarajan oversaw the deregulation of the enormous control apparatus.

The global financial crisis that we have just been through has revived some of the familiar questions that we thought have been settled. Among them is the question, have the regulators gone too far to the other extreme with deregulation? Is it not this faith in 'light touch' regulation that completely blindsided regulators to the bubble building up in the underbelly of the financial sector? Has all this 'freedom' made banking too glamorous, and is not there a compelling need to make banking boring once again? There can be no greater tribute to Dr. Rangarajan's lifetime of work than to look at this issue of 'Should banking be made boring?' from an Indian perspective.

Calls for making Banking Boring

Banks have been at the heart of the global financial crisis and bankers are widely seen as being responsible for the crisis! Quite understandably, there is a deluge of ideas and suggestions on reforming banks, banking and bankers. One of the more influential ideas, one that has generated a vigorous debate, has been the thesis put forward by the noted economist and Nobel Laureate (2008) Paul Krugman that, 'the way to reform banking is to once again make it boring!'

Taking a long-term historical view, Krugman argues that, 'there is a negative correlation between the "business model" of banking and economic stability. Whenever banking got exciting and interesting, paid well and attracted intellectual talent, it got way out of hand and jeopardised the stability of the real sector. Conversely, periods when banking was dull and boring were also periods of economic progress.'

To support his thesis, Krugman divides American banking over the past century into three phases. The first phase is the period before 1930, before the Great Depression, when banking was an exciting and expanding industry. Bankers were paid better than in other sectors and therefore banking attracted talent, nurtured ingenuity and promoted innovation. The second phase was the period following the Great Depression when banking was tightly regulated, far less adventurous and decidedly less lucrative—in other words banking became boring! Curiously, this period of boring banking coincided with a period of spectacular progress. The third phase, beginning the 1980s, saw the loosening of regulation yielding space for innovation and expansion. Banking became, once again, exciting and high paying. Much of the seeming success during this period, according to Krugman, was an illusion; and the business model of banking of this period had actually threatened the stability of the real sector. Krugman's surmise accordingly is that, 'the bank street should be kept dull in order to keep the main street safe.'

The boring banking thesis found an echo in other influential voices. In a speech that attracted wide notice, Mervyn King, Governor of the Bank of England addressed the 'moral hazard' issue: why were banks willing to take risks that proved so damaging to themselves and the rest of the economy? The problem, according to Governor King, was that financial institutions became too important to be allowed to fail. His solution: restrict banking to its traditional 'utility' function—performing basic retail financial intermediation of deposit taking and lending, and providing payment and settlement services; and hive off the riskier financial services such as proprietary trading into a separate entity. In what has come quickly to be known as the 'utility and casino' model, the 'utility' will be heavily regulated and will enjoy implicit government guarantee while the 'casino' will be left to the discipline of market forces.

Closer home, another equally influential voice—Dr. Y.V. Reddy, former Governor of the Reserve Bank of India—weighed in on the issue. In his Guhan Memorial Lecture (October, 2009), Dr. Reddy called for 'back to basics' in banking and urged that banks must curb the tendency towards further financialisation of deposits they mobilise and must focus instead on lending to real sectors of the economy, particularly agriculture and the small and medium industries, that have limited ability to tap the capital markets.

Although neither Governor King nor former Governor Reddy mentioned 'boring banking', in a sense both of them were calling for what can stylistically be interpreted as boring banking.

Krugman's thesis of 'boring banking' is interesting, but also debatable. It raises several important questions. What were the ills of the banking system that caused the crisis? Is making banking 'boring' a necessary and sufficient cure to those ills? How do the several proposals on the table at the international level for reforming banking measure up to the test of making banking boring? And, how relevant is the 'boring banking' perspective in India? Let us address these questions one by one.

Ills of the Banking System that Caused the Crisis

Let me turn first to the ills of the banking system that caused the crisis. I will not go into an extensive analysis of the causes. I will attempt something much more limited—just give a brief synopsis to provide a backdrop for the 'boring banking' discussion.

Glass-Steagall Act, Financial Innovation and Risk Transmission

Many believe that the genesis of the crisis can be traced to the repeal in the United States in 1999 of the Glass-Steagall Act (1932-33) which mandated the separation of commercial and investment banking to protect depositors from the hazards of risky investment and speculation. The repeal opened up opportunities for commercial banks, investment banks, securities companies and insurance companies to consolidate, setting off a wave of innovation. Complex financial products were created by slicing and dicing, structuring and hedging, originating and distributing, all under the belief that real value could be created by sheer financial engineering. The system was characterised by opacity and dissipation of information with no one having a full picture of the extent of risk, how it was getting transmitted across the system and where it resided.

Globalisation of Financial Institutions and Services

A very striking feature of the financial crisis was its global scope with no country escaping unscathed. This should not surprise us. The progressive globalisation of financial institutions and services over the last two decades has led to a complex web of interconnected markets, institutions, services and products. Institutions transcended borders; markets became accessible in real time and financial services were available from everywhere. In short financial markets and institutions declared 'death of distance' and 'conquest of location'. And when the crisis came, it showed that globalisation meant that no country can really be an island.

Proliferation of Quasi-Banks beyond Regulatory Purview

As the pace of globalisation and financial innovation gained momentum, and encouraged by an extended period of monetary accommodation, banks entered into areas of activity that had earlier been the preserve of non-bank institutions. Banks looked for, and exploited, opportunities to shift profitable but risky businesses to entities outside the regulatory purview. To economise on capital requirements, banks developed new structured products to distribute the credit risk, they also found new special purpose entities and vehicles to handle them. The structured investment vehicles quickly spawned a vast 'shadow banking' network that operated and thrived outside the perimeter of bank regulation. With few regulatory restrictions and no coordinated oversight, they were able to take on risks that they did not fully comprehend. And when the Minsky moment arrived turning the financial mania into panic, the risks reverted to the parent banks causing financial turmoil and economic downturn.

The Moral Hazard of 'Too Big, Too Important to Fail' Institutions

The lure of profits encouraged financial institutions to expand, transcending borders and business segments, to exploit economies of scale and scope. And this was facilitated by the implicit faith of the authorities in 'light touch' regulation. Consequently, what we ended up with was large financial conglomerates with footprints across the system. These institutions knew that their failure would result in a systemic collapse, and that they would therefore be rescued at public cost. This acted as a perverse incentive for them to take on risks that we now know were imprudent if not reckless. The moral hazard of 'too big to fail' is therefore reckoned as one of the prime causes of the crisis.

Compensation and Perverse Incentives

Finally, the asymmetric compensation structures in many financial institutions encouraged risky behaviour. The variable components of compensations were anchored to short-term profits, were one-sided (high in good times and at worst zero in bad times) and had little or no risk adjustment. This myopic attitude towards long-term risk provided perverse incentives to bank managements to maximise their current compensations at the cost of shareholders, and to maximise leverage without regard to the tail risks to the institution.

Is 'Boring' Banking a Necessary and Sufficient Solution?

The ills of the banking system listed above raise two follow-on questions. Is making banking boring in the sense that Krugman indicated a necessary and sufficient solution to curing those ills and preventing their recurrence? And what will be the cost of making boring? Both questions cause much confusion, the first because it has too many answers and the second because it has too few. Abstracting from these answers, I will argue that it is neither possible nor desirable to make banking boring.

The narrow banking of the 1950s and 1960s was presumably safe and boring. But that was in a far simpler world when economies were largely national, competition was sparse, pressure for innovation was low, and reward for it even lower. Bankers of the time, it is said, worked on a 3-6-3 formula: pay depositors 3 per cent interest, lend money at 6 per cent and head off to the golf course at 3 pm. From the 24/7/365 perspective of today, that may appear romantic but is hardly practical.

The boring banking concept does not appear persuasive even going by more recent evidence and on several counts. First, recall that during the crisis, we saw the failure of not only complex and risky financial institutions like Lehman Brothers but also of traditional banks like Northern Rock. What this demonstrates is that a business model distinction cannot be drawn between a utility and a casino; and if it can, it does not coincide with the distinction between what has to be safe and what need not be. Second, in an interconnected financial sector, how can a 'boring' bank realistically ring-fence itself from what is happening all around? Let us say a large investment bank, a casino if you will, fails. Because of the inevitable interconnectedness, that will cause a breakdown of trust not just in that particular bank but in the entire financial sector. So utilities cannot expect to insulate themselves against the risks being taken by the casinos. Third, the co-existence of utilities and casinos can also open up arbitrage opportunities. During 'tranquil' periods, financial institutions with higher risk and reward business models will wean away deposits from narrow banks. But when problems surface and stresses develop in the financial sector, the position will reverse with the deposits flowing back into the so-called 'boring banks' triggering procyclicality. Finally and most importantly, what will be the cost of boring banking in economic terms? Does restraining banking to its core function just to keep it safe not mean forgoing opportunities for growth and development?

There have of course been problems in the way banking evolved around the world—problems that were at the heart of the crisis. But clearly the answer is not to adopt Luddite solutions that take us back decades. The solution is to look ahead to what we need. We need to build institutions that go beyond narrow banking and provide the whole gamut of financial services to meet the needs of customers, markets and economies. We need to build on the innovations of the last few decades but in doing so build in also correctives based on the lessons of experience. We need to build a safe and enterprising banking sector that supports growth while preserving financial stability. We need to nurture financial markets and institutions within clearly defined and effectively supervised boundaries. Doing all of this is the basic thrust of the international reform agenda currently under discussion to which I now turn.

International Reform Initiatives: Will they make Banking Boring?

The reform initiatives in the wake of the crisis are intended to rein in the 'irrational exuberance' of the banking sector, keep it safe and healthy, and make banking an aid for growth and macroeconomic stability. What is relevant to our discussion here is that none of these measures is aimed at making banking boring; on the contrary, several of them will likely make banking more challenging and thereby spur innovation of a more value adding and sustainable variety. In order to enable an appreciation of this, let me provide a brief synopsis of the various initiatives under discussion from the macro and micro perspectives.

The Macro Perspective

One clear lesson of the crisis is that regulation and supervision at the institution level is necessary, but not sufficient. Even if each institution is healthy and safe on a stand-alone basis, systemic risk can build up because of procyclical, herd behaviour—what economists call the fallacy of composition. It is therefore necessary to supplement microprudential regulation with macroprudential oversight.

At a macro level, to address procyclicality and contain leverage, three important initiatives are underway: (i) development of capital buffers that banks would be required to maintain to counter cyclical effects; (ii) requirement for institutions to set provisions on a dynamic basis, i.e., building up buffers in good times to be drawn down in bad times; and (iii) developing a metric to contain excessive leverage in banks to supplement the risk-based capital ratio.

A somewhat original idea proposed by Prof. Raghuram Rajan, currently under discussion, is to require institutions to maintain 'contingent capital' to tide over systemic crisis or idiosyncratic problems. This proposal will potentially require banks to issue long-term debt instruments that would automatically convert to equity under specific triggers. This contingent arrangement will accordingly enable banks coming under stress to quickly buffer their capital without imposing any cost on tax payers. All this will not, of course, be costless. The challenge is to design the contingent capital provisions in a way that optimally manages the trade-off between higher cost and lower moral hazard.

An important proposal aimed at mitigating systemic risk is to impose a systemic risk capital surcharge on institutions that pose a higher risk to the system because of their size, complexity or interconnectedness. There is increasing support for such a measure. In fact, Lord Turner, chairman of the UK Financial Services Authority (FSA), went further and argued that, '...should such a capital charge prove insufficient, there should be no hesitation in levying a tax on specific financial transactions.' The Turner proposal is based on the premise that regulation should ensure that the financial sector remains within its 'socially useful' size.

Large, interconnected and complex institutions will be subject to additional regulatory obligations in other dimensions as well. Importantly, such institutions will be required to institute more sophisticated risk management systems, have robust contingency plans and put in place 'living wills' that can steer the course of their orderly exit should problems in these institutions become unmanageable. The Basel Committee on Banking Supervision (BCBS) is working on resolution mechanisms for cross-border financial institutions with an aim to containing risk.

There is a proposal to move over-the-counter (OTC) derivatives to central counterparties and charge differentiated capital for OTC derivatives that are cleared on a bilateral basis. This will contain systemic risk to some extent.

Another lacuna that came into sharp focus during the crisis is that while financial activity is increasingly getting international, regulation remains fiercely national. The growing cross-border nature of banking and banking services underscores the need for a coordinated oversight of banking entities, particularly of large and complex institutions. In an ideal world, we would have global regulation; because we are in a less than ideal world, we are having to settle for a 'global framework' that will mandate minimum consistency across jurisdictions in regulatory principles that would apply to similar markets, institutions, activities and products.

Finally, the emergence of a large shadow banking system, typically with higher than average leverage, has underscored the need for their regulation and the importance of mandating disclosure and reporting requirements. This is coming in the form of expanding the perimeter of regulation to those institutions that are 'near banks' which are currently unregulated or under-regulated.

The Micro Perspective

Let me now turn to the micro perspective which focuses on ensuring the safety and soundness of individual institutions.

First, to ensure that bank exposures are adequately and sufficiently covered by capital, various enhancements to the Basel II capital framework have been finalised. These specifically relate to higher capital requirements for trading book to minimise the opportunity for regulatory arbitrage between the trading and banking books. There are also proposals on the table for improving the quality of capital to ensure that regulatory capital comprises largely elements having a true loss absorbing capacity in a going concern scenario.

Second, recognising that solvency of banks can be threatened by illiquidity as much as by inadequate capital, work is currently under way to develop a global standard for liquidity risk regulation of cross-border banks, and strengthening information sharing on liquidity risk among home and host country supervisors.

Other initiatives under way include promoting compensation structures that reflect the underlying risks taken over a longer term horizon and enhanced oversight of credit rating agencies, particularly where ratings are being used for aligning bank risk to regulatory capital requirements.

Collectively, the measures initiated both at the macro and micro levels to reform the financial sector aim to impart a balanced perspective to banking. The intention is to ensure that the stability of the system is preserved, the integrity of core banking is not violated, retail customers' savings and deposits are not jeopardised and that the costs of riskier business products and practices are internalised to prevent, or at any rate minimise, externalities.

Boring Banking: An Indian Perspective

Let me now turn to Indian banking. The decade of the 80s and 90s and the first decade of this century saw several financial crises around the world, many of them centred in banks. These crises were sometimes country specific, often regional, and in the case of the current crisis, global in scope. And in each case, the banking sector became a drag on the real economy, jeopardised public finances and hurt economic growth. What is noteworthy though is that even as other countries and other regions went through banking upheavals, Indian banking remained safe. This is a reflection, in part of our cautious and prudent regulation, and in part of the relatively lower globalisation of our banking sector.

All this does not mean that the lessons of the crisis are irrelevant for us. Going forward, our banking sector too will acquire an increasingly international character—Indian banks will increase their presence abroad while foreign banks will have larger presence in India. The task for the Indian banks is to learn to compete abroad and to set the terms of competition at home. It is imperative therefore for Indian banks to learn from the successes and failures around the world, study international best practices and adapt them to the Indian conditions. Just as banking around the world is not going to revert to being boring, neither will Indian banking get boring!

In fact, I will go further and argue that boring banking is an oxymoron in the Indian case. Here my intent is to argue not so much from the perspective of a banking model—narrow or full service—but from the perspective of the challenges that Indian banks will have to meet. Meeting these challenges is going to demand lateral thinking, entrepreneurship and management calibre—all a far cry from anything like boring. In order to illustrate this, I will list and explain what in my view are four big challenges that Indian banks will need to address.

First Challenge: Financial Inclusion

Despite its impressive progress, commercial banking in India has not penetrated sufficiently to serve the large mass of rural, illiterate and poor people in any meaningful way. Rough estimates indicate that of the 600,000 habitation centres in the country, only about 30,000 centres are covered by commercial banks. Even this big picture, stark as it is, does not fully convey the true extent of exclusion. Furthermore, even where 100 per cent financial inclusion is claimed, oftentimes it is inclusion only in a nominal sense. Households have bank accounts that remain dormant; few conduct any banking transactions and even fewer receive any credit. What we should attempt is quality financial inclusion which aims not at chasing a target but instead focuses on giving access to at least minimal financial services to the currently excluded.

The RBI has taken several steps over the last few years to further financial inclusion—encouraging 'no frills' accounts to allow access to basic financial services, initiating and then expanding the Business Correspondent (BC) model and the use of mobile phones for extending banking outreach. More recently, we have expanded the categories of entities that can be appointed as BCs and also allowed banks to charge a commission for services rendered by BCs. There are of course formidable challenges to the BC model that we need to address—high maintenance costs, small size of transactions, expanding awareness, improving communication skills and techniques for dealing with semi-literate people in local languages, enlisting the cooperation of the village administrations and overcoming the constraints posed by lack of electricity and sometimes telecommunication access.

What is clear though is that it is not possible to cover a country of a billion plus people, spread over 600,000 habitations, covering vast distances, with poor infrastructure and sometimes inhospitable terrain by traditional brick and mortar branches.

We need to think laterally, harness technology, adopt effective dissemination practices and reach out to all the people across the country to provide at least minimal banking services. Financial inclusion is especially valuable as it will at once promote both growth and equity. I can hardly overemphasise how big a challenge financial inclusion is for banks, for the banking regulator and for the government. Working to meet this challenge can hardly be a boring proposition.

Second Challenge: Financing Infrastructure

Distinct from other large emerging market economies which are typically demand constrained, India has been, and will remain in the foreseeable future, a supply constrained economy. The biggest supply constraint is of infrastructure—physical, social and urban. It is widely recognised that poor and inadequate infrastructure is adding to production costs, denting productivity of capital and eroding the competitiveness of our productive sectors.

The Eleventh Five-Year Plan targets increase in infrastructure investment from around 5 per cent of GDP in 2006/07 to 9 per cent by 2011/12. This translates to cumulative infrastructure investment over the Plan period of over Rs. 20 trillion (US $520 billion). Almost one half of this investment is to be funded through debt, and as much as 43 per cent of this total debt requirement (21 per cent of overall planned investment) is planned to be financed by banks. Regardless of any revision the numbers may undergo, what is clear is that the financing needs of our infrastructure are huge.

A big issue in bank financing of infrastructure is the asset-liability mismatch. While infrastructure typically requires long-term funding, the deposits of banks, their main source of funds, are relatively short term. The problem of asset-liability mismatch in long-term financing is not unique to India; banks elsewhere too face the same problem. But in advanced economies, the long-term finance space is filled by insurance companies and pension and provident funds. If some of the pending legislation gets through, in India too we can expect new sources of long-term financing to open up. But until that happens, the burden of infrastructure financing will have to be met largely by the banks. In order to partly offset this problem, the RBI has, since 2000, allowed banks to enter into take-out financing arrangements with other financial institutions.

To facilitate financing for infrastructure, the RBI has also relaxed the exposure norms. To avoid concentration risk, banks are mandated to restrict their exposures to a maximum of 15 per cent of the banks' capital funds in case of a single borrower and 40 per cent in case of a borrower group. These norms are relaxed in the case of financing for infrastructure by up to 5 per cent in the case of a single borrower and 10 per cent in the case of a borrower group.

A number of recent measures and several in the pipeline should facilitate greater flow of credit to the infrastructure sector. Let me recount a few important ones. First, interest rate futures have been reintroduced recently and these should aid banks in managing their interest risk more efficiently. Second, repos in corporate bonds have been allowed. Third, in the second quarter policy review of 2009-10, we announced the introduction of plain vanilla OTC single-name credit default swaps (CDS) for corporate bonds for resident entities. Fourth, a separate category of NBFCs— infrastructure NBFCs—has been introduced. Fifth, banks will be permitted to build up capital for 'take-out' exposures in a phased manner. Finally, refinancing through the special purpose vehicle, India Infrastructure Finance Company Ltd. (IIFCL), is expected to leverage bank financing for public-private partnership (PPP) projects. These measures, along with existing ones, can be expected to enhance banks' ability to fund infrastructure projects.

Going forward, financing infrastructure is going to be a big challenge for the banking sector. This huge and growing demand of infrastructure finance will have to be met even as banks wrestle with expanding their traditional banking services. Apart from finding the resources, banks will also need to hone their skills in appraisal and management of risks inherent in infrastructure financing. This is a daunting challenge, and hardly fits the description of a 'boring' prospect.

Third Challenge: Risk Management

Let me now turn to the third challenge—the challenge of risk management. In the years ahead, two big forces will define the environment in which Indian banks will be called upon to operate—a rapidly globalising India and a fiercely competitive banking industry. This means in the main that Indian banks will have to upgrade their risk management architectures. In this regard, an important lesson thrown up by the crisis is that in addition to managing more effectively the traditional risks such as credit risk, operational risk and market risk, banks also need to manage some new risks that have proven to be significant such as reputation risk, counterparty credit risk, liquidity risk, interest rate risk in the banking book and incremental risks in the trading book. Expertise in risk management needs to be complemented by strengthening stress testing techniques. Evidently this calls for substantially broadening and sharpening the skill endowment at the institutional level. However, this cannot stop at getting a new toolbox and learning how to use it; it has to extend to changing the mindset. Banks need to develop a culture of risk management at the institutional level. What the crisis has shown is that risk management cannot be done in silos; it demands a more integrated approach with risks and their interconnections across the entire organisation recognised and managed synergistically.

Buffering the capital base of banks is obviously a standard and much needed response to risk management. In this regard, countries around the world are in the process of migrating to the Basel II capital standard. In its current form, the standard provides a menu of approaches from simple to advanced to assess credit, market and operational risks and to calibrate the capital requirement to the assessed risk. Importantly, the standard provides a framework for assessing the new risks that I mentioned earlier.

India is committed to adopting the international best practices though with the sequencing and pacing determined by our domestic conditions. As of March 2009, all Indian banks have migrated to the simpler approaches of the Basel II standard. The task on the way forward is to graduate to more advanced approaches. Towards this end, in consultation with banks, the RBI has now finalised a four-year timeframe starting in April 2010 and ending with March 2014. Moving to advanced approaches is both skill and technology intensive. In the first instance, it will therefore necessarily have to be confined to the larger banks. While the RBI will actively facilitate the transition of such larger banks to advanced approaches, it is expected that the banks themselves will be proactive in preparing themselves to meet the preconditions for the transition in view of the competitive advantages it will offer.

All in all, moving forward, risk management is going to involve pushing the frontiers of knowledge and transforming that knowledge to practical policy. That can hardly fit the description of boring.

Fourth Challenge: Further Improvements in Efficiency

Let me now turn to the fourth and final challenge on my list which is the challenge of further improving the efficiency of banking. But before I look ahead, I need to look back a little. The growth acceleration of the Indian economy during 2003-2008 is attributable to a host of factors. Some of these are tangible such as the deregulation of the industrial sector, liberalisation of external trade and external finance, reform of direct and indirect taxation and elimination of controls on doing business. Some of the factors that contributed to growth are intangible such as improved productivity, higher efficiency and growing entrepreneurism. We often forget to add to this list the contribution made by the financial sector by way of larger and better quality financial intermediation that raised the level of aggregate savings and channelled them to investment. Just one statistic will evidence this—bank credit as a proportion of GDP nearly doubled from 29 per cent in end-March 2000 to 56 per cent at end-March 2009. Even more notable, this rapid expansion of credit has been accompanied by a significant improvement in asset quality which is now close to international norms.

The analysis in the RBI's *Report on Currency and Finance 2006-2008* shows that the Indian banking sector has recorded an impressive improvement in productivity over the last 15 years; many of the productivity/efficiency indicators have moved closer to the global levels. The Report also shows that the performance of public sector banks has converged with that of new private sector and foreign banks. More interestingly, contrary to popular perception, there is also no significant relationship between ownership and efficiency—the most efficient banks straddle all three segments—public sector banks, private sector banks and foreign banks.

Improvement is a never ending business, and there are several tasks on the way forward. The intermediation cost in India is still high, largely due to high operating costs. Non-interest sources of income constitute a very small share in total income of banks in India. Although overall efficiency and productivity have improved, resources are not being utilised in the most efficient manner. There is a degree of stickiness and non-transparency in bank lending rates.

The challenge for Indian banks, therefore, is to reduce costs and pass on the benefits to both depositors and lenders. This will involve constantly reinventing business models and designing products and services demanded by a rapidly growing and diversifying economy. As we noted earlier, in the wake of the crisis, there are proposals at the global level to mandate higher capital standards, stricter liquidity and leverage ratios and a more cautious approach to risk. Admittedly, all these safeguards are necessary, but they will also raise the banks' funding costs. What this means is that Indian banks will need to improve efficiency even as their costs of doing business go up. This is a challenge that will test ingenuity, perseverance, ability to learn and adapt and management skills. And this is going to be anything but boring!

Conclusion

Let me now conclude by summarising the issues that I have addressed here. I have referred to the debate generated by Prof. Krugman's thesis that 'exciting' banking will make for an unsafe and unstable financial system and that an important preventive against future crises is to restore 'boring banking.'

I have argued that making banking boring is neither a cure to the ills that the banking system was plagued with before the crisis nor an appropriate path for the future of banking. Banking has to evolve, grow and innovate in response to the developments in financial markets and institutions. The excitement lies in responding to the challenges that this growth brings.

From an Indian perspective, what banks do and how well they do it is going to be central to accelerating and sustaining our growth momentum. In particular, I have referred to four challenges that the banking sector has to meet head on—deepening financial inclusion, financing infrastructure, strengthening risk management and improving efficiency. These are formidable challenges, and meeting them is going to be an exciting, rewarding and fulfilling opportunity. Perish the thought of Indian banking ever getting boring!

Based on Dr. Duvvuri Subbarao's address at the International Finance and Banking Conference organised by the Indian Merchants' Chamber on 'Banking—Crisis and Beyond', November 25, 2009, Mumbai.

6 Efficiency, Productivity and Soundness of the Indian Banks

Recent Developments

Y.V. Reddy and Swayam Prava Mishra

Introduction

One of the major objectives of the banking sector reforms in India was to promote flexibility, operational autonomy and competition in the system and to raise the banking standards in India to the international best practices (Reddy, 2002). In order to achieve these objectives, several measures have been initiated since the early 1990s. The Indian banking system has been exposed to increased competition with the enhanced presence of foreign banks and the entry of new private sector banks. Banks have also been allowed to diversify into non-traditional activities. The banks have been also subjected to prudential norms in line with the international best practices.

In the above backdrop, this paper assesses efficiency, productivity and soundness of the Indian banks. The objective is to show how the measures of efficiency, productivity and soundness of Indian banks have reflected the pre-crisis and post-crisis periods. The various bank groups, namely, nationalised banks, State Bank of India (SBI) and its associates, other scheduled commercial banks, all scheduled commercial banks and foreign banks are assessed.

The paper gives a picture of the conceptual issues relating to measurement of efficiency and productivity. It also briefly describes the methodology and is subdivided into three parts. It first assesses the productivity and efficiency of the banks based on accounting measures or financial ratios. The economic measure of efficiency and productivity is assessed in the second subsections by virtue of technical efficiency scores. The last subsection assesses the soundness of the banks in terms of capital to risk-weighted asset ratio (CRAR) and asset quality. The paper concludes with note on the indicators.

Conceptual Issues

Productivity is construed as the ability and willingness of an economic unit to produce maximum possible output with given inputs and technology (Kalirajan and Shand, 1994). Higher the output per unit of input, higher is the productivity. Efficiency, on the other hand, measures performance of the bank in a normative sense by comparing it with industry leaders within or across the borders.

The bank which is a multi-product producing unit has specific measures of productivity and efficiency that are broadly of two types, *viz.*, accounting measures and economic measures. The accounting measures refer to various financial ratios that focus on one or more outputs and their relevant inputs to measure the performance or productivity of a banking unit. Efficiency, being a normative concept, is measured by comparing a bank's performance using these ratios against the best practices within or outside the country.

The accounting measures use various ratios where each ratio refers to a particular aspect of bank activity. Since the banking industry uses multiple inputs to generate multiple outputs, a precise inference may not be possible always which is why economic measures of efficiency are used. In this a single measure of firm efficiency is defined to account for multiple inputs. The efficiency measures can be estimated with both parametric and non-parametric approaches.

In this paper, we will be using the Data Envelopment Analysis (DEA) which is a non-parametric method to calculate the technical efficiency.

Methodology

The paper uses data from 2004-05 to 2008-09 and in some cases 2009-10 wherever data is available. The sample covers five bank groups i.e., nationalised banks, SBI and its associates, other scheduled commercial banks, all scheduled commercial banks and foreign banks (in India). The data is mainly collected from the official website of Reserve Bank of India (RBI) (*www.rbi.org.in*). The data is computed from *Statistical Tables Relating to Banks in India* and *A Profile of Banks, 2009-10* (RBI).

Measurement of Productivity and Efficiency using Accounting Measures

In this section four main accounting ratios are used for assessing the efficiency and productivity of the banking units. These are net interest margin (NIM), business per employee, profit per employee and return on assets (RoA).

Net Interest Margin (NIM) or Spread

NIM is defined as the difference between the total interest earned (including from such items as investments) and total interest expended (including on such items as inter-bank borrowings), normalised by assets. This ratio indicates as to how effectively the banks deploy all their funds (both deposit and borrowings) to generate income from credit and investment operations. Lower the ratio, the more efficient is the banking system.

Table 6.1 shows the ratio of NIM to total assets of various bank groups in India during 2004 to 2009. Figure 6.1 depicts the percentage of NIM for 2009.

Table 6.1

Ratio of NIM to Total Assets of Various Bank Groups in India

(Per cent)

Year	*Nationalised Banks*	*SBI & its Associates*	*Other Scheduled Commercial Banks*	*All Scheduled Commercial Banks*	*Foreign Banks*
2004	3.29	2.98	2.42	3.08	3.73
2005	3.13	3.27	2.51	3.08	3.54
2006	2.92	3.22	2.74	3.04	4.05
2007	2.8	2.79	2.54	2.86	4.36
2008	2.28	2.49	2.67	2.58	4.33
2009	2.34	2.39	2.86	2.63	4.32

Source: Computed from Statistical Tables Relating to Banks in India (RBI).

The nationalised banks and SBI and its associates banks almost were at the same levels during and after the crisis. In 2009 they both had the lowest NIM ratios of 2.34 and 2.39 respectively. The NIM ratio of foreign banks has increased during 2006, 2007 and 2008 but slightly declined in 2009. The trend in other scheduled commercial banks showed some variations. However, in 2007 they had the lowest NIM (2.54).

Figure 6.1 shows that the foreign banks had the highest NIM in 2009 (4.32) followed by other scheduled commercial banks (2.86).

Figure 6.1

Net Interest Margin, 2009

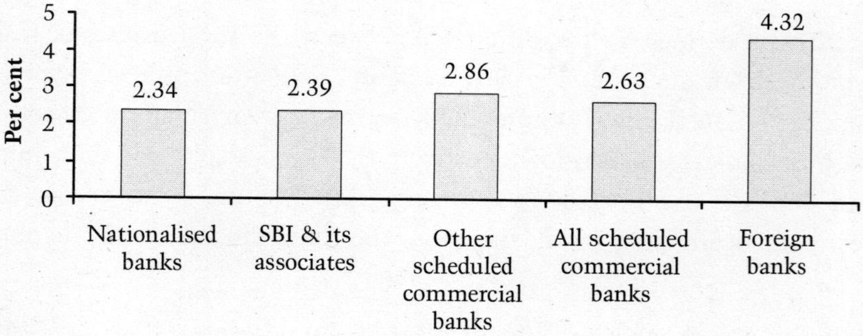

Business per Employee

Business per employee is the total revenue generated on a per employee basis. The productivity of labour can be directly assessed through this ratio. From Table 6.2 it can be seen that by and large there is a rise in this ratio for all banks.

The Business per employee of the nationalised banks, SBI and its associates and other scheduled commercial banks have increased over the years as shown in Table 6.2. However, the business per employee ratio continues to be highest in foreign banks.

Table 6.2

Business per Employee of Various Bank Groups in India

(In Rs. Lakh)

Year	Nationalised Banks	SBI & its Associates	Other Scheduled Commercial Banks	All Scheduled Commercial Banks	Foreign Banks
2005-06	383.07	337.79	670.94	419.8	955.41
2006-07	490.01	436.35	704.19	522.94	974.77
2007-08	618.28	565.06	751.42	643.24	1037.1
2008-09	783.16	650.22	743.85	753.44	1282.74
2009-10	947.4	735.52	798.37	873.32	1445.87

Source: Computed from *A Profile of Banks 2009-10* (RBI).

The business per employee for 2009-10 for various bank groups is shown in Figure 6.2. The foreign banks (1445.87) were the leaders followed by nationalised banks (947.4).

Figure 6.2

Business per Employee, 2009-10

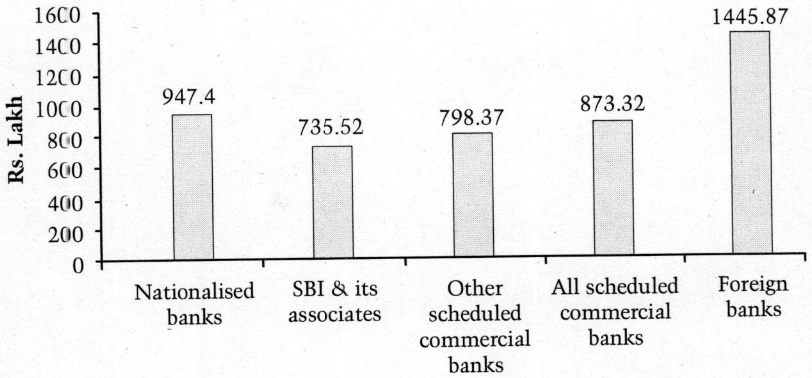

Profit per Employee

Operating profit after depreciation divided by the average number of annual employees is the profit per employee ratio. Profit per employee gives an indication of the ability of labour to generate profit. The higher the ratio, the better is the efficiency of the bank.

Table 6.3 shows the profit per employee among the bank groups in India. The ratio shows an overall increase for all the commercial banks in India, foreign banks being at the top. It is evident from Figure 6.3 wherein in 2009-10 it was almost three times higher than the all scheduled commercial banks.

Table 6.3

Profit per Employee of Various Bank Groups in India

(In Rs. Lakh)

Year	*Nationalised Banks*	*SBI & its Associates*	*Other Scheduled Commercial Banks*	*All Scheduled Commercial Banks*	*Foreign Banks*
2005-06	2.23	2.2	4.5	2.8	13.87
2006-07	2.87	2.57	4.71	3.49	16.13
2007-08	3.77	3.72	6	4.74	19.47
2008-09	4.86	4.43	6.16	5.63	25.39
2009-10	5.74	4.65	7.19	6.05	17.09

Source: Computed from *A Profile of Banks 2009-10* (RBI).

Figure 6.3

Profit per Employee, 2009-10

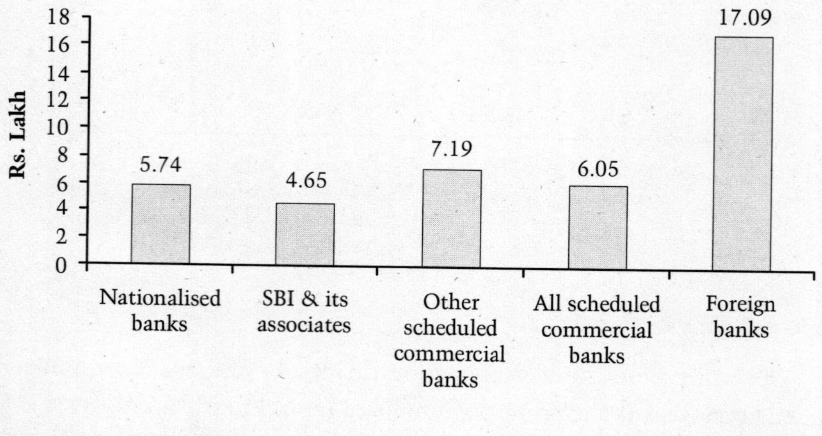

Return on Assets (RoA)

RoA gives an indication as to how much profit a business unit or bank is able to generate per unit of its assets. Higher value of this ratio is indicative of higher profitability. As per Basel II norms, the RoA should be more than one per cent (Ghosh *et al.*, 2004).

The RoA for nationalised banks and SBI group has increased during the study period except 2009-10 where there is slight decline (Table 6.4). The RoA of private sector banks have increased significantly over the study period and in fact it was highest in 2009-10 (1.28) leaving the foreign banks behind (1.26) depicted in Figure 6.4.

Table 6.4

Return on Assets of Various Bank Groups in India

(Per cent)

Year	*Nationalised Banks*	*SBI & its Associates*	*Other Scheduled Commercial Banks*	*All Scheduled Commercial Banks*	*Foreign Banks*
2005-06	0.89	0.87	1.07	1.01	2.08
2006-07	0.94	0.86	1.02	1.05	2.28
2007-08	1.01	0.97	1.13	1.12	2.09
2008-09	1.03	1.02	1.13	1.13	1.99
2009-10	1	0.91	1.28	1.05	1.26

Source: Computed from *A Profile of Banks 2009-10* (RBI).

Figure 6.4

Return on Assets, 2009-10

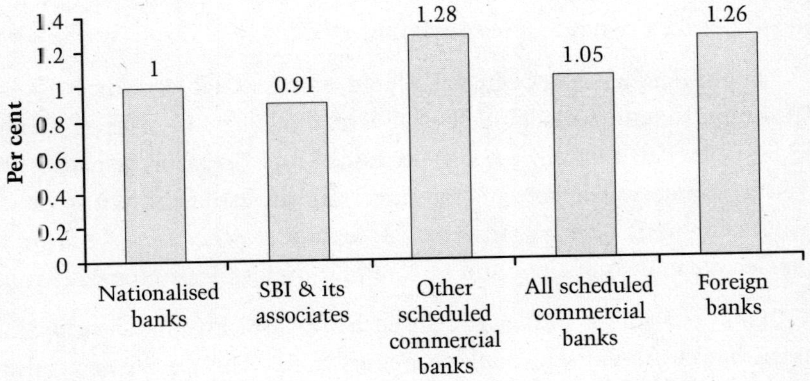

Assessment of Productivity and Efficiency using Economic Measures

The accounting measures cited above have a limitation in that the choice of a single ratio does not provide precise information about various dimensions of the performance of a bank, which uses multiple inputs to produce multiple outputs. This problem is addressed by use of economic measures that capture all aspects of banking operations in a single measure.

There are various techniques for economic measures like parametric and non-parametric approaches. We are using the Data Envelopment Analysis (DEA) method in our study to calculate the technical efficiency scores for the banks.

DEA is a non-parametric method of measuring efficiency of a decision-making unit (DMU) such as a firm or a bank. It employs mathematical programming to construct a best practice frontier from the observed data and to measure efficiency relative to the constructed frontier. It tells the user which of the DMUs in the sample are efficient and which are not. The two main advantages of DEA technique is that it provides bank-level efficiency score and secondly it does not require a prior specification about the underlying technologies.

The major shortcoming of DEA is that it assumes data to be free of measurement error and could therefore give inaccurate results if the integrity of data is not assured (Avkiran, 1998).

The efficiency has been calculated using variable returns to scale (VRS) input-oriented model of the DEA methodology. In order to estimate the best practice frontier, interest expended and operating expenses were taken as inputs, while deposits, advances and investments were treated as outputs for bank group's analysis. A technical efficiency score of 1 is considered as most efficient and a score of 0 implies least efficient bank.

Table 6.5 shows that nationalised banks, SBI and its associates and foreign banks are efficient bank groups in India. The private sector banks showed a little less than efficient score of 0.929 in the year 2007-08. It is significant to note that the technical efficiency score drops for all scheduled commercial banks marginally during the years of stress, namely, 2007-08 and 2008-09, primarily on account of the private sector banks. It lends credence to the popular belief that private sector banks tend to assume more risks than public sector banks in their operations. Overall the technical efficiency scores, for all the bank groups in India in 2009-10 is 1.

Table 6.5

Technical Efficiency Scores of Various Bank Groups in India

Year	*Nationalised Banks*	*SBI & its Associates*	*Other Scheduled Commercial Banks*	*All Scheduled Commercial Banks*	*Foreign Banks*
2005-06	1	1	1	0.993	1
2006-07	1	1	1	1	1
2007-08	1	1	0.929	0.953	1
2008-09	1	1	1	0.991	1
2009-10	1	1	1	1	1

Table 6.6 gives the efficiency ranks for the various bank groups based on their average efficiency score during 2005-06 to 2009-10.

Table 6.6

Efficiency Ranks of Various Bank Groups based on Average Efficiency Score during 2005-06 to 2009-10

Sr. No.	*Bank Groups*	*Efficiency Rank*	*Average Efficiency Score*
1	Nationalised banks	1	1
2	SBI & its associates	1	1
3	Other scheduled commercial banks	3	0.9858
4	All scheduled commercial banks	2	0.9874
5	Foreign banks	1	1

Assessment of Soundness of the Banks in India

The role of regulators in any economy is to limit the systemic risk that arises with the spread of problems related to few institutions to other institutions that are otherwise solvent and liquid. To accomplish this regulators have to ensure the soundness of the banking sector though availability of adequate capital in order to withstand any unforeseen conditions arising out of their operations or any disruptive market movements.

With the growing use of new financial instruments like swaps, options, futures etc., the institutions across the world are very much open to the risk of loss which might exceed the amount recognised in the statement of financial position. Given the integration of financial operations across markets and economies, any contingency in one market or economy leads to spread effects on the other markets. The recent crisis was an illustration of this.

We assess the soundness of the Indian banks through CRAR and since poor asset quality is a major obstruct in the efficient working of a bank, it is also assessed in terms of net non-performing asset (NPA) ratio.

Capital to Risk-Weighted Asset Ratio (CRAR)

The capital adequacy ratio measures the amount of a bank's capital in relation to its risk-weighted credit exposures and is most widely used measure of soundness of banks. It determines the capacity of a bank to withstand the unexpected losses arising out of its operations. The higher the capital adequacy ratio a bank has, the greater is the capacity to absorb the unexpected losses. The RBI guidelines require a capital adequacy ratio of 9 per cent.

Table 6.7 gives CRAR of the various bank groups in India. Here as we can see all are having capital adequacy ratio of greater than 9 per cent. In 2009-10 the other scheduled commercial banks has the highest CRAR of 17.45 per cent leaving even foreign banks behind with 17.25 per cent.

Table 6.7

CRAR of Various Bank Groups in India

(Per cent)

Year	*Nationalised Banks*	*SBI & its Associates*	*Other Scheduled Commercial Banks*	*All Scheduled Commercial Banks*	*Foreign Banks*
2005-06	12.27	11.95	12.42	12.32	13.02
2006-07	12.37	12.3	12.1	12.28	12.39
2007-08	12.13	13.21	14.34	13.01	13.08
2008-09	13.24	13.96	15.23	13.98	14.32
2009-10	13.25	13.46	17.45	14.58	17.25

Source: Computed from *A Profile of Banks 2009-10* (RBI).

Asset Quality (Net NPA Ratio)

The soundness of any bank may be seriously impaired if its asset quality is poor. NPAs requite provisioning or write off which affects bank's profitability and weakens their capital position. So apart from having a sound capital position it is necessary that banks maintain healthy asset quality.

The nationalised banks among other groups had the lowest net NPA ratio as shown in Table 6.8. However, the ratio has increased from 2007-08 to 2009-10. The foreign banks had the highest NPA ratio in 2008-09 and 2009-10.

Figure 6.5 shows in 2009-10 the foreign banks had 1.82 per cent of net NPA ratio followed by SBI and its associates (1.5 per cent).

Table 6.8

Net NPA Ratio of Various Bank Groups in India

(Per cent)

Year	*Nationalised Banks*	*SBI & its Associates*	*Other Scheduled Commercial Banks*	*All Scheduled Commercial Banks*	*Foreign Banks*
2005-06	1.16	1.63	1.01	1.22	0.83
2006-07	0.94	1.32	0.97	1.02	0.73
2007-08	0.77	1.43	1.09	1	0.77
2008-09	0.68	1.47	1.29	1.05	1.81
2009-10	0.91	1.5	1.03	1.12	1.82

Source: Computed from *A Profile of Banks 2009-10* (RBI).

Figure 6.5

Net NPA Ratio, 2009-10

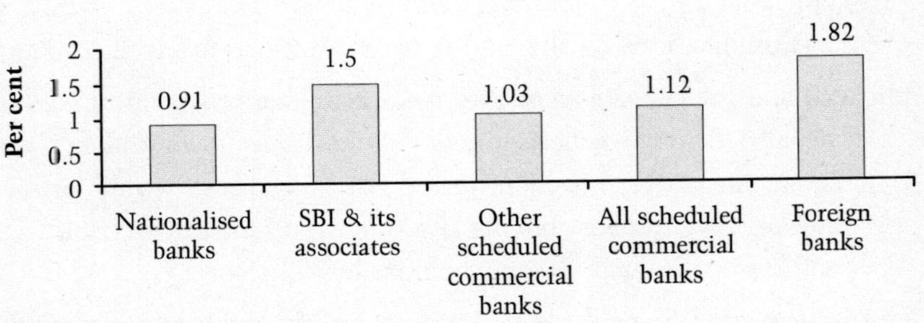

On the Indicators

The above analysis suggests that various bank groups in India display comfortable levels of efficiency, productivity and soundness during the last five years. However, a marginal stress on private sector and foreign banks cannot be ruled out, in terms of some indicators. However, the indicators need to be supplemented with further studies to draw definite conclusions. The limitations of indicators and the areas for further exploration are described below.

(a) Net interest margin (NIM) ratio is a good indicator of the overall performance and efficiency. This measure in the numerator the sum of net income recovered, over the denominator of the assets. In practice, some analysts look at the total net income both of interest and non-interest while some confine to only interest income. Again in the denominator some look at the average performing assets and many others aggregate all assets.

(b) Business per employee ratio needs to recognise the impact of the following—outsourcing (employment of agents); shift in business strategy to focus on retail banking or wholesale banking (which alters the scale of finance); focus on fee-based business (which might not reflect in business—as measured earlier); shift to more active trading (investments, forex, derivatives) which will reflect in turnover and not in outstanding deposits and loans on certain dates. If these are not taken into account, the ratio could show an impressive improvement—even if the efficiency otherwise has moved in the other direction.

(c) The Profit per employee ratio might show an upward trend due to staff reduction via voluntary retirement schemes (VRS), which will have implications on the staff cost paid through deferred severances.

(d) RBI and the banks also pushed towards higher provisioning for NPAs and also through general provisions as back-up for tougher years. These measures which improve the soundness would probably indicate lower return on asset (RoA) or even hide the probable higher profits actually made before such prudential steps.

(e) Business per branch was not analysed in the study, since it needs to recognise significant increase in ATMs, Internet banking and outsourcing (employment of agents). The ratio based on current data could show an impressive improvement—even if the efficiency otherwise has moved in the other direction. This ratio also may not be an useful indicator as there has been a general decline in the opening of regular branches in the last decade in addition to the closing of unviable branches and this would translate into higher business per branch without major growth.

(f) It may also be difficult to segregate the ratios into groups exclusively for measuring efficiency or soundness in view of their intense inter-relationships. The soundness of a bank can not only be based on its CRAR and NPAs. As the crisis has demonstrated, liquidity and investment quality are also critical and often ratios which are comparatively below benchmark ratios do not put a bank into an adverse category if it has helped in the improvement in another ratio or is qualitative.

(g) The issue of liquidity has come to the centre stage after the crisis. Though there was no insurmountable problem of liquidity in Indian banking system during the crisis, with appropriate data, it is possible to analyse the funding pattern (reliance on markets for funding, proportion of wholesale funds, proportion of short-term funds and proportion of cross-border funds) and liquidity positions (mismatches in the near-term and liquid assets ratio).

References

Avkiran, N.K. (1999). "The Evidence of Efficiency Gains: The Role of Mergers and the Benefits to the Public", *Journal of Banking and Finance* 23: 991-1013.

Bhattacharya, A., C.A.K. Lovell and P. Sahay (1997). "The Impact of Liberalization on the Productive Efficiency of Indian Commercial Banks", *European Journal of Operational Research* 98: 332-45.

Ghosh, C.R. *et al.* (2004). *Strategic Models for Repositioning of Public Sector Banks: Creating Global Winner*. Bancon.

Kalirajan, K.P. and R.T. Shand (1994). *Economics in Disequilibrium: An Approach from the Frontier*. Macmillan India Limited.

Mohan, Rakesh (2005). "Financial Sector Reforms in India", *Economic and Political Weekly* 40(12).

Reddy, Y.V. (2002). "Monetary and Financial Sector Reforms In India: A Practitioner's Perspective", Presentation at the *Indian Economic Conference*. USA: Cornell University.

Reserve Bank of India (2010). *A Profile of Banks 2009-10.*

———. (2010). *Report on Trends and Progress of Banking in India 2009-10.*

———. (2008). "The Banking Sector in India: Emerging Issues and Challenges", Volume II, *Report on Currency and Finance 2006-08.*

Sathye, M. (2003). "Efficiency of Banks in a Developing Economy: The Case of India", *European Journal of Operational Research* 148(3): 662-71.

The authors are thankful to Mr. K. Damodaran and Mr. C.R. Muralidharan, for their valuable comments.

7 Macroprudential Approach to Regulation

Scope and Issues

Shyamala Gopinath

I feel extremely privileged in getting the opportunity to be part of this Festschrift being released in honour of Dr. C. Rangarajan. For me, the learning experience that started in the Reserve Bank of India with him as our Deputy Governor, and then the Governor, continues till today. On countless occasions I have drawn inspiration and ideas from his writings and suggestions. Personally I have benefitted immensely from his guidance in negotiating tricky issues during Uruguay round negotiations on trade in services, in particular, in financial services which finally culminated into GATS. We in the RBI fondly remember 'The Philosopher King' with utmost respect for his leadership in steering the country out of the crisis in early 1990s, and laying down the foundation of the subsequent policy framework, which has put the economy on a robust and resilient growth path. There is hardly any area in macroeconomic management or public policy debate that has not benefitted from the visionary and intellectually stimulating work of Dr. Rangarajan. The topic on which I am writing for this Festschrift relates to a new dimension of the post-crisis financial stability framework, in which India, and more specifically the RBI, had already gained some practical experience even prior to global crisis. As a lead adopter of macroprudential measures in the world, and given the exciting debate on the subject that is evolving after the global crisis, I thought this could be an ideal topic for this occasion.

Introduction

Explicit pursuit of macroeconomic and financial stability can be said to be the single most significant take-away from the recent crisis. More than the specifics, the importance of this mandate lies in decisively effecting a course correction with regard to the approach and philosophy for regulation of the financial system. It is being acknowledged that a macroprudential perspective is critical in designing and pursuing microprudential regulation of institutions and markets. Two distinct but highly inter-related constructs have come to epitomise this post-crisis framework: macroprudential regulation and systemic risk management. Both these concepts are philosophically appealing and conceptually sound, but operationally quite challenging. Understanding the nuanced interplay between these would be crucial in designing an efficient operative framework for financial stability.

Systemic Risk Management

Systemic risk is a much broader concept implying probability of sudden disruption to a large part of the financial system, reflected in failure of multiple institutions and freezing of markets, triggered by a common shock and propagated through interconnected exposures and correlated positions. Any framework for containing systemic risks would need to involve the following elements:

- Strengthening the financial system's resilience to economic downturns and other adverse aggregate shocks.
- Sound monitoring of common, correlated exposures among financial institutions arising out of network linkages and developing measures to quantify the contribution of individual institutions to systemic risk.
- Minimising the moral hazard associated with failure of systemically important institutions and finding mechanisms to restrict the contagion impact of failing institutions during crisis.

It is in the above context that the role of macroprudential approach in financial sector policies becomes critical. Macroprudential regulation can be considered as one of the tools of this larger policy framework.

Analytics of Macroprudential Regulation

Macroprudential regulation, as it has come to be generally interpreted, essentially envisages that the key instruments of prudential regulation *viz.*, capital, liquidity and provisioning vary dynamically according to macroeconomic circumstances. The macroeconomic triggers could arise either from the changes in the normal economic cycle or sharp asset price movements. Conceptually, this is supposed to be in addition to stricter prudential standards for capital, liquidity and leverage across the board.

The dynamics of macroprudential regulation is evident when seen in terms of the broad objectives:

(i) To address procyclical elements in the financial system: the basic idea is that cushions should be built up in upswings so as to be relied upon when the rough times arrive—the countercyclical approach. The key measures under consideration, which have countercyclical characteristics and could act as 'automatic stabilisers' are the following:

- Building buffers through capital conservation based on simple capital conservation rules. The objective is to ensure that banks which have depleted capital buffers rebuild them by reducing discretionary distribution of earnings. A buffer range will be established above the regulatory minimum capital requirement and distribution constraints will be imposed on the bank when capital level falls within this range.
- A countercyclical capital buffer that will sit on top of the conservation buffer established as a range to take account of the macrofinancial environment in which banks operate. The buffer will be triggered only when excessive credit growth compared to the long-term trend is judged to be associated with the build-up of systemwide risk. In order to make this buffer effective it has to be combined with jurisdictional reciprocity. The upside of this will be that capital will not be a constraint to maintain flow of credit to the economy during a period of stress.
- Promoting forward looking provisions through a change in accounting standards towards an expected loss approach. Current standards do not permit credit losses based on events that are expected to occur in the future to be included in provisions.

(ii) To provide a mechanism to correct the inherently skewed pricing of credit risk by financial institutions through the cycle: one of the major causes of the recent crisis was that in the pre-crisis boom period there was general euphoria and the financial sector was severely underpricing the risks. In a risk-based capital regime, during booms this directly implied lesser capital for risky activities and hence increased lending to risky sectors and increased trading volumes in riskier instruments. In was only after the crisis had set in that the true extent of risk underpricing became evident. The situation swung to the other extreme after the crisis. The macroprudential tools including the leverage ratio are meant to address situations like this by effectively influencing the costs of credit exposures dynamically.

(iii) To attempt pre-empting asset price bubbles in the economy and limit the build-up of financial risks in the system: asset price booms have invariably been identified with a pre-crisis economic configuration as both symptomic as well as causative factors. Earlier, though, the policy frameworks adopted an approach of benign neglect of asset prices as they saw little role either for the monetary policy or prudential policy in addressing these. The recent crisis however has forced a rethink in this regard. There is now a broad consensus on the need to use credit channel as a macroprudential instrument.

The Group of Governors and Heads of Supervision (GOHS), the oversight body of the Basel Committee on Banking Supervision (BCBS) have recently announced[1] broad agreement on the overall design of the capital and liquidity reform package, though much of the work in regard to countercyclical buffers and forward looking provisions is still work in progress.

The recent BCBS consultative document[2] lays out a broad framework in regard to countercyclical capital buffers, conceptually based on deviation of credit to GDP ratio from its long-term trend. Recognising the different contexts in each jurisdiction, each national supervisory is expected to apply judgment in the setting of the buffer after using the best information available to gauge the build-up of system-wide risk. However, it does not

---

1. BIS Press Release, "The Group of Governors and Heads of Supervision Reach Broad Agreement on Basel Committee Capital and Liquidity Reform Package", July 26, 2010.

2. BCBS Consultative Document, *Countercyclical Capital Buffer Proposal*, July 2010.

envisage addressing sectoral credit issues through such countercyclical measures.

The challenge, particularly in growing emerging market economies (EMEs), would be to reconcile this approach with the risk of credit constraints given the supply-side issues which are qualitatively very different from advanced economies. Generalised credit increase higher than the trend may not, in itself, be a matter of systemic concern in view of the changing structure of economies. The framework in these countries would therefore necessarily have to adopt a more nuanced, sectoral focus. There are challenges in trying to influence asset prices through the credit channel. First, it is really difficult to set an optimum level of asset prices as a target. Second, only bank-financed exposures to asset markets can be influenced through macroprudential tools which may not generally be the dominant funding source.There have been instances where asset prices build-up is due to leverage outside the banking sector. Third sectoral approach will inevitably involve an element of regulatory judgement and discretion.

In this context, it would be pertinent to recount the Indian experience in applying macroprudential elements in view of apparently excessive credit to certain sectors, particularly commercial real estate (CRE) which has been the cause of most banking crises.

The Indian Experience

During the expansionary phase since 2004, the Reserve Bank of India (RBI) had taken various measures to counter procyclical trends. The potential adverse impact of high credit growth in some sectors and asset price fluctuations on banks' balance sheets at various points in time were contained through pre-emptive countercyclical provisioning and differentiated risk weights for certain sensitive sectors. It was for the first time in October 2004 that the rapid growth in housing and consumer credit was flagged as a concern and as a temporary countercyclical measure, the risk weight applicable to these loans was increased by 25 basis points. In the context of continuing high credit growth, the limitations of the prudential framework in capturing the *ex ante* risks of procyclical nature of bank credit were explicitly recognised in October 2005 which triggered an across the board increase in provisioning requirement for standard assets.

To counter the possibility of an asset bubble in addition to concerns about credit quality led to risk weight on banks' exposure to CRE and capital market being increased from 100 per cent to 125 per cent in July 2005. Given the continued rapid expansion in credit to the CRE sector, the risk weight on exposure to this sector was increased to 150 per cent in May 2006. Further, the general provisioning requirement on standard advances in specific sectors, i.e., personal loans, loans and advances qualifying as capital market exposures, residential housing loans beyond Rs. 20 lakh and commercial real estate loans was increased from 0.40 per cent to 1 per cent in April 2006 and further to 2 per cent on January 31, 2007.

The Backdrop of Our Countercyclical Actions

While contemplating the measures, we did not have any disaggregated statistical data or evidence to support our concerns on the potential risks of rising bank exposures to real estate, among other sensitive sectors based on the incurred loss method. However, what we did have was a clear trend in significant year-to-year increase in aggregate bank credit. The Indian financial system is still largely a bank-intermediated system and for this reason, the bank credit channel becomes a key monetary policy transmission instrument. Thus the aggregate bank credit growth has always formed an important variable in the conduct of monetary policy. The credit-deposit ratio, particularly on an incremental basis, has been an important indicator.

In view of the rapid credit expansion in the period 2003-2006, in addition to the countercyclical measures being taken, it was explicitly indicated by the RBI in April 2006 that growth of non-food bank credit, including investments in bonds/debentures/shares of public sector undertakings and private corporate sector and commercial paper, will be calibrated to decelerate to around 20 per cent during 2006-07 from a growth of above 30 per cent. Inflationary expectations had also started firming up and as part of monetary management, the repo rate was increased by 175 basis points in stages to 7.75 per cent by April 14, 2007 from its level of 6 per cent in September 2004. Further, the cash reserve ratio (CRR) was raised by 200 basis points in stages from 4.5 per cent in September 2004 to 6.5 per cent.

Specific Case of Real Estate

From a regulatory perspective, the key observable features that tilted the balance in favour of some kind of pre-emptive sectoral action, aimed primarily at preparing the banking sector to better manage the potential downsides, were the following:

(i) The onsite inspections of banks had started giving indications of the negative fallouts of the euphoria evident in lax underwriting standards and a few frauds that came to light.

(ii) There were emerging signs of underpricing of risks as the real estate prices were spiralling fuelled by ample liquidity and the dominant wealth effect transmittal from the stock market boom. There were clear tax incentives at work here which made utilisation of stock market gains into real estate an extremely tax-efficient arrangement.

(iii) A new factor in the housing credit market that was emerging was the mortgages for investment purposes—the trend for second homes, particularly in metros having a rising population of young, skilled job owners with salaries. Real estate, so to say, had crossed the rubicon to emerge as a true investment asset.

(iv) There was increasing anecdotal evidence of the inventory build-ups of completed commercial as well as residential units. These were clearly signs of real estate having crossed the basic demand-supply equation to an investment asset.

(v) There was a visible steep increase in land prices coming from auction results. Large real estate companies could monetise the huge land banks on the back of the then booming stock market valuations with a simultaneous increase in bank lending for commercial real estate.

It was in the above backdrop that it was decided to make it costlier for banks to finance loans backed by real estate. It was felt that the usual sector-neutral monetary policy instruments would not be effective without posing significant costs to the economy generally. So while the monetary policy instruments were indeed used, the objective of this generalised, gradual tightening was quite different from the requisite stronger action in respect of bank exposures to sectors such as real estate.

It needs to be appreciated that in the Indian context, the sharp rise in bank credit to the real estate was *per se* not a clear indicator of any asset price bubble given the inherent demand-supply dynamics in the economy and the genuine needs of an economy on a high growth path. There was a confluence of positive factors contributing to the development including a decline in inflation and stable inflationary expectations, resulting in decline in both nominal and real interest rates and availability of ample systemic liquidity, contributed no less by the rising tide of capital flows. Concomitantly, there was a shift in funding by the corporates to non-bank sources, including external borrowing, which forced banks to look at diversifying their lending portfolios. This shift also helped in meeting the increasing genuine demands on the commercial real estate front, including the office space largely accounted for by the IT boom and gradual expansion of organised retail to Tier II cities.

The objective, was not to address the asset price bubble *per se* and not to curtail genuine credit needs of the economy but to prepare the banking sector to better manage the potential downsides related to selective sectors. In other words we adopted what is now called the 'expected' as well as 'unexpected' loss approaches.

What are the key inferences? First, that harmonisation of the monetary policy objectives and prudential objectives can give a more complete picture, which may not be possible if banking supervision is separate from central banks; second that macroprudential policy is no substitute for monetary tightening but should rather act as complement to monetary policy and third, that supervisors need to have the necessary independence and flexibility to act timely on the basis of available information, which may albeit be incomplete.

Going Beyond Macroprudential Regulation

As with all ideas which gain currency and wide acceptance in a short period of time, macroprudential regulation runs the risk of being over-applied. However, there is an equally strong risk of making it too narrow in focus. It must be reiterated that macroprudential regulation is just one element of a broader macroprudential approach and needs to be supplemented with other tools to address systemic risk issues. Such tools could be in the form of additional prudential measures applied to all institutions with a systemic objective.

Frankly it would be difficult to make a binary distinction between microprudential and macroprudential policies—ultimately all macro risks translate into micro risks for financial institutions. The critical thing is incorporation of systemic perspective while designing policies.

A recent survey conducted by the Committee on the Global Financial System (CGFS)[3] on macroprudential frameworks in various countries found that though conceptions of macroprudential policy aims and objectives were fuzzy, many countries had used various instruments keeping the broad systemic perspective in mind. The survey also found far more extensive use of macroprudential policies by policymakers in EMEs as opposed to their counterparts in the more advanced nations. It has helped enhance financial system resilience.

The survey clearly shows that the emerging markets were also open to target-specific sectors. The most widely used instruments have been measures to limit credit supply to specific sectors that are seen as prone to excessive credit growth. These included limits calibrated to borrower risk characteristics (caps on loan-to-value (LTV) ratios or debt/income ratios) as well aggregate or sectoral credit growth ceilings and limits on exposures by instruments. Many emerging economies, given their specific context already had placed measures to address specific risks—loan-to-deposit limits, core funding ratios, reserve requirements for liquidity risk and limits on open currency positions or on derivatives transactions for forex risk.

In the Indian context, this perspective was writ large on most of the elements of the prudential framework. The key areas are:

Addressing Interconnectedness

- In regard to wholesale funding markets, prudential limits are in place on aggregate inter-bank liabilities for banks as a proportion of their net worth.

3. "Macroprudential Instruments and Frameworks: A Stocktaking of Issues and Experiences", *CGFS Paper* No. 38, May 2010.

- The overnight uncollateralised funding market is restricted only to banks and primary dealers and there are ceilings for both lending as well as borrowing by these entities.
- Investment by banks in subordinated debt of other banks is assigned 100 per cent risk weight for capital adequacy purpose. Also, the bank's aggregate investment in Tier II bonds issued by other banks and financial institutions is limited to 10 per cent of the investing bank's total capital.
- Exposure limits apply to exposures between banks and non-bank finance companies.

Forex Liabilities

There are limits on the proportion of wholesale foreign currency liabilities intermediated through the banking system, other than for lending for exports. Retail foreign currency deposits from non-residents are subject to minimum maturity requirements and interest rate caps.

Banks are required to hold a minimum of 25 per cent of their liabilities in the form of liquid domestic sovereign securities. This stipulation has worked both as a solvency as well as a liquidity buffer.

The credit conversion factors (CCF) used for calculating the potential future credit exposure for off-balance sheet interest rate as well as exchange rate contracts were doubled across all maturities in 2008. This was done since it was felt that the CCFs as per the Basel norms did not fully capture the volatility in the interest rate and forex markets in the Indian context.

Profits on sale of assets to an special purpose vehicle (SPV) under securitisation are not allowed to be recognised immediately on sale but over the life of the pass through certificates issued by the SPV. Any liquidity facility by the originator or a third party is to be treated as an off-balance sheet item and attracts 100 per cent credit conversion factor as well as 100 per cent risk weight.

The nature and sources of systemic risks are different in EMEs. This part of the world has seen many systemic crises over the past two decades and each of these crises have demonstrated the importance of prudential policy to minimise risks to financial stability and to reduce the impact from disturbances domestically and globally. Financial markets in emerging markets tend to be less well developed and resilient than such markets in advanced economies. This makes the system more vulnerable to even small disturbances and increases the criticality of macroprudential safeguards. It therefore becomes imperative for the systemic stability perspective to guide other realms of economic policy framework as well.

The two specific areas of perceived systemic risk where a macroprudential approach has been used and found useful in India are:

(i) Volatile capital flows: Excessive volatility of capital flows could impose significant costs to the economy beyond the obvious exchange rate impact. There are implications for financial stability in the form of induced risks of asset price bubbles and excessive foreign currency exposures in the financial system and external debt in general. Experience shows that the most volatile components of capital flows have been portfolio flows. These flows as well as debt flows are also procyclical.

While capital account regime in India has accorded substantially large freedom to equity flows—both FDI as well as portfolio flows, debt flows have been attempted to be modulated contextually through a regulatory framework with a combination of quantitative and price-based measures. Calibration of the debt flows into sovereign as well as corporate debt has been the most actively used instrument for this purpose.

(ii) Management of sovereign borrowings: Since the stop to automatic monetisation of government debt in the 90s, market borrowing by the government has been a critical variable in the macroeconomic framework. The stipulation of statutory liquidity ratio (SLR) for banks needs to be seen in this context. Banks have been permitted to hold this mandated investment as 'held-to-maturity'.

Another critical factor, which buffered sovereign balance sheet from vicissitudes of global crisis is that India does not have foreign currency market borrowing and only a limited dependence on foreign investors in respect of domestic currency debt. There is a strong domestic investor base, apart from banks, in the form of insurance and pension/provident funds which has enabled India to elongate the maturity of its domestic debt. The experience in general of emerging market countries has been that foreign investors in sovereign debt prefer short-term investments.

Issue of Systemically Important Financial Institutions (SIFI)

The universally accepted post-crisis approach with regard to management of systemic risks in the financial system accords primacy to addressing the issue of 'too-big-to-fail'(TBTF). The view is that resolution of systemically important financial institutions (SIFI), short of a public-funded bailout, is at the heart of the TBTF issue. SIFIs exaggerate the negative externalities and correlated exposures within the financial system. Their scale, complexity and interconnectedness also implies that their resolvability becomes extremely difficult and hence the 'too-big-to-fail' conundrum.

The real challenge will be to have a non-discretionary framework for quantitatively defining the SIFIs. In November 2009, G20 finance ministers agreed on the criteria for identifying institutions and markets of systemic importance,[4] based on the joint proposals of the International Monetary Fund (IMF), Bank for International Settlements (BIS) and Financial Stability Board (FSB). Three main criteria are proposed:

- Size: measuring the volume of financial services provided by an institution or group. Size—for the purposes of systemic risk identification—is an exhaustive notion covering the exposures, or balance sheet and off-balance sheet risks of the entity in question.
- The lack of substitutability: assessing the financial system's relative dependence on the financial services provided by a single entity to measure the system's immunity to the disappearance of said entity.
- Interconnectedness: looking at the direct and indirect links between financial institutions that will contribute to the spread of systemic risk and its contagion to the real economy.

The efforts at the FSB have since proceeded towards addressing three specific issues: (i) reducing the probability and impact of failure via higher prudential requirements, better supervisory practices, potential limitation on the size, breadth and intra-group connectivity; (ii) improving resolution capacity; and (iii) strengthening the core financial infrastructures and

4. G20 Communiqué, Meeting of Finance Ministers and Central Bank Governors, United Kingdom, 7 November 2009.

markets to address interconnectedness and lessen the risk of contagion in case of resolution.

The specifics of the broad template are still under preparation and it will indeed be a huge challenge for global regulators to arrive at an agreed framework. Given the heterogeneous country situations in respect of banks that are not internationally active, a 'constrained discretion' approach is being discussed which will help country jurisdictions to design a suitable framework for SIFIs. The authorities' choice of a particular measure or combination of measures from the agreed range of policy options will depend on conditions in each financial system and be targeted to the specific risks posed by SIFI institutions in each jurisdiction while agreeing to the broad, internationally accepted principles.

Reducing the probability of failure: Pre-crisis, the twin instruments of effective supervision and market discipline were expected to address the factors endogeneous to the firms that increased their probability of failure—essentially the risk it took on its books. These instruments were found insufficient in doing so. Further, in the new systemically oriented regulatory philosophy, it was believed that apart from being a risk to themselves, many large institutions posed risk to the system at large through significant negative externalities. It therefore became a sort of public good cause to contain the riskiness of these large institutions. The exact mechanism for doing this would be contingent on multiple factors, including size, interconnectedness, complexity, business model and industry structure etc.

Alternate resolution mechanism: In spite of the above regime, if an institution fails on account of systemic stresses, the objective must be to minimise the cost for the taxpayers. Different models have been proposed with the objective to allow the orderly resolution of a systemically important non-bank financial firm, including a mechanism to cover the costs of the resolution. Various approaches that have gained traction in policy deliberations for improving resolution capacity include limits to complexity of internal structures—preference for stand-alone subsidiaries, recovery and resolution planning, use of contingent capital and other instrument to absorb losses as a going concern, a special resolution regime for SIFIs which makes the shareholders and creditors share losses; and a bailout fund, contributed by the same entities expected to be bailed out. In the US, the Dodd-Frank Wall Street Reform and Consumer Protection Act, 2010 envisages a resolution regime which allows the government to impose losses on shareholders and creditors, unlike the normal bankruptcy provisions for other firms where the aim is to reorganise or liquidate a failing firm 'for the benefit of its creditors'.

Strengthening markets and market infrastructure: The singular area of attention in this regard has been to move much of the OTC derivatives market to a central clearing model. There is broad agreement in this regard though few important concomitant issues arising out of risk concentration in Central counterparties (CCPs) will need be addressed carefully, including cross-margining across CCPs or across different products.

There is also the issue of implicit or explicit liquidity support by the banking system to the CCPs in the form of lines of credit or to intermediaries such as brokers and market participants in the form of margins for trades, payment commitments or other forms of guarantees. It is likely that the risk of transactions undertaken through CCP sit in banks/ regulated financial entities books either directly or indirectly and if so it needs to be ensured that they are subject to all the prudential norms and risks are captured appropriately. Ideally, regulators of CCPs should prefer collaterals in the form of liquid securities rather than bank deposits or guarantees.

However, besides the issue of CCPs, there are equally important issues relating to market practices which have bearing on the financial stability. One fundamental issue is the undisputable faith in the benefits of ever-increasing volumes and liquidity in all markets. Shifting to CCPs is only shifting the risks. There is need to regulate all derivatives markets in interest rate, credit and forex products from a systemic perspective—the concept of 'market regulation' as practiced by many emerging countries may perhaps not be so anachronistic.

The regime for credit rating agencies is another such area. In spite of the systemic risk inherent to ratings, current efforts to regulate rating agencies focus mainly on microprudential issues and typically aim at reducing conflicts of interest and cliff effects by lowering use in regulatory and supervisory framework. A moral hazard created by rating agencies is the use of support ratings wherein implicit sovereign support available to systemically important institutions is taken into account to upgrade ratings. It may be necessary to require agencies to provide ratings without assumption of support. Addressing financial stability issues relating to potential procyclicality and systemic risk stemming from rating agencies is, an agenda for future work.

The other important issue, which is going to get accentuated by the move towards CCPs and collateral support arrangements, is the increasing collateralisation of bank balance sheets. Leverage is one part of this aspect—a recent IMF paper[5] clearly brings out the risks inherent in widespread rehypothecation of collaterals in many of the developed markets. The other part is the impact on bank balance sheets of the procyclical collateralisation regimes. If a large part of the good quality collateral on banks' books is locked up for their trading operations, what does it do to the resolvability issues in times of crisis and burden sharing? Both regulation of markets and close monitoring of interconnected exposures would be required to address the underlying risks.

Existing Framework in India for Monitoring Large Financial Conglomerates

The financial system in India is largely bank dominated and the banks are the parents of most of the large financial conglomerates (FCs). Incidentally, those FCs are not owned by any holding companies. Since 2004 there is a framework in place to closely monitor certain large FCs aimed at reducing the probability of failure of these institutions, considered to be systemically important in view of concerns relating to the moral hazard associated with the 'too-big-to-fail' proposition and the contagion or reputation effects on account of the 'holding out' phenomenon.

The current practices being followed in supervision of these conglomerates include off-site surveillance through quarterly returns, regular interactions with the CEOs of the parent companies and other entities in the group, periodic reviews by a technical committee having members from sectoral financial market regulators.

5. Singh, Manmohan and James Aitken (2010). "The (sizable) Role of Rehypothecation in the Shadow Banking System", *IMF Working Paper* No. 10/172, July.

The two-pronged structured processes in the nature of off-site surveillance and the periodic interface with the conglomerates has proved quite robust in assessing the risks faced by these systemically important financial institutions. From time to time these groups have been advised to improve their corporate governance processes and risk management systems especially with respect to the management of credit concentration risks and liquidity risks on a group-wide basis.

Recently other initiatives have also been launched for further strengthening of the regulatory/supervisory approaches for the identified conglomerates. Discussion with the main auditor of the group by the lead regulator is being contemplated. Steps are already underway to tighten the capital adequacy norms for these conglomerates so as to ensure that the amount of capital that the group possesses on a consolidated basis is adequate not only from the discretionary risks that the group entities take but also sufficient from the non-discretionary risks like operational, reputational, strategic risks especially from fiduciary activities.

Perspectives on the Indian Approach

(i) The above approach towards large FCs is focused primarily on a more intensive supervisory process aimed at capturing risk concentrations within the group.

(ii) A differential prudential framework for systemically large institutions has not been considered necessary as the regulatory framework for banks, in general, tries to address issues of excessive risk-taking by individual institutions. The financial system is considerably less complex than most of the developed markets as many complex, high risk products are not allowed or are regulated.

(iii) The sole metric of size has not been found to be much helpful as, apart from the largest bank which is state-owned and a large private sector bank which has a relatively lower market share, the market share of the other larger banks is not that significant. Relative to the needs of the growing economy and the rapid growth in non-FCs, emerging countries will require a larger number of banks with optimal size to meet the increasing demands. The focus has therefore been on differential and intensive supervision of large banks that are conglomerates (which includes the size metric).

(iv) The real concern from the interconnectedness perspective arises from the non-banking financial sector which is regulated by regulators for respective sectors *viz.*, insurance, securities broking, mutual funds, venture capital, housing finance etc. All the other non-banking financial activities are regulated by the RBI as part of a separate regulatory framework.

Many of the non-banking financial institutions (NBFIs) which do not accept public deposits are significantly large and through their interaction with other financial market segments could pose systemic risk. For such entities, a stricter prudential framework on the lines of banks has been put in place.

(v) Going forward, we will have to consider strong SIFI policies drawing on a range of policy levers.

Conclusion

Macroprudential regulation is essentially an inexact science. It has its limitations and needs to be used in conjunction with other policies to be effective. For leaning against the build-up of imbalances, a combination of monetary and macroprudential policies is required. If inflation risks are emerging, macroprudential measures cannot take the place of interest rate increases. Macroprudential measures are well suited to enhance resilience of the financial system but their effect on aggregate demand and inflationary expectations are weak compared to interest rates. It is also important to acknowledge what macroprudential regulation cannot do: it cannot manage economic cycles or target asset prices. It can only provide instruments to respond to these developments to cushion the financial system from potential stresses. It is in this context that the imperative for involvement of central banks becomes evident as otherwise the required synergy between monetary management and macroprudential management will be lost.

The real challenge of macroprudential regulation is strong resistance to countercyclical actions during booms. Having a rule-based approach will to a large extent obviate this problem but this approach has its own limitations. It is difficult to lay down simple rules as the financial system and markets are evolving and banks continue to be a dominant source of funding. Suitability of tools can of course change as the structure of the economy and financial system changes. But regulators may have to rely on continued use of discretionary adjustments.

As the global policy stance remains highly accommodative, there are concerns that the current two-speed recovery will imply short-term volatile capital flows or accentuation of carry trades which increase foreign currency mismatches of the non-financial sector. EMEs will have to address these issues with a range of policy tools.

We also need to be realistic about what capital regulations can do. Banks need capital for lending and to be resilient against shocks. More important is to focus on the business model and continuously monitor leverage and liquidity risks.

Going beyond macroprudential regulation, an issue which will be of critical importance to the EMEs from a stability perspective is the nature of presence of foreign financial institutions. This would determine the exposure of the domestic financial systems to the risk of proxy contamination with problems in global markets. A recent BIS paper[6] attempts to make a distinction between multinational banks and international banks primarily based on their funding models. It argues that from the perspective of stability of banks' exposures to borrowers, local funded positions as in the case of multinational banks are more stable during the crisis than those funded across borders and currencies, as in the case of international banks.

And lastly, the most important issue of the effectiveness and intensity of supervisory process. There is clearly a link between the depth and magnitude of the crisis to the weakness of oversight over the financial system. Stressed environments often reveal weaknesses in supervisory framework and methods which were not readily apparent in times of stability. Regulators and supervisors should be better equipped to not just identify but also take appropriate action pre-emptively to address risks that have the potential to destabilise the system. This brings us to the critical factor of supervisory space. It is possible that, at times the sense coming out of supervisory assessments will be in the nature of potential leads more

---

6. McCauley, Robert, Patrick McGuire, Peter Goetzvon (2010). "The Architecture of Global Banking: From International to Multinational?", *BIS Quarterly Review*, March.

in the nature of anecdotal evidence rather than conclusive evidence. In such a scenario, the supervisors would be prone to making either a Type-I error or a Type-II error in their judgment. It is for the broader political economy and policy setup to provide the tolerance for each of the two errors. This would largely determine the decision-making framework and provide the necessary space for the regulators to take timely decisions given that dynamic judgement is necessary to deal with system risk that is constantly changing.

Excerpted from a paper presented by Shyamala Gopinath, Deputy Governor, Reserve Bank of India, at the ADBI-BNM Conference on 'Macroeconomic and Financial Stability in Asian Emerging Markets', in Kuala Lumpur.

8 The Use of Composite Infrastructure Indices to Catalyse Infrastructure Development

Ravi Parthasarathy

It is widely accepted that the lack of adequate infrastructure acts as a severe constraint to the productive capacities of the Indian economy. It is also now increasingly accepted that inadequate infrastructure exacerbates inequity inequality, and, the perceptions of disparities. Thus whilst there may be a difference of opinion on whether infrastructure should be created in response to demand or in anticipation of demand, there is no denying that the availability of quality infrastructure will act as a significant boost to the productive capacities of the Indian economy as a whole. However, the starting point for such a blue-print will need to be the statistics relating to various types of infrastructure as well as its geographic distribution for policy and planning purposes so as to guide investment decisions. Data relating to infrastructure should be complete, accurate and up to date.

The quality of infrastructure is widely regarded as an essential determinant of growth in the states. Infrastructure in this context is clearly a multi-dimensional feature. Agricultural growth depends upon the availability of rural infrastructure such as the spread and quality of irrigation, land development, extent of rural electrification and the spread of rural roads. In a similar vein, non-agricultural growth depends critically upon sectors such as electric power, road and rail transportation, ports and airports and increasingly telecommunications. Good infrastructure not only increases the productivity of existing resources going into production, it also helps to attract more investment that can be expected to increase growth further.[1]

1. Ahluwalia (2000).

Infrastructure can be categorically classified into three broad groups such as physical, social and financial.[2] Physical and financial infrastructure helps the movement of direct productive activities and thus, improves the use of the physical resource base in the economy. Social infrastructure, on the other hand, improves the human resource base in the country.

'Soft' Infrastructure

All infrastructure businesses have the potential for creating significant impact through socioeconomically relevant activities in the influence area of the projects. The challenge is to systematically build a surround set of socioeconomic projects, ensure flawless implementation and most importantly, analytically measure the impact and loop back into design such impacts.

In a typical infrastructure project, some outcomes are easy to establish and measure e.g., impact on the environment and financial return. However, efforts to measure the outcome on, impact on trade, employment, income levels, access to better quality goods and services, educational facilities, improved communication facilities, etc., are a lot more challenging. Measuring these outcomes will have a significant impact on project design, viability, and risks. At various points in time, there would therefore be both the opportunity and the need for project interventions in the catchments area that will build upon the various externalities generated by the implementation of the specific infrastructure project, and which would significantly improve its impact in the target region.

Realising that the majority of workers at the shop floor level were women with low level of education, the IL&FS Cluster Development Initiative Ltd. (IL&FS CDI) launched a project called SEAM (Skills for Employment in Apparel Manufacturing). The project, which is supported by the Ministry of Rural Development, is targeted at the rural poor, enabling them to benefit from the growing economy while also meeting the skills needed by industry.

Project SEAM seeks to train and place 500,000 rural below poverty line (BPL) youth in the apparel sector in five years. Conceived as a public-

2. Ghosh and De (2004).

private partnership (PPP), it seeks to leverage existing strengths, infrastructure and resources for optimal outcomes, without creating any new buildings or institutions. Trainees for the project are selected from rural BPL families in close consultation with the District Rural Development Agency (DRDA).

The innovative course content, developed in a multimedia format, and translated into several local languages, also incorporates a soft-skill component to enhance the standards of performance. Training is imparted on state-of-the-art machines currently in use in the industry. As part of the course, the candidates are regularly assessed for skills against standards set by Methods Workshop, South Africa, which is also the certifying agency.

As of date, 15 training centres have been operationalised. The centres are located in Andhra Pradesh, Bihar, Gujarat, Karnataka, Maharashtra, Tamil Nadu and Uttar Pradesh. The involvement of the training centre does not end with just providing training to the candidates but involves providing placement assistance as well.

The Indian manufacturing industry is characterised by the predominance of small and medium enterprises (SMEs) located in clearly identifiable sector/product specific geographic clusters. There are at least 350 such important industrial clusters in the country covering the sectors like textiles, leather, pharma and others which contribute significantly to the employment and exports in the country. In addition, there are close to 4,000 artisan and agro processing clusters in the country providing employment to a large cross-section of society. One of the major constraints faced by the SMEs in these clusters has been lack of adequate and quality infrastructure, which has been adversely affecting their competitiveness.

IL&FS has established the Cluster Development Initiative (CDI) as a strategic business unit with the objective of undertaking the cluster development programmes across industry clusters. The Initiative is aimed at enhancing the competitiveness of SMEs through a cluster-based PPP approach. Based on a need assessment, a wide range of services including capacity building, financial, engineering, technology and marketing linkages, are provided to the targeted cluster enterprises in an integrated and commercially sustainable manner.

IL&FS, through the CDI, provides a broad range of turnkey services. The scope of services include:

- Developing appropriate institutional and financial structures for efficient implementation of the project.
- Creating appropriate contractual structures for layout, design, detailed engineering, preparation of cost estimates of the infrastructure facilities, bid documents, selection and appointment of contractors/consulting firms for specific activities to ensure smooth implementation of the project.
- Raising funding for implementation either as public financed project/s or leveraging the budgetary resources of the authority and government to attract private capital in infrastructure project/s.
- Ensuring efficient utilisation of these funds to create good quality infrastructure assets without cost and time overruns.
- Assisting to obtain reimbursement of project-specific funds and/or grants sanctioned by Central and state governments.
- Establishing sustainable systems and contractual structures for effective operation and maintenance of the project.

Pimpri-Chinchwad, located to the west of Pune, is a city in the Pune district of Maharashtra. It consists of the twin towns of Pimpri and Chinchwad which are governed by a common municipal body (the Pimpri-Chinchwad Municipal Corporation or PCMC). Pimpri-Chinchwad is a major industrial hub and hosts one of the biggest industrial zones in Asia. Constantly striving to improve educational and institutional reforms, PCMC with its knowledge partner Science and Technology Park (STP) are focused on enhancing every aspect of school education to meet global standards. Immediate reforms are being taken up for enhanced classroom processes through use of ICT tools and an increase in the efficacy of administrative functions by adoption of web enabled management imformation system (MIS). Transformed and enhanced school and learning environment would not only benefit the holistic development of a child but also improve his/her learning levels.

The PCMC and STP have identified IL&FS Education and Technology Services (IL&FS ETS) as the collaborating partner with the expertise to help realise the school transformation plan and goals in a sustained manner through a PPP. To ensure stakeholder ownership of the project a Joint Appraisal Mission was undertaken by a team of professionals from PCMC, STP and IETS to identify the areas of focus. The upgradation plan as identified by the Joint Appraisal Mission will include:

- Quality improvement and content upgradation.
- Capacity building.
- Special interventions.
- Consultancy for physical infrastructure upgradation.
- IT infrastructure and software.

The sustainable Learning Infrastructure Cycle would have following framework:

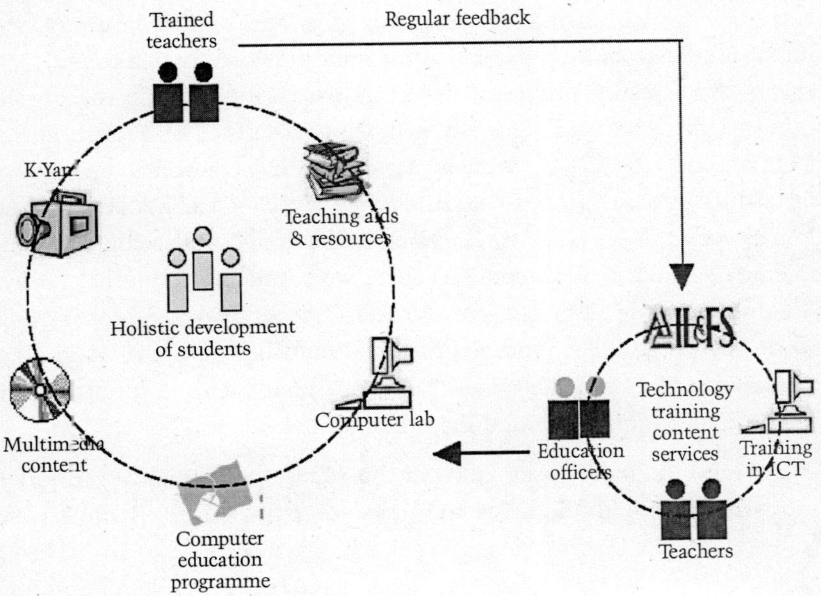

The project will focus on providing quality education from *balwadi* to Xth standard students. Specific interventions are designed to improve the performance of students with special needs. All the 152 schools of PCMC will undergo transformation to meet global standards in all aspects of education such as:

- The learning environment (including school infrastructure).
- Quality improvement in classroom processes.

- Providing blended learning solutions through the innovative use of ICT tools in education delivery and administration.
- Evaluation and impact study of interventions.

Towards a 'Composite' Index

At the outset, however, it must be remembered that India is a heterogeneous country, with substantial differences among its states and within states. While there have been attempts to compute infrastructure indices for states to determine their backwardness, with physical infrastructural index being a major denominator, it is the weights attached to them and the aggregation formula used that has determined a state's position. Thus, horizontal equity (allocations among states) and horizontal transfers have been made a function of a state's backwardness, with physical infrastructure being one of the indicators used in determining such status. As a result, different indicators used to determine the physical infrastructure status of states show different results. The Twelfth Finance Commission (2005-2010) grouped states into five categories, on the basis of an infrastructure index constructed by IDFC.[3] Goa, Maharashtra and Punjab were 'high'. Gujarat, Haryana, Kerala and Tamil Nadu were 'high middle'. Andhra Pradesh and Karnataka were 'middle'. Himachal Pradesh, Madhya Pradesh, Orissa, Uttar Pradesh, Uttarakhand and West Bengal were 'lower middle'. And Arunachal Pradesh, Manipur, Meghalaya, Jharkhand, Mizoram, Nagaland, Assam, Chhattisgarh, Sikkim, Tripura, Jammu & Kashmir, Bihar and Rajasthan were 'low'.

Again, the *India Today* 'State of the States' ranking has a category on infrastructure. This includes the percentage of houses with electricity connections, the percentage of villages connected with *pucca* roads, overall road length, the spread of bank branches, access to energy, communication-related infrastructure and post offices. Here, states are divided into large states and small states. Table 8.1 shows the present ranks.[4] These are ranks, not scores and therefore, depend on how other states are performing relatively. Importantly, it shows how, incrementally, states can improve. This is evident for Tamil Nadu, Karnataka, Andhra Pradesh and Bihar. On

3. Ministry of Finance (2004).
4. Debroy and Bhandari (2010).

the flip side, a state can also slip, evident for Maharashtra, Gujarat and Uttarakhand. Such shifts are particularly evident for large states, less so for the small ones.

Table 8.1

Infrastructure Ranks, 2004-2010

State	*2004*	*2005*	*2006*	*2007*	*2008*	*2009*	*2010*
Big States							
Punjab	1	1	1	1	1	1	1
Tamil Nadu	8	9	5	7	4	6	2
Himachal Pradesh	2	2	2	2	2	3	3
Kerala	7	6	3	3	3	2	4
Karnataka	9	10	7	8	6	7	5
Maharashtra	3	3	4	6	5	4	6
Haryana	6	4	6	4	7	5	7
Andhra Pradesh	11	11	10	10	9	10	8
Gujarat	5	7	9	9	8	8	9
J&K	10	8	11	11	10	9	10
Rajasthan	12	12	13	13	12	11	11
Madhya Pradesh	13	13	12	12	13	12	12
West Bengal	14	14	15	15	14	13	13
Uttar Pradesh	17	16	18	18	15	14	14
Orissa	18	18	16	16	16	15	15
Bihar	20	20	20	20	19	18	16
Assam	15	15	17	17	17	17	17
Uttarakhand	4	5	8	5	11	16	18
Chhattisgarh	16	17	14	14	18	19	19
Jharkhand	19	19	19	19	20	20	20
Small States							
Delhi	1	1	1	1	1	1	1
Goa	2	2	2	2	2	2	2
Mizoram	4	4	4	4	4	3	3
Sikkim	5	5	5	5	5	4	4
Puducherry	3	3	3	3	3	5	5
Arunachal Pradesh	6	6	6	6	6	8	6
Manipur	7	7	7	7	7	9	7
Tripura	8	9	9	8	10	6	8
Meghalaya	10	10	10	10	9	10	9
Nagaland	9	8	8	9	8	7	10

Similarly, the Centre for Monitoring the Indian Economy (CMIE) in its composite infrastructure index, that is based on the seven infrastructure heads of transport, energy, irrigation, banking facilities, communication facilities, education facilities and health facilities, attaches weights to these heads and it links the reforms that started in 1991 to show how the backward states had a backlog of bad infrastructure even before the reforms started. To convey a sense of this historical backwardness and deprivation, Table 8.2 shows this composite development index for major states in 1991.

Table 8.2

CMIE Composite Development Index, 1991[5]

State	*Composite Development Index*	*Rank*
Andhra Pradesh	104.01	10
Assam	104.39	9
Bihar	91.31	13
Gujarat	105.33	8
Haryana	133.12	4
Karnataka	106.12	7
Kerala	162.42	2
Madhya Pradesh	86.66	15
Maharashtra	106.77	6
Orissa	101.45	12
Punjab	171.92	1
Rajasthan	87.27	14
Tamil Nadu	145.62	3
Uttar Pradesh	112.04	5
West Bengal	102.09	11

Again, there are other groups of indices of infrastructure availability for the states for the period 1985-1990. For this, 24 infrastructure variables are classified into eight sectors—agriculture, banking, electricity, communications, transport, education, health and civil administration. The first five sectors are referred to as economic infrastructure and the next two as social infrastructure. But while these studies may differ in individual details, data and methodology, and regardless of how infrastructure is defined and measured, there is certain vigour in them when they term states as backward. Academic work and popular impression have often used

5. CMIE (2000).

the BIMARU (Bihar, Madhya Pradesh, Rajasthan, Uttar Pradesh) nomenclature, with a pun on the word *bimar*, meaning ill or sick. While this is still useful as a starting-off point, the states of Bihar, Madhya Pradesh and Uttar Pradesh have now been sub-divided and Orissa is often worse than some of these four traditional BIMARU states. BIMARU thus becomes BIMAROU. But, there are also significant differences among India's districts, that is, within states. Unfortunately, the non-existence of satisfactory district-level data prevents the computation of infrastructure indices for districts. Of India's 600-odd districts, around 100 are truly backward. The National Food for Work Programme (NFFWP) had a list of 150 backward districts, the Rashtriya Sam Vikas Yojana (RSVY) increased the number to 167 and the National Rural Employment Guarantee Act (NREGA) originally had a list of 200 backward districts. Most of these backward districts are geographically contiguous. Similarly, out of India's 600,000 villages, around 125,000 are truly backward. Infrastructure concerns should address not just backward states, but backward districts and villages within these states as well.

And this is precisely what the Bharat Nirman programme, earlier version being the PURA (Provision of Urban Amenities in Rural Areas), is seeking to do. Bharat Nirman has targets like the following: (a) Water supply—cover 55,000 uncovered habitations and provide safe drinking water to 0.216 million villages affected by poor water quality; (b) Housing—provide 12 million additional houses at the rate of 2.4 million new houses per year, through funds allocated to homeless through *panchayats*; (c) Telecommunication and information technology—increase rural tele-density to 40 per cent and provide broadband connectivity and Bharat Nirman Seva Kendras in all the 250,000 *panchayats*; (d) Roads—provide road connections to the remaining 23,000 villages that have populations of 1,000 and more (500 in the case of hilly or tribal areas); (e) Electrification—provide electricity to 40,000 remaining villages and connections to 17.5 million poor households; and (f) Irrigation—bring 6.5 million hectares under irrigation and another 3.5 million hectares by 2012. Looking at this through a different prism, we see it is nothing but infrastructure development.

A more recent and valuable example is from the northeast. In order to reduce intra-regional disparity and better targeting of schemes and projects in northeastern states the Ministry of Development of North Eastern

Region (DoNER) has prepared a composite 'District Infrastructure Index (DII)' for all the districts of the region.[6] The DII is based on seven broad indicators—transport facilities in terms of road density and road quality, energy, water supply, education, health facilities, communication infrastructure and banking facilities.

The Ministry has used the composite NER DII to give a ranking from 1 to 80 to 80 districts (in all there are 86 districts in eight northeastern states. However, six new districts, four in Assam and two in Arunachal Pradesh have been clubbed with the old districts from which those were carved out, for the purpose of DII). It has also prepared state-wise composite infrastructure index and district ranking on 14 indicators covering the seven broad indicators. Imphal West district in Manipur ranks first while Kiphire in Nagaland ranks the lowest rank 80. Going by the district ranking for banking infrastructure, South Sikkim district has the first rank with 7.07 banks per 100 sq km, while Kolasib district in Mizoram has 80th rank with only 0.02 banks per 100 sq km. The ranking on density and quality of roads has West Tripura district having the first rank with 206.62 km of road per 100 sq km, while Kurung Kumey district in Arunachal Pradesh is ranked 80 with only 2.53 km road per 100 sq km. Similarly Serchhip district in Mizoram ranks first on village electrification with 100 per cent villages electrified while Dhemaji in Assam ranks the lowest at 80 with only 26.01 per cent villages electrified.

Importantly, the Ministry will use the DII for final approval of the schemes and projects submitted by the states to be funded under the Non-Lapsable Central Pool of Resources (NLCPR).

Clearly, it may be appropriate to extend the notion of infrastructure to the social sector as well. Thus, a hospital or a school would constitute the infrastructure facility, which will provide services in the form of health care and education over a period of time.

It is conventional wisdom that the availability of infrastructure spurs economic development. This principle is best illustrated by a comment widely attributed to President Roosevelt: 'America does not have good roads because it is rich: America is rich because it has good roads'. Unfortunately,

---

6. Talukdar (2010).

the level of infrastructure created in India remains well below optimal requirements. Equally important, the development of infrastructure is quite skewed: in fact, the gap in infrastructure development between more progressive states and states that are economically disadvantaged is increasing perceptibly.

The foregoing would inevitably create a self-perpetuating cycle with lower levels of infrastructure development leading to impaired economic growth. It is in this context that it may be desirable to create an infrastructure index for each district or state in the Indian Union. The objective would be to utilise the index so created in order to direct incremental allocation of funds to the states concerned.

A number of indices have been created to reflect the level of economic development within a state:

- The *India Today* index provides valuable statistics e.g., percentage of homes with electricity, per capita LPG connections, etc.
- The CMIE index focuses on key infrastructure areas with a combination of weights relating to each sector. The indicators used for various sectors include surface roads per sq km of area, primary schools per lakh of population, telephone lines per hundred persons, etc.
- The Anant, Krishna, Choudhary (AKC) Index developed by the Delhi School of Economics (DSE) measures infrastructure facilities available in different States in terms of eight sectors and parameters, including administrative infrastructure.

All the three indices have made important contributions in gaining a perspective relating to the level of development across states.

Nonetheless, the *India Today* index and the CMIE index may not have significant utility as far as Central capital allocations are concerned. As an example, more homes may be connected with electricity in State A than in State B. However, the electricity actually consumed in State A might well be less than in State B. These indices provide a snapshot of the present as far as states are concerned, but provide no perspective in relation to their future potential. Most importantly, the parameters and weights used for different sectors remain the same for all states and districts, although the importance of a specific sector would necessarily vary from one region to another.

The AKC index appears to be mathematically more robust, and incorporates regional differences and also assigns weights to different sectors. The AKC index could nonetheless have limitations in that quality aspects are not considered, and no perspective is provided in relation to future potential. As the index is benchmarked with average values at the national level, increases and decreases in absolute value do not imply that the state has in fact evidenced an increase or decrease in the available level of infrastructure facilities. Nonetheless, the AKC index could possibly be the best starting point for creating an infrastructure index that could be utilised for spur economic development.

The approach to the creation of an index for this purpose rests on the premise that the creation of infrastructure is the key driver to enabling a state realise its full economic potential and develop its local economy. Given the foregoing, and based on the demographic variables relevant to a specific state or district, it would be possible to conceive the minimum level of base infrastructure needed in that state or district in order to realise the latent economic potential inherent in that location.

The nature of infrastructure required would necessarily vary from state to state:

- As an example, ropeways and ski resorts would necessarily be of greater importance in Himachal Pradesh, as would be the creation of cold storage depots for the preservation of horticulture products.
- The foregoing would have little relevance in Rajasthan, where the focus would necessarily be on tourism related infrastructure such as museums, as well as water conservation.
- Thus the initial exercise would require the conceptualisation of the base level of infrastructure needed in each state, and in each district within that state.

The resultant list would be the Index 100. The actual level of infrastructure developed or available in that state could be assessed and would be determined at say 25 per cent or 50 per cent as the case may be. The task before the authorities is then to determine in what manner the index could be enhanced through the creation of relevant infrastructure in that state. The principal drawback to this approach is that it is subjective to a degree, and strays from conventional principles that stipulate the use of a uniform measure as the basis for comparative evaluation.

The quantum of funds distributed to states under the aegis of the Finance Commission is based on constitutional principles i.e., it is the right of the state concerned to receive the funds allocated, although a common complaint voiced by states is that the quantum of discretionary expenditure has progressively diminished over the years.

One of the parameters that hampers rapid economic development at the level of states and urban local bodies (ULBs) is the less than adequate institutional capacity to conceive and manage efficient project implementation. If an infrastructure index is used for direction of incremental funds allocation to the states, it may be useful to consider processes and frameworks by which project implementation is also undertaken expeditiously. Given such a framework, it may be possible to see discernible results on the ground as a result of such an initiative over a five-year period.

The 73rd and 74th Amendments to the Constitution gave constitutional status to local self-governments (LSGs) and provided a new, more politically underpinned, universalised platform for decentralised planning from below. However, though it is now nearly 18 years since the amendments were made and there has been progress in implementing some of the mandated provisions such as conduct of elections, the concept of development planning from below has still not taken root, even in the few states in which there is relatively larger devolution of powers and provision of untied funds to local governments.

Each level of *panchayat* and municipalities ought to prepare perspective five-year plan and annual plans as provided in the Constitution, which would be consolidated by the District Planning Committee.

The objective of district planning is to arrive at an integrated, participatory coordinated idea of development of a local area. An essential step in this direction is to ensure that each *panchayat* at any level or municipality is treated as a planning unit and the 'district plan' is built up through consolidation and integration of these plans as well as by considering the development of the district as a whole. It is a two-way interactive exercise, the district being viewed as a convenient local area.

This may be the time to relook at the whole planning exercise and constitute the village or *panchayat* as the basic plan unit. Relevant datasets at the district level and below are therefore essential for Panchayati Raj members as they are expected to participate more and more in planning and the programme implementation. In view of such decentralisation of administrative authority and planning process, requirement of appropriate database at the micro-level makes it imperative to search for alternative data sources.

Information is a basic tool for planning, but information relevant to each area and its population is rarely available. A citizen survey leading to a database for each *gram panchayat* to know more about themselves, developed in a participative manner, is a desirable prerequisite for participatory planning. The process of data collection on citizens could be so dealt with that *gram panchayats* see in it, their own empowerment. This also builds a climate of participation even before the actual planning process starts.

A good design of data collection by the *gram panchayat* will result in:

- The *gram panchayat* will own the data it collects.
- A basic framework will be developed and local initiatives and add-ons encouraged.
- Data collection would involve the local elected representatives. *Gram panchayat* members or their literate assistants could carry out the surveys.
- Data collection is a process, not an event. Data will be continuously refined.
- *Gram panchayats* will begin to act on their findings even before the data is correlated.[7]

Cross-cutting funds or 'semi-untied' funds such as the RSVY and its recent successor, the Backward Regions Grant Fund (BRGF) provide an element of flexibility so that local priorities could be better addressed through convergence with specific purpose grants. *Panchayats* can have the

---

7. Ministry of Panchayati Raj (2006).

freedom to allocate such semi-untied funds for topping up partly funded priorities.

Clearly, infrastructure planning and resource allocation must be done on the basis of the felt needs of the people at the lowest level of governance i.e., at the village level. For that, data collection needs to be done at the *panchayat* level and fed into the system upwards accordingly. This task, many would rightly feel is well-nigh impossible. But the day is not too far away when all *gram panchayats* would be linked and connected. This will not only enable a lot of other things but more importantly, it will enable the collection of data at the grassroots level, thus closing the critical gap at the last mile.

Conclusion

India's economic performance in recent years has been among the best in the world. The significant reduction in the numbers of people living in poverty, leading to a decline in overall poverty, is particularly noteworthy. Despite these improvements, most poverty related education and health indicators continue to show disturbing gender gaps, large rural-urban differences, and wide variation across the states. The pattern of inclusive growth of the economy, with high GDP growth, can be achieved only if this infrastructure deficit can be overcome and adequate investment takes place to support higher growth and an improved quality of life for both urban and rural communities. The visible signs of shortfalls in capacity and inefficiencies include (and is not limited to) increasingly congested roads, power failures and shortages of drinking water. These illustrate the widening gap between demand and supply of infrastructure and also raise questions concerning the sustainability of economic growth in future.

The importance being given by the Government to programmes such as Bharat Nirman, National Highway Development Programme (NHDP), National Urban Renewal Mission (NURM); and Provision of Urban Amenities in Rural Areas (PURA), only reaffirms that the strategy of combating poverty through infrastructure-led growth remains relevant. Therefore, a 'composite' index comprising both hard and soft infrastructure parameters drawn from grassroots level data needs to be evolved to ensure that infrastructure planning is on the right track.

References

Ahluwalia, Montek S. (2000). "State Level Performance under Economic Reforms in India", Paper presented at the Centre for Research on Economic Development and Policy Reform Conference on *Indian Economic Prospects: Advancing Policy Reform.* Stanford University. May.

Debroy, Bibek and Laveesh Bhandari (2010). "State of the States", *India Today.* November 25.

CMIE (2000). *Profile of Districts.* Mumbai: CMIE. October.

Ghosh, B. and P. De (2004). "How Do Different Categories of Infrastructure Affect Development? Evidence from Indian States", *Economic and Political Weekly* 39: 4645-57.

Ministry of Finance (2004). *Report of the Twelfth Finance Commission (2005-2010).* New Delhi: Government of India. November.

Ministry of Panchayati Raj (2006). *Planning at The Grassroots Level: An Action Programme for the Eleventh Five Year Plan.* Report of the Expert Group. New Delhi: Government of India. March.

Talukdar, Sushanta (2010). "Infrastructure Index for North East", *The Hindu,* May 16.

9 Role of Financial Markets in Driving Financial Inclusion

Madhu Kannan

> Access to finance by the poor and vulnerable groups is a prerequisite for poverty reduction and social cohesion. This has to become an integral part of our efforts to promote inclusive growth. In fact, providing access to finance is a form of empowerment of the vulnerable groups. Financial inclusion denotes delivery of financial services at an affordable cost to the vast sections of the disadvantaged and low-income groups. The various financial services include credit, savings, insurance and payments and remittance facilities. The objective of financial inclusion is to extend the scope of activities of the organized financial system to include within its ambit people with low incomes. Through graduated credit, the attempt must be to lift the poor from one level to another so that they come out of poverty.
>
> The country has moved on to a higher growth trajectory. To sustain and accelerate the growth momentum, we have to ensure increased participation of the economically weak segments of population in the process of economic growth. Financial inclusion of hitherto excluded segments of population is a critical part of this process of inclusion. We hope that the recommendations made in this Report, if implemented, will accelerate the process of financial inclusion.
>
> — Preface, *Report of the Committee on Financial Inclusion*, January 2008, chaired by Dr. C. Rangarajan.

Introduction

Growth in telecommunications technology has ensured that Indians living in and around the thousands of small towns, villages as well as large cities cannot miss the glare of scores of TV news channels. Such channels are now available in nearly all the major and minor languages. A common feature of their screens is the ticker at the bottom displaying prices of stocks, indexes (local and global), commodities like gold and silver, and a variety of other information.

From a policy perspective, a couple of obvious questions come to mind regarding the relevance of this information for the average citizen. Is the information on the products and services being pitched of any relevance to the average Indian household? Does the fact that stocks issued by hundreds of Indian companies are being traded actively imply that the average Indian business can access these markets to fund its ideas and operations?

This paper attempts to provide a framework for growing our market infrastructure in a manner, and in a direction, such that we can get closer to replying to both these questions in the affirmative.

Taking Policy Risks

A key challenge for businesses operating in any industry is figuring out how to deliver products and services in an economically efficient (in other words, low cost) manner to potential customers residing in various nooks and corners of the vast land of India. This holds true for providers of financial services, broadly defined to include banks, insurance companies, asset management companies, exchanges and their members, depositories and others. The presumption is that these businesses have figured out the 'products' of relevance to the different niches of the potential customer base living in these nooks and crannies.

Our focus is on figuring out ways to leverage existing infrastructure to develop alternate delivery channels. We believe that innovation happens when individuals and businesses start using tools for purposes not contemplated by the original developers of these tools.

There is a bigger challenge in delivering reliable funding at realistic risk-adjusted costs to businesses and budding entrepreneurs around India. It is broadly accepted that in market-driven economies, new jobs are typically created by small and new enterprises. In a country like India, the average citizen is self-employed—the person selling roasted peanuts in crowded suburban trains, or working on a small plot of land too small to feed the family.

While our formal banking system is mandated to fund what are called priority sector loans, the institutions are clearly not set up to manage the risks involved in funding even the conventional small and medium enterprises (SMEs). The average entrepreneur has to rely on working capital finance from his supplier, or rely on friends and family, and in a absence of that, go to the informal finance sector—also known as the moneylender.

New formalised structures called microfinance institutions (MFIs) have been formed in recent years to serve the needs of this informal sector. But policy and political ambivalence regarding the rates of interest being charged by MFIs indicates that there are continued challenges in the sector. Political discussions tend to ignore the economic reality that for MFIs to be sustainable, credit risk must be embedded in the funding cost.

Forget MFIs; even in the case of large borrowers (think in terms of companies in the BSE 100 index), India has not developed the capability to price credit risk. For reasons related to the interest rate differentials and current view on the currency rates, most of these companies continue to raise funds in offshore markets. Local issuance in the corporate bond market is typically restricted to government-owned institutions which find it more difficult to go overseas to borrow.

The lack of a term structure of rates compounded by the absence of credit spread benchmarks trickles down all the way to the smallest borrower. The solution could lie in new instruments and products, some traded and/or cleared and settled on centralised platforms. Some tentative steps have been taken in the form of a proposal to create a new segment for SMEs, bond futures contracts, and a discussion paper on developing a credit default swap market.

But the pervasive theme in all these initiatives is that of complete risk-aversion. One can argue that maybe it is time to revive the bold approaches taken in the early 1990s when new regulatory frameworks and market infrastructure institutions were created. From the policy perspective, it is timely to challenge our current approaches and adopt risk-adjusted solutions where the downside risk of failure is small compared to the macro benefits to hundreds of thousands or millions of individuals and firms.

Leveraging Exchange Platforms

While India has a long tradition of over 135 years of trading stocks, till about 10-15 years ago, this business was localised to the bylanes of a handful of large cities in India. Quantum growth happened when we leveraged satellite technology to provide investors in the remote corners of the country to the exchanges; the reference here is to the V-SAT technology deployed to avoid reliance on the then expensive terrestrial telephone cables.

While V-SATs helped the development of truly national stock exchanges like BSE and NSE, a key innovation was a decision to convert physical pieces of paper, called share certificates, into demat or electronic records forms.

These two innovations were possible because of bold decisions taken with a view to surmounting key challenges in allowing investors around the country to invest and trade stocks issued by Indian companies.

Accessing Mutual Funds through Exchanges

Another classic example of innovation (in the sense of using a tool for a purpose not covered in the original design document) is in progress—allowing investors to purchase and redeem mutual fund units through the exchanges' networks. In other words, investors can now use the V-SAT and wired lines connecting brokerage firms to exchanges to access mutual fund products.

Mutual funds have evolved globally as a low-cost, efficient way for individual investors to get exposure to specific asset classes, be it equity, debt, commodities, and even non-traditional instruments such as real estate and currencies. There are close to 40 asset management companies registered with Securities and Exchange Board of India (SEBI) offering such products to Indian investors.

The main distribution channel for these funds is the network of investment advisers or independent financial advisers (popularly known as IFAs). While the Tier 1, and large numbers of Tier 2 cities have been well-covered by these IFAs, the same is not the case as one moves outside this range.

Developing a distribution channel is akin to building roads. While tax-payer funds are typically used to create physical infrastructure like roads and railway tracks; not so for soaps, shampoos, cellphones, cars, bread, mutual fund units, insurance policies, banking services, etc. As in the case of banking and insurance, the government might own some of the largest providers of these services, but it cannot use tax revenues to build distribution channels.

In the case of mutual funds for instance, the case for physical infrastructure is weak. What is required is the ability for the fund company to identify potential clients, educate them about specific products, and then have a low-cost way of letting the customer purchase and later redeem the product.

As the cost of developing the infrastructure for any single company is likely to be prohibitive, the fund management industry has been struggling to come up with a common solution, one that could be built, owned, and operated as a utility. This has been the approach in other well-developed markets.

In the meantime, at the behest of SEBI, the fund companies, the RTAs (registrar and transfer agents), and the exchanges have been collaborating to come up with an innovative solution. We pointed out earlier that thanks to V-SAT technology, the exchanges have the electronic infrastructure to the remote corners of the country. Investors can buy and sell shares on exchanges via these networks. Why not allow them to purchase and redeem mutual fund units through the same channels?

While the service providers (fund companies, RTA and exchanges) have to modify their systems and integrate with each other, there is no added cost for the end investor. The innovative thinking comes from realising while the exchange networks were created to trade stocks (by sending buy-and-sell orders to the exchanges), these channels can also be used to communicate, in other words, send purchase and redemption instructions or orders, to fund management companies. The exchange systems have been designed such that they are constantly trying to match buy and sell orders. Routing instructions passively to mutual fund companies was not part of the original design.

The mold has now been broken; systems have been modified, connectivity between exchanges, fund companies and their RTAs have been established. From a policy perspective, this is a huge development. It is time to re-energise the tired phrase, build it and they will come.

One can argue that the products designed by the fund industry are targeted at the educated investor living in Tier 1 and 2 cities. Most of the funds are actively managed, which in turn means that their expense ratios are high. The fund industry has not been rushing to offer mutual funds in tiny pouches (which would be akin to shampoos in tiny packets for Rs. 5 each!). But if the financial services industry is serious about having products of relevance to the potential customers residing in the far corner of the country, then it ought to be studying the product design practices of fast moving consumable good (FMCG) companies.

Selling a financial product, be it banking, insurance, or mutual funds, will never be as simple as walking to the corner store to purchase a sachet of shampoo. But true financial inclusion will happen when service providers design products with the end customer in mind. The innovation in distribution will help ensure that the fund companies no longer need to worry about distributing the products to the customer.

In terms of offering lower cost products, there are numerous ideas being explored by the fund industry. Passively managed index funds benchmarked to indexes such as the Sensex and the BSE-100, target funds with asset allocation structures varying with time to retirement, etc. Offering products with low expense ratios make sense only if the corpus under management attains a large minimum size, say about Rs. 1,000 crore.

Given the high savings rate in the country, most of which now seems to be going into gold and bank accounts, there is a huge opportunity for the financial services industry to offer products such that Indian citizens can invest their savings in a more diversified and economically meaningful manner. Moving away from gold, for instance, could make these resources available for funding capital investments and fuel the double digit growth rates essential for moving millions of Indians out of poverty.

Mobile Finance

The development of the facility to invest in mutual funds and insurance policies through the exchange platforms has raised an obvious question: In a country with over half a billion cellphones, why are we not aggressively pushing mobile banking, mobile payments, mobile trading and mobile investments?

Mobile trading, in other words, buying and selling instruments listed on exchanges, has recently become a reality in India. This development was held back due to lack of regulatory clarity. While the technology has been available for a long time, exchanges and brokerage firms were not keen to push the facility without clear regulatory guidance. One could argue that this is another illustration of our risk aversion to innovation.

Regulatory policy development was stymied by concerns about the security of the network (or lack thereof). Proponents of mobile trading won their arguments and allayed the security concerns of the regulators by pointing out that regulations lagged technology.

Policy on Internet-based trading allowed an investor using a laptop to connect to the exchanges using a wireless modem. But if the SIM card from the modem was removed and inserted into a mobile phone, policy did not allow the investor to connect to the exchanges.

Safe from the constraints of regulation, cellphone technology has advanced such that the new phones bear little resemblance to the brick-sized version of phones of the 1980s. The term 'smart phone' does not do justice to these instruments. As they are used extensively for browsing and for email, phone manufacturers, network operators and application providers have developed robust security systems.

September 2010 finally saw the launch of mobile trading in stock exchanges. For a few years now, firms have been using the medium to inform and educate their customers about investment opportunities; they can now use the technology to provide access to markets and products.

As in the case of distributing mutual funds through the exchange platform, the ability to transact using mobile phones, in other words, accessing markets instead of just accessing information, can serve as a catalyst for increasing penetration of financial services to Tier 3 and 4 cities, as well as the lower segments of society residing in Tier 1 and 2 cities

While it is tempting to picture the newspaper vendor tracking Infosys stock on his mobile phone and buying and selling his stock through a few key strokes, a more realistic outcome is less jazzy, but a lot more relevant to improving the financial well-being of our citizens.

Are our Policies and Processes Truly Inclusive?

It is a truism to state that economic opportunities have grown substantially thanks to mobile phones. The fisherman headed to the shore calling multiple market centres to check for best prices before deciding on which port to land is part of modern Indian folklore. The more enduring theme is that of the newspaper recycler taking calls on his cellphone to pick up trash from customers' homes.

While regulatory bodies sometimes are hesitant in allowing certain types of activities to be transacted using new technologies, the average Indian, the target we are trying to include in modern financial services, clearly has a much higher level of comfort. Their daily sustenance seems to be dependent on business via cellphones.

Continuing with our theme of leveraging available technologies and network capabilities to develop new distribution capabilities, the launch of the mutual-funds-through-exchange platform plus mobile trading, opens up a host of new possibilities. The range of potential opportunities will simply increase once mobile banking and mobile payments are allowed.

Unfortunately, current rules for opening and operating a mutual fund account are clearly designed to exclude potential investors, for example, those without bank accounts. If we are really serious about financial inclusion, we should endeavour to get rid of this rule.

The old newspaper recycler should be allowed to open a savings account without ever visiting a bank, or being subject to know-your-customer (KYC) norms more stringent than that required for getting a pre-paid SIM card. Once this account has been set up, he should be able to deposit his daily savings into his account through a process similar to that for recharging his pre-paid card. Out of this account, he should be able to transact in a wide range of financial products including mutual fund units, insurance, etc.

The microfinance industry has demonstrated the potential for extending formal loan products to the average Indian. But micro savings and investment products, as well as micro insurance products, have yet to see the light of the day.

Clearly the inability to distribute and service such products is a likely reason for this. But with the opening up of mobile transactions, along with new forms of connectivity between intermediaries and fund companies, there is no reason why we should not witness a flood of new nano-sized product offerings.

One can argue that our current rules and processes ignore the fact that we are still a cash-based economy. A majority of our citizens do not have, and might never ever open, a bank account. The evidence is clearly visible when one moves from big cities to Tier 3 and 4 towns. A city like Mumbai will have at least one ATM in every block. In a town like Tiruchirapalli, one can travel for a few kilometres without coming across an ATM.

From a policy perspective, the options are stark. Financial service providers can wait for banks to increase their branch network, or they can leverage existing technology networks to reach the unserved segments of the market.

Funding Private Enterprise: SME Experiment

The fact that SMEs have difficulties raising capital from reliable sources is well-documented. While debt funding will typically be the preferred option for any business, the fact that these businesses do not have access to equity capital markets has been of concern to policymakers for a while now.

There is strong empirical evidence that new jobs are typically created in tiny, SMEs. Speak to any new businessman and the lack of access to reliable sources of capital is a common refrain. So from a policy perspective, we have strong interest in ensuring that we have a supportive environment for the creation, sustenance and growth of new businesses.

There is a joke that if you attend a banking industry function in Mumbai and loudly announce that you are looking to raise Rs. 1,000 crore, a score or more of bankers will form a line to shake hands with you and to exchange business cards. But ask for Rs. 10 crore, and there will be hardly anyone interested!

So the challenge from a policy perspective is to create a market infrastructure such that someone looking to raise a relatively small amount of money can access the equity capital markets. One can argue that in modern markets, entrepreneurs look upto venture capitalists (VCs) for funding. While this might be true for the US and some parts of Europe, and even Bangalore, VCs tend to have restricted reach—they are located in specific parts of a region, and specialise in specific sectors and industry. Moreover, for various reasons, the VC culture has really not taken off in India yet.

So we clearly have to work towards creating alternate sources of equity capital. With this goal in mind, SEBI has been working closely with exchanges and the banking community to develop a framework for the creation of a specialised, SME-focused segment. The broad outlines of the framework are:

- It is applicable for companies with market capitalisation of Rs. 25 crore or less.
- SEBI approval of the prospectus is waived.
- The onus is on exchanges and merchant bankers to screen prospective listings.
- There is a minimum underwriting and market making responsibility for the bankers—to ensure sufficient liquidity in the secondary market.

Though the framework has been in place for a while now, we are yet to see a rush by companies and their bankers to list stock on the SME segment. Clearly there is a lot more work to be done before we get the magic formula to facilitate equity capital funding to our SMEs.

Sticking to theme of bold experimentation, it is tempting to prod the regulators to allow the exchanges and the banking community to suggest alternative frameworks for SME markets. The new regulations are clearly focused on mitigating any risks to the investor.

But while seeking to protect the retail investor, which is an important goal, have we gone too far such that the typical SME can no longer afford the new facility? Can we take a 180-degree turn and focus on a structure that reduces the cost of capital for the SME sector?

For instance, the requirement that the merchant bankers make provision for market making for at least two years assumes that liquidity will be a critical variable in an investor's pricing and evaluation model. Returning to our earlier discussions regarding the absence of an organised venture capital service, can we think in terms of a market model wherein the goal is to bring together investors with a VC's mind-set and SME businesses?

Venture capitalists and private equity investors do care about liquidity but not in the same sense as someone looking to apply for the Coal India public offering. Discussions related to the SME segment typically refer the London AIM (Alternative Investment Market). The interesting thing about AIM is that there is hardly any secondary market trading in the shares listed on it. If immediacy is not critical for the investor, then why have regulations in India insisted on it as a precondition for any listings to take place?

There is a cap of Rs. 25 crore on the market capitalisation or paid-up capital of the companies seeking to be listed on the SME segment. Instead of thinking in terms of absolute ceilings, which tend to become restrictive thanks to inflation, can we design rules such that retail investors are kept away from this market? Perhaps only institutional investors and high net-worth investors (HNIs), who can afford to invest at least Rs. 1 crore and above should be allowed to subscribe to shares listed on this segment.

Interestingly, there is a relatively huge market comprising structured products (non-convertible equity linked debentures with capital protection), listed on exchanges and sold to HNIs and others. There is hardly any trading in the secondary market; any transactions are typically by 'appointment'.

Gaps in the Market Structure

For monetary policy to be effective there should be a well-functioning transmission mechanism. In other words, if the central bank reduces the repo rate, it should have an immediate chain impact on a series of interest rates and thus the cost of capital for businesses and households. If the central bank changes one of its target rates, there is an immediate ripple effect on all overnight, 1, 3, 6, 12-month and 2, 5, 7, 10, 15-year rates.

In other words, we need a term structure of interest rates, one wherein rates along different points in the maturity structure are determined by idiosyncratic and systemic factors.

Such a schedule of rates at which banks can actually lend and borrow does not exist in India. In terms of funding rates, we have the overnight rate, 90-day T-bill rate, 6-month and 12-months commercial paper and certificates of deposits, and then the government bond tenors of 5 and 10 years.

If a bank wants to make a two-year loan to a corporate, or even a one-month loan, there is no benchmark rate to reference. Various survey based rates are published but surveyed rates are not funding rates, in the sense that no one is actually willing to lend or borrow at those rates.

Globally, the interest rate swap market is an important funding source for companies. This market typically references 1 or 3-month Libor (US$, Sterling, Euro or Yen) rates. In the absence of such rates, credit tends to be mispriced in India—either too cheap (with government debt), or prohibitively expensive (loans to small businesses).

Benchmark rates are determined by transactions in standard instruments in the money and bond markets. There is very little systematic policy discussion on the development of such instruments. The limited effort in recent years is a concept note on the introduction of interest rate futures on the exchanges.

A major challenge is that the pace of introduction and development of this market is controlled by the regulators. While there is strong interest from market participants in both short-term rate and bond futures contracts, the regulators have only authorised one product so far. The first instrument introduced was the 10-year bond futures contract with a cheapest-to-deliver structure. After some early efforts to generate trading from market participants, interest has dissipated. Post the failure of the first experiment, there is now talk of introducing cash-settled bond and short-term interest rate contracts.

The process for developing benchmark rates and successful trading instruments is more an art than a science. In fact, formation of market consensus over a specific instrument as the preferred benchmark is itself a random event. With these dynamics, plus the vital needs for benchmark rates, policy should proactively support experimentation by the exchanges. Let the exchanges more freely develop their own products and see if they can attract participation. Any downside risk is likely to be offset by the long-term benefits from the development of deep and liquid markets.

Conclusion

Sustained and broad-based economic growth can happen only when low-income households and the smallest businesses have access to financial services at reasonable costs. Thanks to some bold policy moves in the early 1990s, we have been relatively successful in developing a broad array of liquidity and funding pools. But access to these pools is still restricted to high-income households and large corporations.

As the benefits of economic growth trickle down, there is a huge opportunity to improve the financial well-being of hundreds of millions of Indians by offering them access to saving and investment products.

The average Indian is self-employed. Most of the new jobs are typically created by tiny SMEs. These businesses lack access to reliable sources of finance. From a policy perspective, we have a strong motivation to experiment with various market models to ensure that appropriate or relevant funding sources are developed.

Policymakers should explicitly acknowledge the importance of experimentation and be willing to shoulder the moderate risks of failure implicit in experiments. The old newspaper vendor is willing to risk his meagre capital to buy a cellphone and pay the monthly charges with the expectation that this technology will help him grow his business. Accordingly, regulators and politicians should be willing to take policy risks to ensure that our markets and institutions remain relevant to this vendor. Our success or failure will be determined by the positive impact we bring to this vendor's life.

10 Credit Markets and Financial Inclusion

Kartikeya Desai and Nitin Desai

Dr. C. Rangarajan is one of India's most eminent and influential economists. As a Professor at IIM-Ahmedabad, as Governor of the Reserve Bank of India (RBI), as Chair of the Twelfth Finance Commission (2005-2010) and as Chair of the Economic Advisory Council to the Prime Minister (PMEAC) he has pioneered many innovations in policy analysis and development particularly in the sphere of macroeconomic thinking and the management of the financial system. He has played a key role in the policy innovations that led to the transformation of the financial sector and the relationship between fiscal and financial authorities during the 90s. It is a privilege to pay tribute to his many achievements with this contribution on an issue of financial policy of such importance and relevance.

Financial inclusion could mean many things but one feature that is always present in any definition is the widening of access to organised credit to households and enterprises who otherwise have to rely on informal sources like moneylenders. The rapid expansion of cooperative rural credit which started in a big way soon after Independence, the nationalisation of banks and the subsequent expansion of the branch banking network, credit planning through the priority sector obligations on banks and a host of other measures are examples of this dimension of finance policy. The most recent manifestation of this concern about credit delivery for the underprivileged is the rapid expansion of micro-credit and the introduction of the business correspondent (BC) framework to extend savings and other banking services to the financially excluded population.

The interventions to promote credit delivery to underprivileged households must be looked at as interventions to correct market failure. That means that the operating philosophy and the structure of the schemes to promote financial inclusion must be based on a good understanding of how credit markets operate and the precise market failures that need to be corrected. Hence in what follows we deal first with the nature of credit markets, a history of financial inclusion regulation in India and then go on to an evaluation of the most recent attempt at promoting financial inclusion which is the complex of institutional developments that are subsumed under the heading of microfinance, the successes and stresses of this model in credit delivery and the resultant implications for regulation of microfinance and financial inclusion in India.

The Nature of Credit Markets

A commodity market can be conceptualised in terms of a homogeneous product where some sort of auction establishes a market-clearing price and exchange takes place between anonymous buyers and sellers at this price. This is what Walras called the tattonment process. Every buyer who wants to buy at the market-clearing price is able to fulfill his demand and every seller who wants to sell at this price can dispose off the amount he wishes to offer.

The market for credit or loanable funds is sometimes portrayed in the same way as a commodity market with a downward sloping demand curve and an upward sloping supply curve, both showing quantities as a function of the interest rate. This is quite misleading.

The market for loanable funds is different in several essential ways. A financial asset can be defined as a legal contract between two counterparties with a defined cash flow over a defined time period. What is traded in this market is a promise to pay a sum in the future against the receipt of a sum today, a trade between current utility and future utility. The future is inherently uncertain and financial transactions involve a variety of risks. There is the systemic market risk if a whole class of borrower is affected by some natural market event like a drought or a price collapse. There is the possibility of an individual borrower running into temporary difficulties with repayment because of a liquidity crunch and there is the credit risk of a wrong evaluation of the borrowers capacity. A further possibility, not too far away in India, is the legal and institutional risk of not being able to enforce contracts and unpredictable changes in government policy that affect the terms of the contract. In the final analysis the central issue for the lender is the protection against default.

If the penalty attached to default is low then the demand for funds would be very elastic at almost any rate and the supply of funds would be very low and inelastic. This is not just a theoretical possibility as the main point of due diligence by a lender-supplier in this market is to assess whether the borrower-demander is a crook or a dreamer with an unrealistic idea of his capacity to repay. Because of this two things happen which are different from a commodity market where the relationship between buyer and seller ends once the goods are exchanged or sold. First the trade takes place with provisions to guard against default which link the buyer and seller over time. Second, as a consequence, the buyer and seller cannot remain anonymous since trust and confidence, which lie at the heart of this transaction in promises require a direct and continuing relationship.

There are of course many institutional measures which can and are taken to make this lending transaction smooth—the pledging of collateral, mortgaging of assets against future liabilities laws relating to debt liability and debt recovery and credit ratings to allow lenders to gauge the risk of default better. But none of this changes the fundamental feature of this market that the lender-seller chooses buyers-borrowers he will deal with in a way that is not necessary in a product market. Hence in the market for loanable funds the supply of capital is allocated by lenders to known and specific borrowers. The well-behaved demand curve that is usually portrayed can, at best be thought of as a curve that aggregates the demands of borrowers whose credibility can pass muster with some lender. It would have to exclude the demand from those who are deemed to be potential cheats or unrealistic dreamers. In this sense, not everybody who wishes to borrow at the prevailing interest rate goes away satisfied.

The fact that lenders choose borrowers is even clearer when the transaction is not in terms of a simple promissory note but is tied to a particular purpose or project for which the borrower seeks funds. This would be the case for bank lending for working capital, mortgage loans for housing, project lending for new fixed investment and even new equity offerings for corporate finance. The lender now has to judge the merits of the purpose and the credibility of each offer and then choose amongst them.

Financial intermediation develops to create the possibility of a more anonymous relationship between the ultimate savers and investors. Intermediate financial products, generally involving the securitisation of debt, can operate on a more anonymous basis. Even these involve assessments of credit risk which are specific to particular borrowers. But these assessments can be standardised or the future payments guaranteed by some trusted entity, for example a market committee.

The central point to recognise from this stylised description of the market for loanable funds is that in all situations capital is allocated by each lender. In this sense credit is always rationed. The real question then is by how many people? If there are many lenders, with differing perceptions of risk, or differing degrees of risk aversion, then the options available to a borrower become wider. Rejection by one lender need not mean rejection by all.

This variation in the behaviour of suppliers is crucial for competitive outcomes in this market in a way that has no counterpart in product markets. If every seller of rice in the market has the same objective function it really would not matter much. But if all lenders had identical assessments of risk and degree of risk aversion then the market would operate as if a single entity is rationing credit on the basis of assessments about the future which may turn out to be wrong. The effective functioning of credit markets requires that the class of lenders is not wholly homogeneous.

Financial intermediation also leads to a strong connection between different financial markets. Because of this piecemeal interventions in one market can have unforeseen repercussions in other markets. A closely related point is the possibility of contagion from a market which faces a serious systemic risk to others which do not as each leveraged lender working on a thin margin tries to hedge his bets before others do the same.

One further point needs to be made. The market for credit, which is a trade between current and future promises to pay, is the link between finance and growth. Growth involves a link between the present and the future through the mechanism of savings and investment. Hence what matters most is the impact that the operation of credit markets have on savings and investment, which link current and future consumption in the real economy.

Hence any analysis of credit markets must recognise five fundamental principles:

- A credit transaction is inherently a futures transaction and somebody somewhere is bearing the risks of an unknown future.
- Credit markets do not operate in a simultaneous market-clearing mode, they are highly interlinked and this generates opportunities for arbitrage.
- These markets depend crucially on the existence of a financial services industry which implies that transaction costs are a central feature of these markets.
- Market functioning depends crucially on the institutional arrangements for enforcing contracts and preventing fraud.
- The link between credit markets and growth processes must focus on the impact that these markets have on savings and investment.

These basic lessons from how credit markets operate can help us understand some of the main lessons from the successes and failures of the microfinance model in India and other efforts at financial inclusion of the last 40 years.

History of Financial Inclusion Regulation in India

On the face of it, India has a deep financial system. Financial assets amount to about $2 trillion or about 160 per cent of GDP in India compared to ~$4 trillion for emerging Asia (ex-Japan and China) and $12 trillion for China, ~230 per cent and 280 per cent of GDP (2008).[1] India also has a very large network of bank branches—185,000, of which more than half are in rural or semi-urban areas.[2] As a result, India compares favourably in terms of branch density. However, India's deep financial system is very uneven and has been relatively unsuccessful in improving access of poor people to financial services with over 50 per cent of the

1. McKinsey Global Institute Report (2008). *Global Capital Markets*.
2. Reserve Bank of India (2010). *Bank Report*.

population still not having any formal saving option, borrowing money largely from informal sources at exorbitant rates (50 per cent-100 per cent APR), paying upwards of 5 per cent commission to transfer money domestically, and for whom penetration of life insurance and pension schemes is negligible. Overall it can be said that meaningful financial inclusion has been a strategic gap in India's development chronicle.

There have been various regulatory interventions in India to facilitate financial inclusion including bank nationalisation in 1969, the RBI's thrust on no frills accounts, simpler know-your-customer (KYC) norms, liberalised branch authorisation policy for scheduled commercial banks in rural areas, priority sector lending and policies on the use of intermediaries such as business correspondents/business facilitators (BCs/BFs). Together these efforts have contributed significantly towards the goal of financial inclusion.[3]

- Localised banks: Historically, the regulatory framework has encouraged smaller regional banks—local entities such as cooperative banks, deposit taking non-banking financial companies (NBFCs) and regional rural banks (RRBs)—to drive financial inclusion. However the regulator's experience with these entities has highlighted the risks of poor governance, connected lending, geographic concentration leading to vulnerability to natural calamities and downturns. Other bottlenecks include the fact that small entities also tend to absorb disproportionate share of supervisory resources and often do not have the scale and ability to invest in adoption of ICT solutions that are essential for accessing mainstream payments systems.
- Priority sector lending (PSL): All domestic commercial banks are required to allocate 40 per cent of their lending to the priority sectors, defined as disadvantaged sections of society as well as agriculture and allied activities. Credit extended by banks to SHGs, and NBFC-MFIs for on-lending to priority sector categories is included in the definition of PSL, though recently the regulator has indicated that

3. Speech delivered by Usha Thorat, Deputy Governor, Reserve Bank of India at the Tenth Annual International Seminar on *Policy Challenges for the Financial Sector* co-hosted by the Board of Governors of the Federal Reserve System, the International Monetary Fund, and the World Bank at Washington, June 2-4, 2010.

for-profit MFIs would gradually be removed from the list of entities eligible for PSL funding.

- Branch licensing: The RBI has linked statutory approvals for branch licences in more lucrative centres to the number of branches opened in underbanked districts and states, thus encouraging banks to open up branches in underpenetrated areas.
- No frills accounts and simpler KYC norms: In 2005, the RBI directed all banks to offer at all branches the facility of 'no frills' accounts, or accounts allowing nil or low minimum balances and charges and having limited facilities. At the same time, the RBI has provided for simpler KYC norms for small value accounts where the balances in the account do not exceed about $1,000 and where the annual credits in the account do not exceed about $4,000, and for small remittances and payments not exceeding $1,000.
- Unique ID initiative: Recently, the government has constituted the Unique Identification Authority of India (UIDAI) initiative to issue a unique identification number (UID) with biometric recognition to every resident of the country. This exercise is expected to provide a significant boost to financial inclusion efforts through addressing the challenges relating to client authentication.
- Business correspondent (BC) framework: The RBI issued the BC guidelines in 2006, paving the way for branchless banking through agents. The guidelines were significantly relaxed in 2010 with permission for for-profit corporates to participate as BCs.
- Payment and settlements: Subsequent to the notification of Payment and Settlement Systems Act, 2007, payment services have been opened up in India for non-bank service providers. Recently, the RBI has issued several payment licences including to pre-paid card issuers and other non-bank intermediaries involved in setting up payment systems.

While all these are significant policy measures, perhaps the most important attempt at delivering financial inclusion from the credit delivery perspective for more than a decade now has been the self-help group or SHG model. The SHG approach to microfinance was pioneered by the National Bank for Agriculture and Rural Development (NABARD) and is today one of the most widespread microfinance programme in the country. Under this model, typically an NGO forms homogeneous groups consisting of 12 to 20 members. These small groups are encouraged to meet frequently and collect small thrift amounts from their members. Through group dynamics, decision-making and funds management, the sense of empowerment is promoted. The group is not merely a savings and loan association, but serves as a collective conduit that provides a platform for a range of issues such as watershed development, awareness building and family planning.

However, on the savings side of financial inclusion, despite the substantial efforts of the last 40 years and these ambitious policy initiatives, success has been limited. Out of 600,000 villages in India, only 32,000 have access to a bank branch. Less than 50 per cent of the population across the country has bank accounts. In 2010, as part of the renewed priority placed on financial inclusion, the government has required banks to reach all 100,000 habitations in India with a population of over 2,000 by March 2012. The RBI has directed banks to draw up a roadmap by March 2010 to provide banking services through a banking outlet, not necessarily a bank branch, which has encouraged banks to work to a variety of BCs and BFs, whose regulations have been recently relaxed to allow entry for for-profit corporates.

The Microfinance Model in India

Microfinance is best thought of as a credit market development that handles the risks involved in loans to small borrowers who cannot provide a collateral and reduces transaction costs so as to make the delivery of small amounts of credit viable. The microfinance business model is designed to address the challenges faced by the traditional financial services sector in fulfilling the credit requirement of the low-income segment at an affordable and sustainable cost. Most MFIs follow the Joint Liability Group (JLG) model, which consists of 5 to 10 women who act as co-guarantors for the other members of their group. This strategy provides an impetus for prudent self-selection of reliable and fiscally responsible co-members. Moreover, the JLG has an inbuilt mechanism that encourages repayment in a timely fashion as issuance of future loans is contingent upon the prior repayment record of the group.

The poor, like the rest of society, need financial products and services to build assets, stabilise consumption and protect themselves against risks. Microfinance serves as the last-mile bridge to the low-income population excluded from the traditional financial services system and seeks to fill this gap and help alleviate poverty. Microfinance loans serve the low-income population in multiple ways by: (1) providing working capital to build businesses; (2) infusing credit to smooth cash flows and mitigate irregularity in accessing food, clothing, shelter, or education; and (3) cushioning the economic impact of shocks such as illness, theft, or natural disasters. Moreover, by providing an alternative to the loans offered by the local moneylender priced at 50 per cent to 100 per cent annual interest, microfinance prevents the borrower from remaining trapped in a debt trap which exacerbates poverty. The microfinance model is designed specifically to help the low-income population overcome typical challenges such as illiteracy, lack of financial knowledge and deficiency of collateralisable assets. At the same time, the model takes advantage of existing community support systems and networks to encourage financial discipline and ensure high repayment rates.

The fundamental reason behind the Indian microfinance industry's impressive growth is that it is fulfilling a critical need of its target audience, the low-income population, which has thus far remained unaddressed by the traditional financial services sector. Currently, a total population of 1.2 billion is being served by 185,000 bank branches, 12,000 cooperative bank offices, 15,000 RRB branches and 100,000 primary agriculture societies. This density of financial services, however, belies the availability of financial services to low-income households, which make up a significant chunk of the Indian population.

The reasons behind the formal financial sector's failure to reach such a large segment of the Indian population are manifold and operate in a self-reinforcing manner. The principal prohibiting factor is that banks face extremely high fixed and variable costs in servicing low-income households, resulting in high delivery costs for relatively small transactions. Much of the low-income population is located in rural areas that are geographically remote and inaccessible. For this population, the cost of visiting a traditional bank branch is prohibitive due to the loss of wages that would be incurred in the time required. Concurrently, from a bank's perspective, the cost of operating a branch in a remote location is financially unfeasible due to the low volume and high cost dynamic. Moreover, low-income households are not interested in the same products that are usually utilised by the rest of the population because they have different immediate needs, lower financial capacities and variable income streams. The unsuitability of existing credit products for low-income households is exacerbated by a general unavailability of collateralisable assets. Additionally, the low-income population is often illiterate and lacks financial knowledge, making it nearly impossible for it to even contemplate availing existing financial services, which provide no ancillary support to mitigate these challenges.

It is also important to note the key differences between microfinance and uncollateralised sub-prime consumer lending, the prime differentiator between the two being that a microfinance loan does not inherently assume a higher chance of default and does not subsequently charge a higher rate of interest. The rate of interest arises from the higher operational costs associated with smaller loan sizes and remote delivery. This assumption is backed by a process of verifying the intended use of the loan and the repayment capacity of the client and given veracity by the low default rates on microfinance loans in India. Moreover, unlike sub-prime borrowers, microfinance clients do not have unattractive credit histories, but rather the complete absence of a credit history, which is not a precondition for determining creditworthiness.

Microfinance as a Credit Market Intervention

One can explain the relative success as well as the stresses within the microfinance model in terms of the key principles of credit markets articulated above, as well as suggest some implications arising from this for financial inclusion regulation.

The first point—that a credit transaction is inherently a futures transaction and somebody somewhere is bearing the risks of an unknown future—suggests that effective functioning of micro-credit delivery requires multiple types of lenders (government, private and NGO) with different risk perceptions so that different types of borrowers can be accommodated. It also requires uniform, national regulation to avoid systemic risk. In the

Indian context, the for-profit (NBFC) and non-profit (SHG) models have existed and thrived simultaneously addressing different types of borrowers as well as the same segment. While SHGs are providing multiple valuable services, from a financial services delivery perspective, the MFI model has proven to be more efficient and scalable—having grown its base from 10 million to 27 million customers from 2007 to 2010, while SHGs have grown considerably as well, from 38 million clients to 60 million in 2010.[4] While both for and non-profit microfinance models have grown dramatically in scale, regulation has remained divergent—with the private MFIs regulated by the RBIs at the national level while non-profit MFIs regulated by state governments and NABARD. While a uniform, national-level regulator would prevent state-level political risk and bring non-profits under increased supervision and accountability standards similar to NBFC-MFIs, it would somehow need to take into account and reconcile two different economic models.

The second principle—that credit markets do not operate in a simultaneous market-clearing mode and generate opportunities for arbitrage—has even greater application in the micro-credit market, which contains more scope for arbitrage due to the large unsatisfied demand as well as uneven supply and credit rationing decisions of the varied lenders. In India, MFIs as well as SHGs have focused on southern states due to their suitability for micro-credit delivery and created a situation of over-lending in some of these markets. In Andhra Pradesh in particular, the microfinance industry has concentrated nearly a third of its total portfolio, creating a situation of severe over-lending, culminating in the repayments crisis of October 2010 precipitated by an intervention by the state government effectively preventing microfinance operations. Regardless of the causes of the events in Andhra Pradesh, preventing contagion or a larger liquidity crisis are the primary responsibility of the national regulator. Providing liquidity support to the sector and avoiding systemic risks, given its strategic importance to the financial inclusion agenda and links with the banking system, as well as an overhaul of microfinance regulation addressing the causes of the crisis like in Andhra Pradesh to

4. Microfinance India: State of the Sector Report 2010.

prevent future instances of market failure, ought to be the two principal objectives of regulation.

The third point—that credit markets rely on the existence of a financial services intermediary which can reduce the transaction costs—explains the success of the Indian microfinance model in credit delivery. Comparing the Indian microfinance model in the global context highlights the relative success it has achieved. With one of the highest growth rates globally since 2002, the microfinance in India has emerged as relatively socially conscious (having one of the lowest average loan sizes of around $150 as well as the lowest yield on portfolio) as well as financially sustainable (returning healthy profits and return on assets through high levels of operational efficiency despite these lower ticket sizes and interest rates). The success of the Indian model can be seen from the fact that most of the refinancing for microfinance in India comes from the domestic banking system, highlighting confidence in the underlying business model and expectations of future growth and returns, rather than through development financing that is responsible for funding microfinance in other countries in Africa or Latin America. Any regulatory perspective towards financial inclusion should appreciate the importance of private microfinance companies and while providing for appropriate regulation—capital adequacy, governance, reporting, and customer protection standards as well as other prudential norms commensurate with increased oversight—avoid regulating interest rates, an action that would effectively cripple private intermediation.

The fourth idea—that credit markets' functioning depends crucially on the institutional arrangements for enforcing contracts and preventing fraud—suggests that the success of the microfinance model is due to institutional arrangements such as joint liability, standardised products, weekly collections, and ongoing audit, which become critical to establish trust between borrower and lender in the absence of collateral or legal recourse mechanisms present in formal credit delivery. In the Indian context, it is precisely through these types of alternative mechanisms that MFIs have reduced transaction costs to deliver efficient and scalable financial product distribution platforms. However, the commercial intent inherent in a for-profit model has resulted in an inability to establish a meaningful relationship with the customer beyond the standardised credit transaction. It needs to be recognised from a regulatory perspective that, despite servicing the poor or bottom of pyramid segment, for-profit microfinance faces the same incentives as any other business and cannot be expected to shoulder a social responsibility in the absence of a regulatory requirement, or one imposed by lenders.

As a result, beyond an inability to diversify product offerings, there have been two types of market failure arising from a purely commercial, standardised and process-driven approach to credit delivery. First, because they are competing for the same clients' borrowing requirements and do not have access to a common credit database, lenders will not voluntarily share information with each other, creating systemic risks of over-lending in attractive markets. Secondly, a competitive incentivisation of staff-based targets and collections can lead to aggressive growth as well as as recovery practices. All of these have been seen to be the key causes of the Andhra Pradesh crisis and highlight the need for a national credit bureau and implementation of a code of conduct for microfinance operators. They also show the potential of the unique ID initiative to enable authentication and identification of clients required for a credit bureau and remote branchless banking.

The fifth proposition—that what matters most is the impact that the operation of credit markets have on savings and investment—highlights the relative disappointment that while the microfinance model has been relatively successful at credit delivery it has not succeeded at delivering savings, pension and insurance and thus holistic financial inclusion. Partly this can be due to regulatory prudence—MFIs not being allowed to raise deposits or act as for-profit BCs—but also due to the MFIs' own focus on driving growth of credit and inability to innovate their business models adequately. From a regulatory perspective, the key challenge is how to allow microfinance companies to participate in the banking system by raising deposits or act as corporate BCs to provide savings and also encourage their participation in formal insurance and pension provision by bringing them into relevant regulatory frameworks. Government budgetary support required to incentivise the banking sector to support the business correspondent roll out would also help provide a major push for the savings side of the financial inclusion goal.

Implications for Financial Inclusion Regulation in India

Given the important role of non-bank intermediaries and entities such as for-profit MFIs in providing innovative and low-cost financial inclusion solutions, any policy framework for financial inclusion in India also has to consider how to regulate such entities effectively. This becomes especially important given the liquidity risks as well as possible risk of contagion created by the effective ban on the microfinance model in Andhra Pradesh in October 2010. Indeed, that is the expectation with the report to be issued by the sub-committee of the RBI headed by Y.H. Malegam in January 2011, which is required to address this situation and make a systemic attempt at addressing the credit delivery challenge to achieve financial inclusion in India.

While MFIs have scaled up their operations and achieved substantial commercial success, many of them have indeed drifted away from their social mission—which can be seen in the uneven geographic spread of microfinance across India, with many MFIs choosing to focus on the southern states like Andhra Pradesh (the epicentre of the current repayment problems and also headquarters to many large microfinance companies) rather than venture into underpenetrated markets, and the lack of product diversification, with most MFIs currently offering only a limited basket of highly profitable simple loan products. But the success of the model in achieving scalability cannot be denied—in just a few years Indian MFIs have brought over 25 million low-income women and their families into the formal financial system and out of the clutches of unregulated moneylenders and unscrupulous relatives, over 70 million families if we include non-profit MFIs. Also, in a global context microfinance in India is one of the most socially conscious and professional, because of the low average ticket size of loans, the relatively lower interest rates charged and the professional background and social motivation of many MFI promoters active in the sector for the last decade.

It is important to understand that even among for-profit NBFC-MFIs, which are governed by the RBI and distinct from NGO-MFIs or the SHG system, there are two models of microfinance—high return on assets (RoA) and medium RoA. High RoA MFIs that are focused on the efficient delivery of a limited suite of credit products will have lower operating expense ratios and, despite pricing their loans at relatively lower yields, still be able to generate healthy. However MFIs that are more focused on expanding to virgin markets, developing new products needed by customers and improving the level of service—all of which happen at some initial hit to profitability—will tend to have lower RoAs and need to charge higher interest rates to cover their costs, especially if they have not yet reached scale. Thus an interest rate cap would have the perverse effect of causing most damage to those MFIs that are doing a better job of achieving social-commercial balance and benefit those MFIs that are following the business-first approach to microfinance. The interest cap becomes even more untenable considering the increasing operating costs MFIs need to incur to avoid over-lending and to improve training and systems to prevent aggressive collection practices, as well as their increased borrowing costs from the proposed removal of PSL.

While financial deregulation is important, it is not enough. There is plenty the government can and should do to regulate the microfinance sector—not just by accelerating the setting up of a credit bureau, but by issuing a set of simple and enforceable requirements for governance, transparency, HR and customer protection and putting in place a microfinance regulator with enough teeth to ensure compliance and punish the guilty. Most important of these, it can codify customer protection principles—which already exist and are followed on a voluntary basis—and enforce their implementation through the new regulatory framework, which ideally should cover not just for-profit MFIs but all entities engaged in microfinance operations.

The critical market failures related to over-lending, collection practices and profiteering can be addressed through simple but fundamental reform of the microfinance sector without undermining the business model. The RBI and Government should take a strategic view of financial inclusion instead of a tactical approach and act on the opportunity to turn the micro-credit liquidity crisis into fundamental reform of the financial inclusion regulatory framework in India. We must remember that financial inclusion is not the same as poverty alleviation, which involves a more holistic intervention beyond providing credit—for example, livelihood support or vocational training. And it is this fundamental mismatch of expectations—often driven by MFIs themselves who claim to be reducing poverty rather than just addressing the inclusion issue—that causes a backlash when MFIs profit excessively while the clients continue to remain poor. MFIs themselves need to recognise and be reminded by regulators that they are doing a social business and thus profit optimisation, rather than maximisation, ought to be their objective.

From the perspective of the regulator, ultimately if the microfinance model in India is allowed to fail, in addition to the effect on the lenders themselves and the banking system, it is clients who will suffer, both in terms of decreased availability as well as cost of credit. Taking into account the basic lessons from operation of credit markets and their application to the microfinance delivery model in India, we have the opportunity to harness the strengths of this model in delivering financial inclusion while still addressing its market failures through effective regulation.

The views expressed here are personal.

11

Reinventing NABARD

K.G. Karmakar

It is indeed an honour to be invited by Skoch Foundation to contribute an essay in honour of Dr. C. Rangarajan, an intellectual giant who has adorned many national level institutions as Professor of Economics at IIM, Ahmedabad, as Deputy Governor of RBI and then as its Governor for a full term, and as Governor of Andhra Pradesh and now as Economic Adviser to the PM—he has held all these posts with dignity, intellectual ability, courage of conviction and above all, compassion. The various reports he has prepared for RBI and GoI are known for their excellent suggestions and he has actually expanded the horizon of intellectual discourse. I was fortunate to be associated with him for the introduction of the SAMIS (Service Area Monitoring and Information System) while in RBI in 1991 and for the *Report of the Committee on Financial Inclusion* in 2007. I have benefited immensely by interacting with him as he is always accessible and is willing to discuss freely on topics of mutual interest. Integrated rural development is close to his heart and hence this paper on 'Reinventing NABARD' so that a reality check and course correction is possible.

Introduction

Besides occupying a geostrategic position in Asia, India is in the process of rediscovery of its potentials and strategic positioning in view of its consistently high economic growth and its potential as a responsible power. However, for some years, agriculture and rural development had not been given adequate attention and hence the rural economy could not deliver the expected results. With food security issues, financial inclusion and rural poverty alleviation as also socioeconomic focus on rural unemployment and sustainable environmental development, National Bank for Agriculture and Rural Development (NABARD) has been grappling with these issues. When NABARD was created in 1982, the operating environment was very different, compared to what it is today in terms of economic policies, sectoral importance in terms of contribution to GDP, etc. The functions of NABARD were that of a refinancing agency and the same had its relevance then. Over the years, the economy has opened up since 1992 and the role of NABARD has also undergone a sea change from refinance to that of an agency that facilitates integrated rural development and balanced growth.

It is this ever-changing environment, which coupled with the felt needs of rural India, which has enabled NABARD to take up activities such as rural infrastructure financing, SHG-bank linkage programme, watershed development, Wadi (Water Demand Integration), etc. Many of these initiatives were directed towards developing the rural credit market by reducing the possible risks, whether by enabling collateral free lending to the poor or by bringing in peer pressure in SHG-bank linkage or by ensuring recharged water table through watershed development. Since 1982, NABARD has been reinventing its role and enriching the same in tune with the changing environment as necessary for any financial institution to remain relevant.

With economic reforms since 1992, it was felt that the role of institutions like NABARD would become irrelevant. However, given the challenging rural economic scenario in India, NABARD has a much more important role to play than ever for while the share of agriculture in GDP continues to reduce, the number of people dependent on the agriculture sector, has remained largely stagnant.

The Arjun Sengupta Report on the unorganised sector in 2008 and the Suresh Tendulkar Report in 2010 reveal the extent of very poor rural people who have continued to be largely excluded from all developmental initiatives!

To ensure that we are on the right track, it would be essential to identify the appropriate areas for sustained intervention. Based on the present scenario and within the framework of what is expected to happen in the near future, certain areas can be identified as key areas for development. They are:

1. Food security and agricultural credit.
2. Creation of appropriate rural infrastructure.

3. Skills development and rural livelihoods.
4. Renewable rural energy issues.
5. Environmental sustainability concerns.
6. Rainwater harvesting and wasteland development.
7. Nurturing rural financial institutions.
8. Financial inclusion by 2015.
9. Microfinance and regulatory issues.
10. Mainstreaming the marginalised.

These are some of the key areas which need to be addressed with due commitment backed by proper plans, design and implementation. Each of the above issues are discussed in detail.

Food Security and Agricultural Credit

The major challenge before NABARD is to source cheap funds so as to enable farmers access cheap funds (i.e., at 4 per cent interest rate) as per the Farmers Commission Report on Suicides (2007). With no sheltered funds available, it is difficult for NABARD to access funds from the money market and ensure cheap refinance to banks for agricultural rural development. Commercial banks use refinance as a treasury tool for liquidity rather than for financing of agricultural projects. The major agricultural projects spanning state/districts for proper utilisation of forests, plantations are no longer planned and this has affected agricultural productivity. Also, biotechnology has not been utilised to harness quality seeds/planting material and our productivity levels *vis-à-vis*, USA/China etc., are poor. Poor productivity in pulses and oil seeds is another serious failure on the technological front as is the inability to enhance irrigation beyond 40 per cent over the last 50 years, despite huge investments. The need for micro-irrigation techniques on a massive scale needs no further emphasis if we are to save our water resources. Our animal husbandry and fisheries sectors need massive investments so that rural farm incomes are made risk-proof and diversified agriculture with emphasis on cash/ horticultural crops is possible. The major challenge is to enhance the profit margins of farmers and to reduce the farmers' risks in largely rainfed farming. Emphasis on reducing post-harvest losses, grain warehouses, agri-markets, along with more joint liability groups, farmers' clubs (from 60,000 to 1,00,000 by 2012) and farmers' associations to play the aggregator's role, are essential and all states must proactively be working with NABARD to achieve these, though proper use of the Mahatma Gandhi National Rural Employment Guarantee (MGNREG) Scheme, Rural Infrastructure Development (RID) Fund and other agricultural subsidies so that food security issues are adequately addressed. The lead bank scheme of 1970 needs to be reviewed and revamped for better targeting of rural development schemes so that it enables quicker financial inclusion.

Rural Infrastructure

Rural infrastructure in terms of irrigation structures, bridges, schools, godowns, roads, medical facilities, etc., are the key to sustained and sustainable growth in the rural economy. For example, one cannot expect rural industries to increase without proper infrastructure such as electricity, bridges, trained manpower, transportation facilities and proper roads. Over 30 per cent of the fruits and vegetables are wasted and the value of agriculture produce goes down because of lack of proper connectivity. Studies suggest that a significantly large number of Indian children are anaemic due to lack of food and nutrition issues. We are endangering the physical and mental development of rural/urban children who are not getting proper nourishment and in fact many people go to bed on a hungry stomach. This is because anaemia reduces supply of oxygen to the brain. In order to address such seemingly innocuous problems which would become a problem of unmanageable proportions, it would be necessary to ensure food security and proper medical facilities because without such facilities one would not even be aware of the fact that such a problem exists. In the process we may lose out on the demographic dividend which we expect to benefit over the next 20 to 30 years, as we would have the largest proportion of under 25 population compared to other ageing countries. The rural economy can be revitalised if adequate rural infrastructure is built up on an urgent basis. The Agricultural Debt Waiver and Debt Relief Scheme (ADWDR), 2008 and the MGNREG scheme have enabled the growth in the economy despite economic slowdown in USA and Europe. We need to invest in rural India. Micro-irrigation systems, roads/bridges and cold storages/warehouses are urgently needed today!

Skills Development and Rural Livelihoods

The imbalance created by reduction of GDP share in agriculture without any perceptible reduction of labour dependent on the sector, has led to increasing income disparity in rural areas which needs to be addressed with due care. The only way to tackle the problem is to enable rural people to enhance their incomes, given better earning opportunities and appropriate training. This could be in farm/non-farm activities or it could be linked to industrial needs. While we have executed hundreds of entrepreneurship development programmes, the basic capacity to be an entrepreneur does not exist in every person. Creation of rural jobs is the responsibility of the industry sector and the availability and supply of trained manpower from rural areas could become an area of prime concern. Moreover, just as outsourcing from developed countries to India gave a fillip to our economy, the next big thing could be outsourcing from urban India to rural India because the cost of manpower in urban India is fast catching up with the rest of the world. It may take some more time, say, another 10 years for the cost advantage to get neutralised but 10 years is probably just enough time to gear up the training needs of the rural workforce. Let us not ignore the fact that all farmers are not equally good at farming. There are lazy farmers, untrained farmers, and also very innovative farmers. Who is really training farmers! Some banks have started Rural Development and Self Employment Training Institutes (RUDSETIs) and the Ministry of Rural Development (MoRD) is also setting up RUDSETIs in all districts. Can training of agriculturists in modern farming and scientific practices be taken up? The handloom sector is in a serious crisis situation as looms are being abandoned with the consequent loss of various skills handed down from generation to generation. Can the revival of this sector be taken up seriously? The handloom sector provides the second highest employability after agriculture in rural areas. Educated rural children do not want to take up agriculture, in view of the drudgery involved. Can we make farming more scientific, more profitable by ensuring the use of biotechnology, seed technology, machines, entrepreneurship etc., to retain young and educated people in rural areas?

Employment and livelihoods very closely linked with education and skills development. This would not only address the problem of widening income disparity between rural and urban areas but also prevent urban migration. NABARD is experimenting with linking industrial employment requirements with various NGOs, linking industrial employment requirements with skills development of the rural people. Designing a suitable infrastructure for training and selection of the people with the right attitude and aptitude for work, becomes the key to such an effort. However, there are problems with displacement which many people are not able to cope with easily in the changed environment of the urban areas and are forced to go back to their roots. While training also covers these areas to develop the necessary psychological skills to cope with urban shocks, it is a tedious and drawn-out process. There would however, be only a limited number for employable youths in industry to absorb in urban areas as per their requirements. It would be ideal for the rural educated youth to have employment opportunities in rural areas itself, as this would have multiple benefits including less stress on urban infrastructure which is being stretched to its limits. How to ensure that educated youth take up scientific agriculture and rural development issues, is a major challenge today. The National Rural Livelihoods Mission (NRLM) which is restructuring our approach to rural livelihoods is a step in the right direction and the entire banking system needs to be involved in ensuring the success of the NRLM so that on a cluster basis, there are various employment opportunities available to the youth and those in need of employment.

Renewable Rural Energy Issues

In order to sustain development in rural areas as well as to give agriculture a much deserved boost, rural energy requirements are bound to increase exponentially and these needs have to be addressed. If we look at the energy requirements today in urban areas and compare the same with that available 15 years ago, the problem can be understood very easily. Along with mall-type consumerism, which is fast catching up in rural areas, the need for renewable rural energy is bound to increase. In addition, there would be requirements for setting up small and micro-enterprises in rural areas which provide the key to employment generation. Moreover the requirement of energy has to be met through 'green' energy. It has to be either through solar and wind energy or through some other sources like fuel cells, micro-hydel plants etc., which would enable production of 'green' energy. It is just not possible for a population of the size in India to go the

American way in terms of energy production as our model of development has to be self-sustaining. Moreover, the same has to be made an economically viable proposition for the rural masses. RRBs in Uttar Pradesh have tried this successfully by financing solar lanterns which has enabled housewives increase their work hours for producing *'chikan'* works and in turn earn more. It has also helped the children in the homes to devote more time for studies in the evenings. The rural solar energy mission of the GoI permits 30 per cent capital subsidy and interest rates of 5 per cent for purchase of solar cell powered lamps, mobile charging units etc., for individual or community-based units. This project should be a boon for rural India and SHGs are geared up to utilise this scheme. Besides, wind power, mini-hydel plants in hill regions, gobar gas plants, agricultural waste gasifiers, biodiesel and ethanol blending etc., are being encouraged in rural India and these need to be better targeted so that the resource poor regions get priority status for subsidised 'green' energy projects.

Environmental Sustainability Issues

Whatever we do in the name of rural economic development, has serious effects on the environment and sustainability issues have to be at the top of our agenda. Studies have shown that to achieve the present levels of agricultural and rural development, we are drawing heavily, without replenishment, from the existing natural resources. In fact if a profit and loss account is drawn up taking into account what is borrowed from the existing resources, the same would indicate massive losses. In other words, further development has to be through regenerative processes in order to prevent any more environmental degradation. This would not be only in terms of energy requirements but also in terms of production of food grains to meet the rising demand. The world has to find out ways to get out of the use of chemical pesticides and fertilisers and wasting precious freshwater and groundwater resources. While it did show us a way for increasing food grain production, it is amply clear that Green Revolution technologies are not a sustainable way for development. The level of degradation of the soil in places like Punjab which has been the centre of cereals production based on cheap electricity and water, hybrid seeds and chemical fertilisers, is there for all to see and it has taken just 50 years to destroy the future. Besides the watershed and Wadi programmes which have tried to address environmental concerns, the renewable rural energy project, the Umbrella Programme on Natural Resources Management (UPNRM), the setting up of the Natural Resources Management Centre at Kolkata are all major steps taken to prevent faster environmental abuse. The effects of SHGs, the clean development mechanism (CDM), carbon fund issues and the need for understanding global warming and climate change issues and their efforts on farmers, System for Intensification (SRI) methods for paddy, wheat, sugarcane etc., are all steps in the right direction. Much more basic research needs to be supported on these issues by NABARD from the R&D Fund, rural innovation fund and other funds created to assist the rural sector.

Water Harvesting and Watershed Development

Despite receiving much rain from the southwest and northeast monsoon winds, much of our freshwater resources flow into the sea while our groundwater resources are being depleted at an alarming and unsustainable rate. Dark water blocks have emerged where water is being mined and the ecological disaster is in the offing. Freshwater resources are being wasted by using inefficient pumps for unsustainable crops. The Gujarat model for water use and conservation needs to be replicated. Large-scale use of rainwater harvesting structures, drinking water availability in all villages with the Narmada Dam and the Sardar Sarovar projects, salinity ingression dams in coastal areas to conserve freshwater resources, micro-irrigation and efficient irrigation techniques, are all being tried so that the water-deficient state is able to ensure profitable agriculture on a commercial basis for its farmers. Another precious resource is our arable land which is more than that of China. But every village has land which is not being utilised and which is loosely called wastelands. Proper land use policies and planting of bamboo, aromatic grasses and medicinal shrubs and bushes should be encouraged so that land resources are properly used and rainwater conserved in underground aquifers. While NABARD has been working in the area of watershed development and it is also on the priority list of Central/state governments, a lot has to be done to ensure that we do not reach a point of no return. It would also mean educating rural people about judicious water use and using systems which would reduce water requirements for crops, etc.

Nurturing Rural Financial Institutions

To maintain agricultural credit flows and the pace of rural development at acceptable levels, it is essential to have efficient and strong rural financial institutions (RFIs). For 2010-11, the targeted agriculture credit flow is Rs.375,000 crore with 72 per cent disbursed by commercial banks, 18 per cent by cooperatives and 10 per cent by RRBs. While commercial banks are regulated and supervised by RBI, NABARD has been nurturing the weak RRBs and cooperative banks over the past 28 years with some success. With the implementation of the Vaidyanathan Committee reforms for the short-term cooperative credit structure (STCCSs)/long-term cooperative credit structure (LTCCs), the rural cooperatives are set to improve their operations and business levels on a profitable basis, without bureaucratic and vested interests affecting their viability. The 196 RRBs have been reduced to 82 large-sized RRBs and only 3 RRBs are operating at current losses while 27 are having accumulated losses. While the supervisory wing of NABARD is efficient, the institutional development efforts need to be boosted so that the computerisation efforts of RRBs and cooperatives are able to switchover to the core banking solutions (CBS) mode urgently or else they will fail to hold onto their rural clientele. The second phase of mergers of RRBs is overdue as all RRBs could be merged on a state-wise basis. The northeast region needs a boost as their cooperatives and RRBs are functioning at below viability levels.

NABARD's off-site supervisory system needs an urgent overhaul once the CBS of cooperative banks and RRBs are stabilised. The treasury functions, audit systems, Alco mechanism, vigilance and inspection mechanism and risk management systems need to be toned up in RRBs and cooperatives. The quality of supervision over RFIs will have to be strengthened by NABARD and with the proposed regulatory role over MFIs necessary preparatory steps will have to be ensured. We do not need new institutions but we must ensure that the existing institutions perform their financial intermediation and outreach functions, efficiently and effectively so that rural financial inclusion is possible by 2015.

Financial Inclusion

Financial inclusion is a key to the solution for many of the endemic problems of poverty alleviation though this needs to be developed with other supporting mechanisms. For example, just by providing money, one would not be able to educate or train the younger generation. What is needed along with money is the facility to educate, train and implement employable skills at reasonable costs. While financial inclusion is important, it is just one of the means and not an end by itself. With the *takavi* loans in 1793 and the cooperatives in 1904 (based on the German Raiffeisen model), the country has tried out financial inclusion and created various institutions to speed up the process. NABARD has been working on this through the SHG-bank linkage programme much before the term financial inclusion was coined. A logical move would be to carry forward the good SHGs to the level of formation of producer groups/producer organisations or promote micro-enterprises. This would require in marketing skills, entrepreneurship skills, financial skills in terms of skills development, income generation and manpower deployment. Our experience shows that financial empowerment is a slow process and starts with thrift/savings, preparing slowly with group formation, micro deposits, SHG-bank linkage, micro-credit and then micro-enterprises either on a group or individual mode before graduating into individual accounts with banks, etc. Any efforts to bypass the process or to increase the pace, has its own pitfalls as can be seen in the recent developments in the microfinance sector. While it is easy to say that the poor need money, it also has to be understood that the same has to be judiciously used, especially in this era of consumerism when the demarcation between need and want is getting blurred. Setting up MFIs in overbanked areas, is not to be encouraged and preference should be for their proliferation in unbanked or underbanked areas. High interest rates (>25%) is to be avoided. Our target is to ensure that by 2015, all adults have a bank account to meet various financial requirements. The Financial Inclusion Fund and the Financial Inclusion Technology Fund, needs to be utilised more efficiently.

Microfinance and Regulatory Issues

There are two major models of microfinance in the country, the SHG-bank linkage programme and the MFI model (for-profit/non-profit). While the average growth rate has been about 30 per cent for the first model over the last five years, it has been 80 per cent for the second model. But the MFI model has been under a cloud over the last six months due to suicides, high interest rates, coercive recovery measures, outstanding issues, social boycotts and multiple SHG membership issues, corporate governance issues and a whole host of supervisory and regulatory issues which need to be sorted out. The Microfinance Regulatory Bill is proposed to be introduced after the Malegam Committee Report by the RBI is finalised and studied. Certain contentious issues like a cap for interest rates (as in Bangladesh), multiple regulatory institutions (RBI for non-banking financial companies (NBFCs) and Section 25 companies and NABARD for NGO-MFIs and Registrar of Cooperative Societies (RCS) for cooperatives), priority sector status for MFI loans, etc., need to be sorted out urgently. Too much regulation for an emerging sector which enable the poorest of the poor to access savings/funds, would not be in the interests of the poor rural people. The SHG-bank linkage programme needs to be revised with the help of all banks and give it a new direction to meet the challenges of financial inclusion and poverty alleviation over repeated cycles of SHG lending. The average loan size of Rs.5,500 per SHG member is clearly too less to enable poverty alleviation.

Mainstreaming the Marginalised

Those at the bottom of the pyramid, the tribal people comprising 9 per cent of Indian population, the weaker sections of the society—women, SC/ST, economically backward people in the 256 districts identified as backward due to resource problems etc., have always been marginalised as the poor have no voice or force and their economic issues and rights are rarely discussed. However, the RTI Act (2005), the MGNREG Scheme (2008) and the prepared Food Security Bill, have been important landmarks and have certainly empowered the poor and poverty rationalism. Economic empowerment of the poor through appropriate systems and structures are very important and NABARD has over the years consistently innovated in creating appropriate structures. The village watershed committees which take all technical/financial decisions in our watershed programmes, the Wadi committees, the SHG, the Joint Liability Group (JLG), The farmers' clubs, the farmers' associations, the SHG federations, the village development programmes, the grain banks, the 16 funds created by NABARD over the years, has strengthened NABARD's efforts to build up rural India. The rural entrepreneurship development programmes, the

RUDSETIS/RSETIs are important developments as also the rural *haats* and rural malls encouraged by NABARD to improve the non-farm sector by creating employment opportunities. All Banks need to join hands with NABARD and the NGOs working in rural areas so that a people's movement for self-development alongwith empowerment emerges. Dependency is not to be encouraged and NGOs also should have an exit policy after some years of intervention.

Conclusion

All the above factors have been considered by NABARD in the past though probably not on a large scale barring financial inclusion and watershed development. Given the future needs as explained above, it is apparent that NABARD focus on as many rural issues and areas as is possible. Given the capacity of the organisation, it may not be possible for us to address all these issues single-handedly. For example, rural sanitation and rural drinking water supply are issues where few bankable models have emerged though many attempts have been made by NABARD. Cheap rural housing especially for SHG members is another area where NABARD has failed to bring out a viable financing model. Moreover, there are full-fledged organisations both at the state/central and corporate levels for addressing these issues. In addition, the type of funding requirement for addressing these areas can be intimidating. NABARD as an institution, can play a pioneering role in experimenting and developing sustainable models in order to enable the corporate and government machinery to take up the same. Moreover, if we can showcase such experiments as sustainable models, the same could be aggressively pushed as commercial proposition by the banks and financial institutions. Due to NABARD's desire to have a low-level self-advertising system, there is a lot of misinformed criticism about NABARD being ineffective and a 'dinosaur' among developmental financial institution (DFIs) NABARD continues to be a clean and transparent organisation and has never been involved in any scam which regularly besets the financial sector. It continues to function only in rural India which has few champions and its work especially in the SHG/MFI sector; watershed/Wadi development, RRBs/cooperative development and supervision have been exemplary. The decline of refinance as a tool for directing agri/rural credit flows urgently needs a redesign of its refinance instrument. NABARD's project financing capabilities have been redirected from the agricultural sector to the rural infrastructure sector and needs fine tuning, if our country's agricultural sector is to be strengthened. NABARD needs to reposition itself as the knowledge centre/domain specialist for the agricultural/rural development sector. NABARD's staff strength is under stress and the retirement of the senior financial/technical specialists between 2009-2012, will be a big blow and suitable replacements will have to be sourced urgently. NABARD has been a profitable organisation since its birth in 1982 but it has never been a 'commercial' organisation where every financial transaction has to be profitable. It remains the only DFI dedicated to rural India and remains committed to growing the RFIs at times, with losses to its own balance sheet. Its staff continues to be innovative and dedicated to rural India and very professional in their approach to integrated rural development. Our country can emerge with double digit growth figures only if rural India is enabled to grow at faster rates and if agricultural growth at a minimum of 4 per cent of GDP is ensured.

12 Technology and the Financial Inclusion Imperative in India

Banking and Dr. Rangarajan: The Philosopher King

K.C. Chakrabarty

It is only fitting that a festschrift is being brought out in honour of Dr. C. Rangarajan (born 1932) celebrating his life and achievements. Dr. Rangarajan is a man who needs no introduction and writing an essay on the life and achievements of a multi-faceted personality like him makes the task extremely difficult in that one does not know where to start and where to end. He is a renowned economist and a distinguished former Member of Parliament. Prior to his appointment as the Governor of RBI, he held charge as Deputy Governor for over a decade, a position I am fortunate enough to now hold. He was also a member of the Planning Commission and a member of the Tenth Finance Commission (1995-2000). He is a monetary economist par excellence, a development practitioner, an administrator who wields a gentle touch, the proverbial iron hand in a velvet glove and so much else besides.

His tenure as Governor of RBI saw unprecedented central bank activism to put in place a comprehensive set of measures to strengthen and improve the competitive efficiency of the financial sector. New institutions and instruments were introduced and changes in exchange rate management culminated in the establishment of a unified exchange rate. In the field of monetary policy, his tenure saw the historic memorandum signed between the Bank and the Government whereby a cap was put on the automatic finance by the Bank to the Government in the form of ad hoc treasury bills.

Currently, he is the Chairman of the Prime Minister's Economic Advisory Council (PMEAC). He is also the Chairman of the Madras School of Economics, and the Founding Chairman of the C.R. Rao Advanced Institute of Mathematics, Statistics and Computer Science (AIMSCS).

He is the author of numerous books. But above all, we consider Dr. Rangarajan as our eternal teacher and Guru, and for any problem in the financial sector we go to him for consultations. His contribution to the financial sector is immense and is difficult to quantify or measure. He is also the visionary who brought technology into the banking system. In fact, Dr. Rangarajan is the person credited with ushering in two path-breaking changes in the banking system. First was that of technology adoption in the banking system and the second was financial inclusion, and as a visionary he foresaw the importance of their integration. He brought the conceptual framework for both technology and financial inclusion. But for him, the radical transformation in the banking system that is so pervasive today such as anywhere anytime banking would not have been feasible. But for him, we would not have been able to visualise so early that inclusion is not possible without the help of technology. If today, the mainstream financial institutions are capable of meeting the financial inclusion challenges, it is primarily due to their technology adoption status.

Dr. Rangarajan has chaired numerous committees which have made far-reaching recommendations but there are a few committees under his chairmanship without alluding to these, an essay on him remains incomplete. Therefore, to put things in their correct perspective, it would be in order to briefly recap some of the recommendations of committees chaired by him on technology and financial inclusion.

Committee on Mechanisation in the Banking Industry (1984)

During a period when the financial sector was grappling with the problem of poor credit delivery and poor reach of the banking system and when the labour unions were strong; fearlessly and with a vision for the future, Dr. Rangarajan brought in computerisation in the banking industry introduced first as mechanisation in the banking system. He chaired the Committee on Mechanisation in the Banking Industry (1984). This was a period when there was resistance and supreme reluctance on the part of the labour unions to adopt mechanisation. However, his vision, patience and sagacity prevailed which brought in a sea change ushering in an era of mechanisation in the financial sector. The recommendations included setting up of service branches by banks as well as asking banks to be in readiness for adoption of magnetic ink character recognition (MICR) technology.

A phased plan was drawn up for computerisation and mechanisation in the banking industry over a five-year timeframe of 1985-1989. The focus by this time (justifiably) was on customer service and two models of branch automation were developed and implemented:

- Front office mechanisation where front desk operations were computerised while back office work was done manually, and
- Back office automation covering mechanisation of general ledger and back office operations while the front office work was done manually.

Both the models provided the customer with error-free accounting, regular statements of accounts etc. Considering the contemporary level of computerisation, these were major achievements but did not go far enough and the pace of their implementation was tardy, to say the least, with compromise and conciliation through the trade unions.

Committee on Computerisation in Banks (1988)

In 1988, Dr. Rangarajan also chaired the committee on computerisation in banks. Having gained experience in the earlier mode of mechanisation, the committee under his chairmanship drew up a detailed perspective plan for computerisation in banks and for extension of automation to other areas like funds transfer, electronic mail, BANKNET, SWIFT, ATMs etc. The committee recommended the following roadmap for computerisation over the next five years:

- Around 2,000 to 2,500 large branches located at high activity (urban and metropolitan) centres to be fully computerised.
- Inter- and intra-bank transactions using the BANKNET set up by the RBI, and
- Installation of a network of cash dispensers/ATMs at strategic locations such as airports/railway stations etc., on a shared basis by banks.

The committee under his chairmanship also made studied recommendations on the 'Single Window Concept', 'all bank credit cards', credit clearing/giro system, office automation, etc. In fact, this report was the most comprehensive roadmap for bank automation considering the state of the technology at that time. It is only now that the true impact of those early initiatives is being felt and all credit must go to Dr. Rangarajan's foresight.

Committee on Financial Inclusion (2008)

Even though, post-nationalisation of banks in 1969 and in 1980, the branch banking network has improved considerably, it had not been able to reach out to all parts of the country, especially to the villages. Thus, many of our villages still remained without availability of banking services. The number of bank customers had not increased. Therefore, considering the extent of financial exclusion in the country, the Government constituted the Committee on Financial Inclusion under the Chairmanship of Dr. Rangarajan, the recommendations of which brought financial inclusion to the centre stage.

However, even before the Committee on Financial Inclusion was set up, Dr. Rangarajan, as the Governor of RBI, played a key role in taking banking to the poor in the form of the landmark development of credit-linked self-help groups (SHGs). The SHG banking linkage programme was initiated in 1992 which tried to facilitate the flow of bank credits to SHGs. The pilot phase was followed by the setting up a working group on NGOs and SHGs by the Reserve Bank of India (RBI) in 1994, which put forth a wide ranging set of recommendations on SHG and bank linkage as a potential innovation in the area of banking with the poor. Explaining the rationale behind the policy decision, Dr. Rangarajan in one of his speeches illustrated that despite the expansion of the organised banking system deep into rural areas, a very large number of the poor continued to remain outside the fold of the formal banking system. The then existing banking policies, systems and procedures were not well suited to enable the poor to approach the formal system. Thus began the search for an alternative delivery mechanism which would better meet the requirements of the poor and especially the women members of such households. It was then the idea of organising SHGs started to take shape. SHG is a group of about 10-

20 persons from a homogeneous class (affinity group) who come together for addressing the common problems. They collect voluntary savings on a regular basis and use the pooled resources to make small interest bearing loans to their members. The process helps them imbibe the essentials of financial intermediation including prioritisation of needs, setting terms and conditions and accounts keeping. Dr. Rangarajan considers bank-SHG linkage model and business correspondents (BCs) as two important pillars of achieving financial inclusion.

The Committee on Financial Inclusion under his chairmanship studied the entire gamut of issues related to financial inclusion in India and observed that the overall strategy for building an inclusive financial sector should be based on:

- Effecting improvements within the existing formal credit delivery mechanism.
- Suggesting measures for improving credit absorption capacity especially amongst marginal and sub-marginal farmers and poor non-cultivator households.
- Evolving new models for effective outreach, and
- Leveraging on technology based solutions.

The Committee gave a formal definition for financial inclusion and stated that, 'Financial inclusion may be defined as the process of ensuring access to financial services and timely and adequate credit where needed by vulnerable groups such as weaker sections and low income groups at an affordable cost.'

It identified that financial inclusion is ultimately nothing other than the delivery of banking services, at an affordable cost to the vast sections of disadvantaged and low-income groups. Universal access to public goods and services is the *sine qua non* of an open and efficient society. As banking services are in the nature of a public good, it is essential that availability of banking and payment services to the entire population without discrimination be the essence of public policy. It may include a basic no frills banking account for making and receiving payments, a savings product suited to the pattern of cash flows of a poor household, money transfer facilities, small loans and overdrafts for productive, personal and other purposes, insurance (life and non-life), etc. While financial inclusion, in the narrow sense, may be achieved to some extent by offering any one of these services, the objective of 'comprehensive financial inclusion' would be to provide a holistic set of services encompassing all of the above.

The committee under his chairmanship made several significant recommendations which have been since implemented.

- The Committee suggested that financial inclusion must be taken up in a mission mode as a 'financial inclusion plan' at the national level.
- A 'financial inclusion technology fund' has been set up at NABARD with a corpus of Rs. 500 crore and in the budget for 2009-10 the corpus has been increased by another Rs. 100 crore.
- All commercial banks (including regional rural banks (RRBs)) have been advised to provide access to credit to at least 250 hitherto excluded rural households at each of their existing rural and semi-urban branches.
- The committee suggested targeted branch expansion in identified districts, product innovation, incentivising human resources, expansion of the BC model, support for RRBs, and greater role for NABARD in microfinance.
- The committee recommended leveraging technology to open up channels beyond branch network and create the required banking footprints to reach the unbanked so as to extend banking services comparable to those dispensed by bank branches.

The Government has identified financial inclusion as a national priority and has been giving directions to achieve the objective of inclusive growth for equitable development. The Government's role, apart from being a driver, is also supportive. For the technology solutions to be in place, there needs to be good infrastructure support in the form of adequate digital and physical connectivity, etc., which can be provided by the Government. Our objective is to take banking services to everybody to meet their entire savings, credit and remittance needs initially, and needs for all other financial products and services subsequently. It is initially focused on villages with population above 2,000 but the banks need to plan to cover villages with population below 2,000 in an integrated manner over a period of next 3 to 5 years. The objective is move to universal financial inclusion to provide banking services to the entire population residing in urban and metro centres.

It may not be viable to open a brick and mortar branch in each village of the country. We have about 6 lakh villages in the country, and we have to work our way out to provide banking services in these villages. Now, with the advent of technology this dream is not too far and it should be possible to reach out to all villages using ICT-enabled financial inclusion. Technology however must be adapted to our needs. It must be indigenised. The basic question is the ability of the banks to understand, adapt and use technology to optimise gains, reduce operating costs and build in sustaining revenue streams. The success of the T model ford motor car—the most popular vehicle of its time—even in countries like India was in no small measure due to the adaptability and innovation on the part of the Indian mechanics who ensured quick and reliable solutions when something went wrong. Fixing a problem/glitch when it happens thus becomes the weakest link in providing efficient customer service. The moral of the story is simply to remind that technology is a good servant but a bad master, so banks should ensure that they ride on technology and leverage its benefits to the full and not that technology should be allowed to dictate their business strategy. Thus, to reiterate, while adopting technology, it has to be borne in mind that the solutions available are robust, secure and amenable to easy problem resolution.

Banks in India have achieved some progress but let me sound a word of caution—the task is mammoth and the pace of work will have to be relentless and sustained. RBI's efforts have been to remove all regulatory bottlenecks for facilitating greater financial inclusion. Our broad strategy for achieving planned, sustained and structured financial inclusion is through a planned approach to the entire gamut of issues whose detailed steps are as follows. Banks have been advised to formulate a board approved Financial Inclusion Plan (FIP) for the next three years. A uniform model has not been imposed so that each bank is able to devise its own strategy in line with its 'business model' and comparative advantage. FIPs must be integrated with the normal business plans of the banks. RBI has freed interest rates and has also allowed banks to charge their customers for other transactions. We believe that banking for the poor is a viable business opportunity but a cost-benefit analysis needs to be done by the banks to make financial inclusion congruent with their business models. Banks must view financial inclusion as a viable business model, a huge business opportunity and perfect their delivery models. The RBI had permitted banks to utilise the services of BCs to provide banking services. Banks can use individuals, NGOs, and several other select entities as their BCs. BC based delivery model has been made more flexible and inclusive over the years. Recently, banks were permitted to engage companies registered under the Indian Companies Act, 1956, excluding non-banking financial companies (NBFCs), as BCs in addition to the individuals/entities permitted earlier. Using appropriate technology, the BCs can be effectively used by the banks to provide services in far off places.

However, for effective implementation of the financial inclusion strategies, banks must fix technology aspects first including completion of core banking solution (CBS) in all their branches and those of sponsored RRBs, and seamless integration of front-end devices with the back-end systems. Without this, it would not be possible to scale up the activities. There is a need to increase the bouquet of products currently being offered. During discussions on their FIPs, banks have been advised to provide a minimum of four products to the account holder, *viz.*, a) A savings cum overdraft account, b) A pure savings account, ideally a recurring or variable recurring deposit, c) A remittance product to facilitate electronic benefit transfer (EBT) and other remittances, and d) Entrepreneurial credit products like a General Purpose Credit Card (GCC) or a Kisan Credit Card (KCC). Apart from these minimum basic products, banks can offer any other product like insurance, mutual funds, etc., to the account holders. On the issue of coverage, we have clarified that for a village to be considered covered by banking services, either a bank branch has to be present or a BC has to be visiting/present in that village. There must be a bifurcation between villages with more than 2,000 population and those with less than 2,000 population. The plan needs to cover in an integrated manner both categories of villages. The name of the BC/branch covering a particular village needs to be indicated on the banks website. There has to be a special focus on financial inclusion at urban and metro centres through a functional approach. Thus, as mentioned earlier, RBI's endeavour has been to remove all regulatory bottlenecks for facilitating greater financial inclusion and involve all stakeholders in the process. Governments, both

Central and state, NGOs, technology vendors, industry associations, insurance and mutual fund companies, society at large, etc., would be required to chip in their contributions to make the effort bear fruits.

With the arrival of appropriate technology and the realisation that poor are bankable, banks are willing to greater financial inclusion. However, so far without appropriate technology, they could not have done so even when willing. It is not their willingness but the lack of ability to deliver which is coming in the way. Another issue which surfaces is that the cost of achieving financial inclusion is too high. In reality, costs can easily be borne by banks. Overall cost of financial inclusion will not be more than Rs. 3,000/4,000 crore per year. State and Central governments can obviously provide a helping hand. Thus, the basic problem is not the cost or willingness, but the absence of business model and ICT-based delivery model. Technology coupled with appropriate delivery model will bring about inclusion.

In conclusion, the financial inclusion efforts in our country have become possible due to two landmark developments related to technology and inclusion, the conceptual framework for which was laid down by Dr. Rangarajan. He is a colossus who towers over the banking industry. He not only gave us the dream of financial inclusion but also initiated technology adoption much earlier to make it a reality. It is his passion to achieve universal financial inclusion and there can be no greater tribute to the master than to transform his vision into a reality through relentless efforts. Financial inclusion indeed needs to be taken up in a mission mode with the involvement of all the stakeholders. It is a special privilege for me to contribute to this volume. I thank Sameer Kochhar for allowing me to pay homage to the great visionary. I have been a fortunate recipient of Dr. Rangarajan's goodness and have had the good fortune of having shared ideas and experiences with him. He is a visionary, an eternal teacher and Plato's 'Philosopher King'.

13 Managing Sovereign Risk

An Integrated Approach for Sovereign Assets and Liabilities

Udaibir S. Das

Dr. Rangarajan has been a long time a mentor and teacher. Even before I met him first in 1992, I had been reading his work. That first meeting when I briefed him in the context of the parliamentary enquiry on irregularities in securities and banking transactions was a tough but memorable encounter. In a style that I was to become familiar with later, he asked precise and demanding questions that were belied by his quiet demeanor. Soon afterwards, when he became the Governor of the Reserve Bank of India I became his Executive Assistant. I worked with him for almost his entire term as the Governor, until the middle of 1996, before I moved as Policy Advisor to the Governor of the Bank of Guyana and later to the IMF.

With his phenomenal capacity to ask the right questions and seek economically sound explanations, Dr. Rangarajan demonstrated the value of speeches and statements to start a policy debate. Some of the benefits of reforms India enjoys today were initiated during his time and through the debates he started and the decisions he took. These include the use of monetary policy as a flexible instrument of economic policy, rationalisation and reform of the interest rate regime, adoption of internationally accepted prudential norms, entry of private banks, and most of all on the issue of the use of the central bank balance sheet for direct fiscal financing so as to give the central bank autonomy in the conduct of monetary policy.

I have remained associated with Dr. Rangarajan after 1996 as his insights and conceptual thoughts have a universal appeal and are easily applied to diverse contexts and problematiques. My current paper broadly draws on Dr. Rangarajan's ideas about the central bank balance sheet, reserves, and balance of payment management, and what he later elaborated as the dynamics of debt accumulation in India, good governance of government accounting systems, and fiscal federalism. The idea of an integrated approach to sovereign asset and liability management (SALM) elaborated below supports what he said at a conference in June 2005 in Hyderabad. He had emphasised the need for institutional changes to tackle structural problems in government finances, and for restructuring of public finances. SALM could be thought of as an operational to reap tangible benefits for India's macroeconomic and financial stability, help in its balance sheet preparedness to manage a systemic crisis, and mitigate the associate financial costs. An integrated management of assets and liabilities could also help policymakers to better adjust to global shocks, and to determine more clearly as to which investment opportunities show the highest growth potential as the economy continues to evolve.

The Context of Sovereign Assets and Liabilities

The 2008-2010 global financial and economic crisis has heightened the need for policymakers to carefully identify and manage the direct and indirect consequences of 'sovereign risk'. Indeed, past crises have been triggered by a rapid decline in sovereign assets, or a build-up in sovereign liabilities and debt. But, this round of crises has brought out the critical importance of how assets and liabilities directly under the control of a sovereign are managed. The structure, composition, and institutional capacity to manage balance sheet risks considerably influence market perceptions about the soundness and solvency of the sovereign and how it interacts with macroeconomic and financial stability.

Sovereign assets and liabilities have historically received attention as a crucial component of a country's macroeconomic and financial policy framework. However, they are, susceptible to risks and uncertainties, and face exposures to terms-of-trade shocks and changes in the refinancing terms of debt, volatility in domestic and international capital markets, as well as climatic shocks and demographic patterns. This exposure grows as economies internationalise.

These susceptibilities have been reinforced by the recent expansion in sovereign balance sheets expansion that has taken place in developed economies, and the spread of contagion fears in Euro area countries through the interplay between sovereign and financial sector balance sheets. At one level these economies may appear to face lower risk exposure than emerging market countries given the depth of their real and financial sectors. However, as their balance sheets expanded and assets and liabilities came under closer scrutiny of investors, market, other sovereigns, and multilaterals, several uncertainties surfaced. Financial sustainability of these economies came to be questioned, and doubts arose as to how contingent liabilities relating to the financial sector will be managed alongside steps needed to minimise liquidity and solvency risks facing the sovereign. A phenomenon that also got amplified through this process was the systemic interconnectedness between sovereign and financial sector balance sheets.

As policy focus moves towards how best to balance the defence of financial stability while safeguarding fiscal solvency, a formal integrated balance sheet approach toward sovereign assets and liabilities (SALM) becomes a useful operational policy tool. Although a SALM approach has been used in the past to identify debt-related vulnerabilities, a more formalistic approach allows for monitoring the impact of movements in exchange rates, interest rates and commodity prices on a country's sovereign level financial assets and liabilities.[1] For commodity-exporting countries, the balance sheet approach could highlight the potential risk management needs within the framework of a comprehensive medium-term fiscal strategy. This approach can help countries identify and manage emerging financial challenges, such as an unfunded pension liability, and how it affects the balance sheet as a future claim on financial resources to be managed.

The SALM framework could help policymakers reduce risk exposures from a financial portfolio perspective. On the liability side, debt management aims at minimising debt service cost subject to a prudent level of risk. On the asset side, management goals aim primarily at accumulating adequate levels of fiscal and foreign exchange assets to buffer

1. The European exchange rate crisis in 1992 and the Mexican crisis in 1994–95 are examples of how possible maturity and currency mismatches in sovereign balance sheets can make countries vulnerable to external shocks.

against domestic and external shocks. It may also involve the design and management of investment portfolios for sovereign wealth funds (SWF), or other dedicated sovereign investment funds, so that they can offset the impact of domestic and external shocks on the sovereign balance sheet.

At an operational level, a SALM approach can help understand the financial characteristics of the sovereign balance sheet and identify sources of costs and risks as well as correlations among these sources. If the financial aspects of the assets and liabilities can be matched or hedged by the application of prudent but active risk management practices, then a stronger policy focus could become possible on preserving the sovereigns' net financial position. In a short to medium-term perspective, a financial strategy could be developed to reduce risk exposures. In a longer term perspective, a sovereign could implement economic development strategies to diversify the economy in a way that can help to improve the structure and composition of the sovereign balance sheet. Therefore, specifying a SALM sovereign strategy, within a medium-term macroeconomic framework, could become an integral part of a country's overall economic strategy.[2,3]

Sovereigns always run the risk that guarantees may be called, or announced lending facilities may be used, loans may not be repaid, and assets may not retain their value. The impact of these uncertainties can be tracked better by examining components of a sovereign balance sheet. From a risk point of view, a SALM approach facilitates a more comprehensive approach, than just the flow of fiscal accounts, to determine the budgetary impact of various interventions by the sovereign in the real or the financial

2. A recent IMF paper to its Executive Board suggests that a comprehensive balance sheet approach is required to understand and manage the fiscal impact of public interventions in the financial sector. This approach should encompass all public entities involved in providing support. Sovereign asset-liability management (SALM) should derive from a clear medium-term macroeconomic strategy, which specifies the path from stimulus to consolidation—timely articulation of such a strategy will be important for sustaining confidence. To effectively manage the full extent of risks, including off-balance sheet contingent risks, and maximise balance sheet protection, the SALM strategy must be informed by a robust risk assessment, such as through stress testing (IMF, 2009).
3. Sovereign ALM entails a comprehensive approach where the desired structure and composition of the state's financial liabilities is determined taking account key characteristics of all of its financial assets, regardless of which public institution holds them.

sector. The resulting financial portfolio effects can then be considered both in terms of their (short-term) fiscal costs, but also in terms of the potential risks they pose to sovereign net worth and creditworthiness.

Sovereign Risk and SALM[4]

'Sovereign risk' is traditionally defined as the probability that a country, unable or unwilling to meet its financing needs and payment obligations, will default on its financial obligations debt. Debt sustainability analysis suggests that ultimately this probability will be a function of the country's primary balance, as well as the interplay between the growth of the economy and the average cost of funding. This definition fits well most of the crisis that hit emerging markets during the 80s and the 90s.

However, the 2008-2010 global financial and economic crisis has amplified the scope and notion of what constitutes sovereign risk. Apart from its fiscal risk connotations, sovereign risk also impacts the behaviour of capital markets, investors, central bankers, debt managers, financial regulators, and financial stability authorities. Sovereign debt securities, for example, have assumed risk characteristics that are affecting benchmarking, valuation, asset allocation methods, and financial stability evaluation.

A redefinition of sovereign risk is thus underway with greater emphasis being placed on the risk management aspects of sovereign assets and liabilities. Stronger focus is being placed on the structure and composition of assets and liabilities, linkages with the financial sector and debt capital markets, and on asset allocation methods:

- *Balance sheet approach and contingent liabilities.* Even in those countries where liabilities appear to be on a long-term sustainable trajectory, sovereign risk may be affected by a number of other factors: assets may register a significant contraction in value or announced lending facilities may be used or guarantees may be called.

---

4. An excellent account of the phenomenon of sovereign risk and sovereign spreads is provided by my colleague Vincenzo Guzzo in his recent paper "Sovereign Spreads: Global Risk Aversion, Contagion, or Fundamentals?" *IMF Working Paper* No. 10/120 (Washington: International Monetary Fund).

- *Portfolio vulnerabilities.* In addition to balance sheet considerations, measures of sovereign risk should fully reflect key vulnerabilities in the structure and the composition of debt portfolios, such as significant dependence on short-term borrowing or excessive reliance on foreign capital.
- *Refinancing risk.* A debt maturity profile with disproportionate near-term rollover requirements can accelerate the transformation of solvency concerns into funding problems. Increased dependence on short-term borrowing can rapidly balloon future interest costs for debt rollover, particularly where inflationary expectations are also changing.
- *Investor base.* The absence of a deep domestic buyer base for sovereign debt introduces heavy reliance on foreign demand, which is naturally more volatile than local sources.
- *Sovereign risk and financial stability.* The current financial crisis has provided a stark reminder of the close linkages between sovereign risk, the financial system, and the potential for cross-border spillovers. Spreads on sovereigns perceived to face greater challenges rose rapidly in the wake of sovereign and bank funding difficulties. Similarly, markets began to differentiate among banks with the greatest exposures to those economies.
- *Spillovers effect and an adverse feedback loop.* In countries perceived as most vulnerable by markets, an adverse feedback loop developed, with widening sovereign spreads raising concerns about bank exposures. In turn, this feedback loop drove up counterparty risk and led to higher funding costs. Interbank markets also began differentiating between types of Euro government collateral and the borrowing institution's country of origin. With each cycle, the affected sovereign's ability to backstop the financial system came into further doubt, as rising funding costs raised the magnitude and likelihood of bank interventions.
- *New characteristics of some debt securities.* Some sovereign bonds are now likely to be perceived as less suitable for inclusion in asset portfolios, regardless of their likelihood of default or restructuring. This shift will have profound potential implications for asset

allocation. First, investors will begin to exclude from their portfolios sovereign bonds which no longer exhibit specified characteristics. Second, the price of such sovereign bonds might have to fall significantly to make them attractive within a broader asset-allocation context.

Ultimately, sovereigns have begun to face risks arising from various channels similar to those in the private sector. These risks, if not managed properly, can affect operations for both sovereigns and the private sector. In the case of sovereigns, the risks could put their balance sheets under debt stress and/or expose them to external vulnerability. For the private sector, companies may not have adequate cash flow to meet either their operating expenses or debt obligations, or may become undercapitalised.

Nevertheless, the risk management practices of the sovereign and private sector differ in complexity and precision, available tools, and systemic importance. First, balance sheets used by the private sector clearly specify assets, liability, and equity. The existence of international accounting standards simplifies the comparison between companies. In the case of sovereigns, the lack of a clear-cut definition of a sovereign balance sheet, inaccurate reporting—often containing assets and liabilities that are difficult to quantify with precision—and hurdles to consolidate all components of an overall sovereign balance sheet make active risk management difficult to implement.

Second, risk management tools available to private firms may not be available to sovereigns who are often ill-equipped to use financial derivatives to manage their risks. Since domestic interest rate, exchange rate, and inflation rate are linked to macroeconomic policy objectives, sovereigns may not be in a fair position to use derivatives to hedge. The purchase of credit derivatives, especially to cover credit exposure relating to its own debt (as underlying instruments), could be controversial from a sovereign's stance.

Finally, the risk management practices of the sovereign could have systemic implications, more so than those of individual private entities. In a worst case scenario a sovereign under debt distress could trigger a financial and economic crisis. In contrast, a financially well-managed sovereign with sound macroeconomic policies, friendly business environment, and high credit ratings could mitigate the risk management burden of its private sector, such as, by reducing the risk premium for international market access. Also, some sovereigns, especially where the private sector is not sophisticated enough, may become risk managers of last resort by providing implicit guarantees on private sector—especially, foreign exchange—exposures.

Defining SALM Objectives

The elements of SALM depend upon the stated economic policy objectives. The balance sheet definition, analytical framework, targets, and instruments are usually chosen in light of the economic policy objectives to be achieved through SALM. Hansen (2003) presents a useful overview, which categorises the objectives in seven groups: (i) to neutralise the impact of the size and composition of the government balance sheet on economic welfare; (ii) to minimise the expected deadweight losses of taxation; (iii) to minimise the risk of unstable fiscal and monetary policies; (iv) to minimise the agency cost of government; (v) to maximise opportunities for efficient risk sharing in a setting with incomplete capital markets; (vi) to provide optimal risk management in the presence of asymmetric information; and (vii) to minimise efficiency risks.

The most common theoretical approach to SALM is based on the idea that taxes may create economic distortions. Hence, in order to maximise social welfare, the government can adopt an SALM strategy that minimises the impact of these distortions. If taxes are distortionary, the government will try to structure its portfolio so that all diversifiable risks are hedged in order to reduce taxation costs. In cases where a rise in taxes yields proportional welfare losses, the optimal strategy for the government is to minimise the average long-term tax and choose a balance sheet portfolio with the highest return, even if this implies exceptionally high leverage.

For a sovereign, risk could loosely be defined as the possibility that services delivered have to either be significantly reduced for a given level of taxes, or that taxes will have to be increased to maintain a given level of government services. Both decisions can be implemented in response to different situations, including sovereign illiquidity and insolvency. More formally, the government's objective, and by association, its risk definition, could be derived from the two streams of economic literature that deal with the optimal combination of taxes and debt. The tax-smoothing and the default risk literature provide a well-defined objective for the government: to manage assets and liabilities in such a way as to minimise the need to raise taxes or the need to curtail services when faced with unexpected shocks causing a permanent fall in cash flows revenues or a rise in the value of liabilities.

It has been argued that sovereign debt managers do not attempt to smooth taxes, as suggested by theoretical economists, but are mostly concerned with the variability of interest expenditures. The reason for this divergence between theory and practice is that debt managers are responsible only for achieving the sovereign debt management objectives—ensuring that government's financing needs and payments obligations are met at the lowest possible cost over the medium to long run—not necessarily achieving sovereign's overall objectives.

An optimal sovereign liability or debt structure depends on the correlations between output, inflation, and the interest rates. With a normal yield curve the government will achieve a stable fiscal position if it issues short-term debt when output and inflation are lower, because cash flows are likely to be sufficient to cover only low interest payments given the fiscal constraint. If output and inflation are positively correlated, the government's optimal debt strategy could include the issuance of an inflation-indexed bond, which will offset cyclical deficits.

Other well-known sovereign liability management objectives are also consistent with deficit smoothing. In countries employing the best debt management practices, the main objective is to minimise the cost of government financing and debt service by incurring a prudent degree of risk (IMF and World Bank, 2001). To the extent that the variability of the debt servicing costs is reduced in this process, the variability of the budget deficit can also be minimised. For example, a macroeconomic model relating debt-servicing costs to the government budget deficit allows to assess the smoothing properties of the debt management strategy. In practice, this has been achieved through simulations of the ratio of the debt servicing costs to GDP, as GDP typically co-varies with the government primary fiscal position. In this case, a smooth ratio of debt servicing costs to GDP ensures low variability of the overall fiscal position.

When the composition of sovereign debt is endogeneously determined, other elements of the sovereign balance sheet—such as the international reserves—could come into play. A number of emerging market and developing countries still suffer from the 'original sin', which allows them to issue only short-term local currency debt. They may also suffer from other institutional constraints—a very narrow investor base or undeveloped government securities market—which limit a sovereign's ability to select the optimal composition of liabilities. In such cases, the composition may be driven by demand considerations, which may amplify the sovereign balance sheet risks. Other components of the sovereign balance sheet—most commonly international reserves—could be used to offset such balance sheet risks.

A key objective of the sovereign in holding international reserves is to smooth intertemporal consumption. To appreciate this role of international reserves in operational terms one would need to focus on the consolidated balance sheet of the sovereign. This would require accounting for all existing and contingent liabilities of the sovereign, and balance sheet risks stemming from the exchange rate regime. In emerging market countries with relatively open capital accounts and integrated financial systems, reserves are more appropriately measured in terms of short-term public and private debt by residual maturity. Additional considerations determining reserve adequacy are the strength of a country's economic fundamentals (possible exchange rate overvaluation, current account balance), the notional value of short-term public sector derivatives positions, and possible weaknesses in the banking system that may lead to passing foreign currency liabilities to the government.

- The composition of international reserves, therefore, should depend on the type of shocks that they are meant to offset. Usually, a portion of highly liquid reserves is determined through an assessment of the potential liquidity needs based on balance of payments stress tests and past interventions. Countries that have limited international market access may structure their reserves so that they match the currency of denomination of their future imports. In countries where reserves provide coverage for short-term debt, their currency composition should match the currency composition of their short-term debt. Industrialised countries with flexible exchange rate regimes, that maintain international reserves for precautionary purposes to intervene in times of market turmoil, often maintain international reserves with a diversified currency structure.

Risk-return considerations are gaining increasing importance in sovereign asset management, along with the traditional objective of maintaining ample liquid reserves to meet balance of payments and intervention needs. There has recently been a significant growth in the level of total foreign exchange reserves. This growth implies an opportunity cost for central banks who are not yet adopting more active investment strategies for the portion of their reserve portfolio having a low probability of being used for macroeconomic or policy purposes. The challenge then becomes how to apportion the portfolio between a liquid part that could be used for balance of payments and intervention purposes and another part for investment purposes, while also managing currency, interest rate, credit and operation risks.

In principle, when sovereign asset (reserves) are greater than sovereign liabilities (debt), they could be used to buy back debt, thereby reducing the size of the sovereign balance sheet. The benefit of such a strategy could be to minimise the risk of possible currency and maturity mismatches and to lower the carry cost of reserves, since coupon payments to investors in sovereign bonds are likely to exceed returns on international reserves. If reserves are excessive even after debt redemption and buy-backs, they could be used to set up an investment or a sovereign wealth fund (SWF). Cases where an investment fund appears to be a sensible solution include: (i) a local economy that cannot absorb additional spending without overheating; (ii) windfall profits that are likely to disrupt the domestic economy; (iii) an uncertain future, especially in countries that are rich in natural resources; (iv) a country with a small asset base that may need to be diversified.

As SWF-type assets grow, their objectives may change to hedge risks originating in different components of the sovereign balance sheet. For example, a SWF may originally be set up as a stabilisation fund to smooth fiscal revenue or sterilise foreign currency inflows in a natural resource exporting country. As the assets in the fund continue to grow beyond the level needed for the purpose of stabilisation, the authorities may carve a portion of the assets, revisit the objectives, and redesign the structure of the

SWF to broaden its objective. This often leads to assets being split into several tranches for different purposes, or the creation of separate funds with different objectives. During the 2008-2010 crisis, several countries with SWF-type arrangements made active use of their assets to mitigate the impact of the crisis on the overall sovereign balance sheet and to maintain macroeconomic and financial stability.

Reducing Balance Sheet Risks: Reduce/Eliminate Foreign Currency and Maturity Mismatches

Asset and liability management focuses on the risk exposure of an entity as a whole, which is sometimes referred to as its economic exposure. In the case of SALM, this means the exposure of the economy as a whole or, the risk exposure of the aggregate bundle of goods consumed. A more practical working definition is the exposure to changes in exchange rates, interest rates and commodity prices of the country's net cash flows from international transactions.

Foreign Currency Mismatches

Foreign currency exposure has two dimensions: (i) liquidity risk—the ease or difficulty of obtaining foreign exchange; and (ii) balance sheet risk—the sensitivity of the borrower's net wealth or net income to changes in the exchange rate. In practice, it is difficult to distinguish these risks because liquidity may dry up easily for borrowers with encumbered balance sheets.

Sovereign liability managers should clearly state the objectives of foreign exchange risk management within a well-defined SALM management framework. The desired output should be a strategic benchmark portfolio that defines the optimum structure of debt, including the optimum share of foreign-currency debt in total debt. Obviously, a benchmark portfolio changes with changes in policy objectives, structure of the debt, and other macroeconomic and financial stability conditions.

In a liability management framework, the optimum currency composition of debt is usually determined by the minimisation of projected debt servicing costs (assumed overarching objective of debt management in most countries) subject to constraints regarding (i.e., not exceeding) certain foreign exchange, interest rate, credit and liquidity-risk levels (secondary objectives).

If a SALM framework is employed, the optimum currency composition of debt could be determined by an optimisation that takes into account both the minimisation of projected debt servicing costs and maximisation of the return of the country's assets (in particular, international reserves and projected primary balances) subject to constraints regarding specified risks and the country's asset-liability structures. The latter approach, in essence, espouses the view that the currency composition of the sovereign liabilities should closely match that of the assets in a sovereign's balance sheet.

Maturity Mismatches

Liquidity risk is less common in the case of local currency debt and, therefore, most measures of interest rate exposure focus on balance sheet risk. The sensitivity of the borrower's net worth (or net income) to changes in short-term interest rates depends on the average maturity of the debt, the extent to which the coupon on long-dated debt is linked to short-term interest rates, and the structure of assets and other liabilities on the balance sheet of the borrower.

When gauging financial stability based on assessments of interest rate and currency mismatches, it is important to take into account the impact of derivative transactions on the transfer of economic risk and, hence, there is a need to also account for off-balance sheet exposures.

Achieving Other Secondary Objectives

SALM objectives should be always consistent with the overall macroeconomic policy framework. However, in addition to the primary SALM objectives outlined above, other secondary objectives may be explicitly or implicitly included in a SALM framework. Usually, secondary SALM objectives include the achievement of various public policy goals (attainment of a better credit rating, correction of externalities, provision of certain public services, income redistribution and poverty reduction).

Defining Relevant Assets and Liabilities

There are two main challenges in defining relevant assets and liabilities in a SALM framework. The first relates to the choice of the relevant accounting practices. The value of assets and liabilities depends on which accounting measure is used: mark-to-market valuation or historical price. As is well known, bond prices move inversely with interest rates. Changes in exchange rates affect the market value of external debt. Therefore, mark-to-market valuation will lead to a larger fluctuation in the value of debt, as compared with the use of historical prices. For contingent liabilities, such as unfunded pension funds, the value depends on assumptions regarding the discount rate, expected return, life expectancy, and inflation rate. In terms of assets, at least for some of them, the market value and historical value will yield a significant gap. For example, the equity in loss-making state-owned companies, if evaluated using market values, may be much lower than evaluated using historical values.

The second challenge is to determine items of assets and liabilities that should be included in SALM. A narrow definition of SALM, used in many developing and emerging market economies, includes international reserves and foreign currency debt. As foreign currency debt has to be served with foreign exchange, a SALM approach would enable the decision-makers to assess whether their debt currency structure is consistent with the financial characteristics of current and future foreign reserves. Moreover, foreign reserves can be used to hedge currency and interest rate risks on the foreign currency debts. The analysis of the risks could then focus on the unhedged. If the netted position results in net reserves, decision-makers can assess the size, maturity, and currency composition of net reserves, and draw up the cost of holding net reserves.

Most broader definitions include all sovereign financial assets and liabilities, but exclude the non-financial ones. There are two reasons that non-financial assets and liabilities are excluded in SALM. The first is that non-financial assets and liabilities do not generate cash flows, and thus is difficult to measure their price sensitivities to changes in economic variables such as interest rates and exchange rates. The second is that in order to use market valuation, assets and liabilities should be able to be approximately measured using market variables, which is not easy for non-financial ones.

Broader Definitions of a Sovereign Balance Sheet

In general, there are several unambiguous items of financial assets and liabilities to be included in a broader definition of the sovereign balance sheet. A comprehensive sovereign balance sheet incorporating all of these elements is provided by Merton (2007) (Table 13.1). It is based on economic, rather than accounting principles, and underlies the analysis of the intertemporal objectives of the sovereign by including future incomes and expenditures. It also emphasises the consumption smoothing.

On the asset side, a country's foreign reserves and long-term funds in foreign currency, such as SWFs should be part of sovereign assets. Cash, securities, loan, and receivables owned by the government are also sovereign assets. Equity in state-owned companies with profits should also be counted as sovereign assets. On the liability side, sovereign debt should be included in SALM regardless of whether it is issued by the central bank or the government. Values of debt change with changes in interest rate, exchange rate, or inflation rate. For example, inflation will dent the real value of non-indexed domestic debt, while the depreciation of local currency will inflate the value of external debt measured by local currency.

Other items such as contingent liabilities should also be included in SALM, although they may be more difficult to quantify. It is increasingly acceptable that contingent liabilities should be factored into SALM. It has been argued that contingent liabilities are a potential source of government cash outflow, which has to be met through either increasing borrowing or selling assets. Evaluated under SALM, contingent liabilities are more likely to be honoured during economic recessions, when the borrowing requirements are expected to be high. However, it is often difficult to value contingent liabilities as their valuations depend on many assumptions, including probability of defaults and recovery rates. This becomes particularly complex in the event of financial or corporate sector bailouts.

The present value of government budget could also be included in the SALM framework. Given that a sovereign's largest asset is the ability to collect taxes, it is reasonable to add the present value of government revenues to the asset side of SALM. For the same reason, the present value of government expenditures should also be part of liabilities. The inclusion of the present value of government budget entails an asset-driven borrowing and liability-driven investment strategy. The government has to assess whether the debt-service costs from new debt can be met by the returns of current assets and future cash flow from revenue. The investment decision will be examined against the need to serve debt.

Table 13.1

Stylised Economic-Risk Balance Sheet of the Sovereign

Assets	*Liabilities*
Present Value of Incomes from:	*Present Value of Non-discretionary Expenses on:*
Taxes	Social and economic development
Fees	Economic development
Seignorage	Government administration
Balances of:	*Balances of:*
Cash	Monetary base
Currency reserves	Government debt
Investments (pension and wealth funds)	In domestic currency
	In foreign currency
	Pension liabilities
Government-owned enterprises	
Infrastructure	
Real estate	
Other assets	
	Contingent claims (explicit and implicit)
	Guarantees to banks and non-banks
	Guarantees on retirement income
	Guarantees on social welfare
	Net worth
	Net financial worth

Source: Merton (2007).

The conventional items of a sovereign balance sheet are typically included in the contingent claims analysis (CCA). In a common sovereign balance sheet of the CCA approach (Gapen *et al.*, 2005), sovereign liabilities include foreign currency debt, domestic currency debt, and base money, where their prices can be observed in the markets. In this framework, the market value and volatility of sovereign assets can be derived from option pricing formulas that take the market price and volatility of domestic and foreign currency liabilities, risk-free interest rate, and time as inputs. Given that the value of liabilities should be observed from markets, contingent liabilities are moved from the liability side to the asset side with a negative sign (Table 13.2 and Figure 13.1).

Figure 13.1

Overview of CCA for the Sovereign

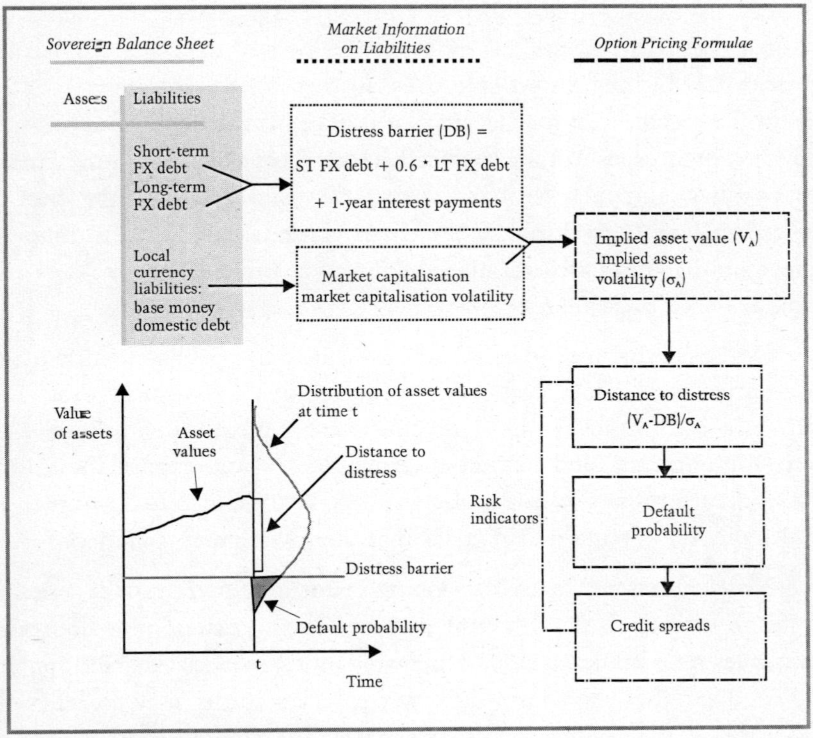

Source: Adapted from Jones and Gray (2006).

Table 13.2

Stylised Sovereign Balance Sheet in the CCA

Assets	*Liabilities*
International reserves	External debt
Net fiscal assets (discounted value of primary fiscal surpluses)	Equity
Value of monopoly over issue of money (seneiorage, or zero for countries using another country's currency as a legal tender)	Domestic debt
Other assets-less guarantees	Base money

Source: Papaioannou and Souto (2007).

Methodologies

Many governments use some form of SALM in which they try to identify risks and vulnerabilities of the sovereign assets and liabilities, without necessarily identifying an economic form of the sovereign balance sheet or establishing SALM objectives. In these cases, governments often determine specific debt management or reserve management strategies that reduce certain exposures and reduce balance sheet vulnerabilities, without necessarily quantifying the risks. Further, they may use a balance sheet in conceptual terms to visualise the inter-relationships between different assets and liabilities to determine the direction in which these assets and liabilities need to be changed.

One issue that most of these governments may readily recognise is the need to maintain a low level of foreign currency and short-term debt. The rationale is that government revenues are typically denominated in domestic currency, and foreign currency debt would expose them to a consequent currency risk. Short-term debt is to be avoided in order to reduce the rollover and refixing risks that the government could face.

Nevertheless, in many developing countries, international reserves could be directly linked to debt service. To the extent that domestic companies have limited access to financing in international markets, public and total external short-term debt by residual maturity may coincide. In this case, it may be reasonable to match the currency and maturity structure of reserves with that of the public debt, as a simple natural hedging strategy. However, as local currency government debt markets develop and the country becomes more financially integrated, public debt may take a decreasing share in external debt. Then, the objectives of reserve and debt management would become increasingly more complicated and difficult to coordinate.

Various formal approaches are also used to obtain an optimal allocation of reserves and/or an optimal debt structure. The mean-variance approach is primarily used to determine an optimal allocation of assets, based on a prespecified upper limit on portfolio volatility. Also, the two variants of the mean-variance approach, the Value-at-Risk (VaR) and Cost-at-Risk (CaR) approaches are commonly used to determine an optimal reserve portfolio (VaR) or an optimal debt structure (CaR) with a certain probability. Note that all optimal solutions from mean-variance type approaches depend on exogeneously determined (ad hoc) levels of risk to be assumed by the government. In essence, the mean-variance framework assumes that there are preconceived (e.g., by the government—the Minister of Finance, or the governor of the central bank) value amounts for the various types of risk that are imposed on the selection process for the optimal allocations.

When, instead of a prespecified level of risk, the government's objective function regarding risk and return (for the various asset strategies) and risk and cost (for the various debt strategies) is to be taken into consideration in determining optimal allocations, then the Multivariate Adaptive Regression Splines (MARS) method could be a useful one to use. Finally, when the criterion for deciding on optimal allocation is minimisation of credit risk, i.e., default probability, then the Contingent Claims Analysis (CCA) approach may be the most suitable.

Technical Issues in SALM Modelling

In implementing the SALM framework, the modelling of variables such as interest and exchange rates and other macroeconomic variables is important for estimating the risk exposure of a country as a whole. This is because the net worth of the country is driven by the evolutions of these variables. For example, if the country is holding net financial assets, the domestic/foreign interest yield curve movement and/or the exchange rate movement will have an impact on the value of these assets. If the country is holding net liabilities, these movements will also affect the value of liabilities. Other macroeconomic variables, such as output gap, inflation, and short interest rate should be taken into account. For example, the term structure of interest rates is influenced by developments in the macroeconomy and vice-versa, the short-term interest rate—a policy rate—is controlled by the central bank to conduct its monetary policies and the government's funding requirement is influenced by macroeconomic developments.

A way to estimate a sovereign's risk exposures is to generate risk indicators from stochastic simulations driven by changes in interest rates, exchange rates, and other macroeconomic variables. These risk indicators are, then, determined by the generated probability distributions and specific confidence levels. In essence, these indicators allow estimating gains and losses originating from market movements with a certain probability.

Institutional Requirements

Coordination between the Government and the Central Banks

As mentioned before, the SALM framework should first and foremost ensure consistency with the overall macroeconomic framework. For effective implementation there should be a level of institutional coordination between the entities that manage sovereign assets and sovereign liabilities, and appropriate supporting legislation that institutes policy guidelines. Given the different institutional objectives and the necessary degree of coordination between the entities involved, possible institutional frictions may arise in applying the SALM framework. In case institutional constraints render an integrated asset and liability management strategy impossible to implement, second best options need to be considered. One option may be the separation of the central bank's balance sheet and objectives from the sovereign's balance sheet and objectives. However, the rationale for this separation and its implications should be clearly examined including specifying the conditions under which the central bank balance sheet can be used for SALM purposes or for managing various components underpinning a sovereign's financial networth.

In the context of a stable macroeconomic environment, where the central bank and the government have a well-established understanding to follow consistent fiscal and monetary policies, the role of the SALM manager could get simplified. In this case, a CAR approach—taking basic indicators such as GDP, the inflation and interest rates as given—may be sufficient to achieve the main sovereign objective. Some countries refer to this situation as a steady-state and have found that incorporating more sophisticated macro models and the central bank's balance sheet into the SALM approach has a very low pay-off—in terms of a set of new policy choices—and a high resource cost.

However, if the central bank conducts quasi-fiscal operations, managing a consolidated balance sheet including the central bank becomes necessary, because the financial viability of the central bank may have sustainability implications for the sovereign. In some emerging and developing countries, the central bank has conducted such quasi-fiscal operations in the process of resolving banking crises. In practice, the liabilities that a central bank takes over in such cases should be recognised as contingent liabilities of the sovereign government. Hence, if the central bank is responsible for bailing out financial institutions by issuing debt to recapitalise them, the central bank balance sheet should be managed jointly with the balance sheet of the government.

The issuance of central bank debt may raise governance issues since, unlike government debt, it is usually not subject to legislative approval. In many countries, especially when the government does not have a financing need, such debt is issued for monetary policy/sterilisation purposes. Quite often the banking system is a captive investment base for such debt and its sustainability depends on the central bank's ability to make regular payments. Because of the systemic implications that might ultimately impact the government's balance sheet, such central bank liabilities may have to be managed in a coordinated manner between the government and the central bank.

Similarly, coordination between the central bank and the government is warranted in the case of a (commodity-based) country with large fiscal surpluses that are being held at the central bank, particularly if the government owns a dominant share of the central bank liabilities. In this case, the government balance sheet is directly affected by the risk management practices of the central bank.

Debt Capital Market Development

For an SALM approach to succeed in generating optimal outputs, a minimum development of domestic capital markets (principally, with regards to depth and liquidity) and financial intermediation (in particular with regards to the investor base) is presumed. If constraints in capacity building and financial infrastructure exist, possible asset and/or debt allocations suggested by the SALM framework may not be feasible because domestic markets cannot accommodate them. This could especially be the case for countries that do not have adequately developed yield curves both in terms of benchmark issues and maturities, and their investor base is limited, possibly due to restrictive regulations or small population size of the country and limited growth prospects. These issues may significantly restrict the scope and usefulness of a SALM approach for many, especially developing, countries.

Concluding Observations

Several countries are actively moving towards developing their asset or liability management strategies at the sovereign level. Some countries are already carrying out partially coordinated SALM. Typically, this involves integrated management of the net position on Central government debt and cash reserves thereby setting objectives and risk constraints only in account of these balance sheet items. In other cases, the allocation of assets between alternative portfolios and funds may take account of the sovereign's broader priorities and objectives, but not specifically of balance sheet risks.

As the SALM objectives are frequently specified on a narrow set of balance sheet items (net Central government debt and cash reserves), the risk considerations from an asset management perspective involve minimising liquidity and credit risk and, in some cases, interest rate risk. From a liability management perspective, considerations for minimising interest rate risk, refinancing risk, and currency risk prevail among debt managers. Duration and modified duration are used commonly in both asset and liability management. VaR is used more commonly by asset managers, while CaR by liability (debt) managers. Asset managers also use scenario analysis and stress tests more often than liability managers; and counterparty limits are common to prevent credit risk by asset managers. With respect to liability management, ratio analysis—and in particular the refixing ratio—is commonly used to monitor risks.

Given the prevailing fragmentation in the management of sovereign assets and liabilities, coordination between various institutions involved in SALM is not common at present. While mirroring each other, the objectives of managing assets and liabilities need better coordination. The main objective of sovereign liability management is to ensure financing of the budget at the lowest possible cost subject to an acceptable level of risk.

The objectives of the sovereign asset management are to ensure that cash balances meet commitments and to maximise the purchasing power of the long-term capital given moderate level of risk.

In the most integrated case, decision-making authority for both assets an liabilities is assigned to one agency or ministry—e.g., the ministry of finance—who delegates responsibilities for day-to-day management—e.g., to the central bank—and coordinates the planning and execution of the borrowing and investing programmes. In other cases, the mandates of the agencies in charge of SALM may be set following coordination or a delegation by a responsible ministry—treasury or the ministry of finance. Another more common coordination mechanism is instituting regular meetings between the agencies involved in SALM.

Clarity about macro-goals is a precondition for articulating an appropriate SALM framework. Given the high level of uncertainty, risk assessment must play a central role in informing the SALM strategy. Such assessments require elaboration of alternative scenarios which encompass short- and long-term costs and stress test for various macroeconomic shocks. The potential volume of new liabilities should be analysed, using, for example, quantitative methods such as the CCA framework. Information about the risks associated with the management of the sovereign balance sheet should be published as transparency and accountability are key to maintaining confidence with the application of a SALM approach.

Involvement of multiple institutions that comprise the sovereign balance sheet blurs accountability. Combining the management of sovereign assets and liabilities under one framework may also not always be optimal from an institutional point of view. It should be noted that, so long as the roles, objectives and resources available to each institution are clearly defined and consistent, then a comprehensive sovereign balance sheet approach would remain consistent with maintaining the degree of independence of each institution.

Hence, either in the near-term or as part of disengagement, a goal of SALM must be to re-clarify institutional responsibilities. This may require redistributing assets and liabilities across the institutions. The debt management strategy needs to be robust to the risk that contingent liabilities will materialise. More generally, as the characteristics of acquired assets are clarified, and assessments of likely holding periods updated, the SALM strategy should be reviewed to see if ALM considerations require a change in the structure of the debt portfolio.

The SALM process, indeed, is a long drawn-out one and depends on country's structural and institutional peculiarities. A lot of technical assistance and support may be needed, at a global level, to help put in place consistent and comparable sovereign balance sheets. Such a system could, however, go a long way in helping policymakers take into account the financial aspects of their decisions, mitigate distortionary spillovers, and to be better prepared for a systemic event.

References

Caceres, Carlos, Vincenzo Guzzo and Miguel Segoviano (2010). "Sovereign Spreads: Global Risk Aversion, Contagion, or Fundamentals?", *IMF Working Paper* No. 10/120. Washington: International Monetary Fund.

Cassard, Marcel and David Folkerts-Landau (1997). "Risk Management of Sovereign Assets and Liabilities", *IMF Working Paper* No. 97/166. Washington: International Monetary Fund.

Das, Udaibir S., Michael G. Papapioannou, Guilherme Pedras, Faisal Ahmed and Jay Surti, "Managing Public Debt and Its Financial Stability Implications", *IMF Working Paper* (forthcoming). Washington: International Monetary Fund.

Das Udaibir S., Yinqui Lu, Michael G. Papaioannou and Iva Petrova, "Sovereign Asset and Liability Management: Conceptual Issues", *IMF Working Paper* (forthcoming). Washington: International Monetary Fund.

Gapen, Michael T., Dale F. Gray, Cheng Hoon Lim and Yingbin Xiao (2005). "Measuring and Analyzing Sovereign Risk with Contingent Claims", *IMF Working Paper* No. 05/155. Washington: International Monetary Fund.

Hansen, Eric (2003). Objectives, "Targets and Instruments for Crown Financial Policy", *New Zealand Treasury Working Paper* No. 03/21. Wellington: New Zealand Treasury.

International Monetary Fund (2009). *Crisis-Related Measures in the Financial System and Sovereign Balance sheet Risks.* SM/09/210. Prepared by Fiscal Affairs and Monetary and Capital Markets Departments. Washington. July. Available at: *http://www.imf.org/external/np/pp/eng/2009/073109.pdf.*

International Monetary Fund and the World Bank (2001). *Guidelines for Public Debt Management*.

Jones, Matthew T. and Dale F. Gray (2006). "Measuring Sovereign and Banking Sector Risk in Indonesia: An Application of the Contingent Claims Approach", Selected Issues Paper, *IMF Country Report* No. 06/318. Washington: International Monetary Fund.

Merton, Robert (2007). "Observations on Sovereign Wealth Fund, Reserve, and Debt Management: A Country Risk Management Perspective", Presentation at the *First IMF Roundtable of Sovereign Asset and Reserve Managers*. Washington, United States. November.

Papaioannou, Michael G. and Marcos Souto (2007). "A Toolkit to Measure the Market and Credit Risk of a Portfolio of Government Bond Securities: User's Guide". Washington, D.C.: International Monetary Fund. May. (*mimeo*).

The views expressed in the paper are mine and should not be attributed in any way to the IMF, its Executive Board, its Management. I thank my colleague Michael Papaioannou for his partnership in developing these ideas. More analytical and empirical work is clearly needed as the lack of adequate data remains a serious constraint for this type of an approach. The models developed thus far have been applied primarily to open-economy settings. However, I see several important lessons of a SALM approach for policymakers in emerging market economies seeking to improve policy tools, impart accountability, and improve the operating environment for managing assets and liabilities and the operating environment. The paper draws upon a forthcoming IMF Working Paper 'Sovereign Asset and Liability Management: Conceptual Issues' by Udaibir S. Das, Yinqui Lu, Michael G. Papaioannou, and Iva Petrova.

14 Securities Market Development

Indian Experience and Some Lessons for Future

Ravi Narain

Introduction

As an academic, policymaker and administrator, Dr. C. Rangarajan has been closely associated with the development of India's financial markets. He has been a mentor to many of us and his vision for the financial market reforms continues to shape the thinking and career of many younger professionals.

Prof. Rangarajan played a leading role in the broad-based reform programme that India embarked upon after the Balance of Payments (BoP) crisis in 1991. In the history of capital market developments in India, the events and reform initiatives in the following two decades have been most remarkable, accelerating the market activities to a pace that was never witnessed before. The market development during this period kept pace with and duly supported the rapid economic growth that India achieved. Currently, India is among the fastest growing economies of the world and the optimism for achieving sustained double digit growth in the foreseeable future has grown substantially.

As India moves into a high growth trajectory, sustaining such high growth in the long term has become a policy objective. At this juncture, the recent global financial crisis has focused the attention of policymakers in India, as elsewhere in the world, to the vulnerabilities arising from the financial sector. While the resilience of the Indian economy to the crisis has been lauded, there are fears of a more severe impact on economic growth should there be a similar crisis in future as India's financial sector gets further integrated into the world economy. What has fed this fear is the fact that the crisis was the most acute in countries where financial markets are among the most developed. Based on this fear, there is a growing view that to sustain economic growth and reduce vulnerabilities to shocks emanating from the financial sector, we need to view every initiative to make the financial system more diverse and sophisticated with some degree of skepticism.

It is our contention that this may not be the most appropriate lesson from the crisis for India, although we recognise that there is need for caution in developing financial markets. The global financial crisis was a result of multiple factors, and one of these was a regulatory environment that trusted the market to 'take care of itself'. Financial market innovations, and a permissive, even lax, regulatory culture speeded up and gave potency to what was set in motion by global savings imbalances and fiscal and monetary policies followed by major economies.

It is not our intent to comment on the deficiencies in regulatory environment that may have contributed to the global financial crisis. Our aim is to shift focus to our domestic experience of capital market development. While there has been considerable progress in some parts of our markets, certain other parts have lagged behind, which have implications for India's growth prospects. (The linkages between capital market development and growth are briefly outlined in Box 14.1). We try to identify the underdeveloped segments of the securities market that are critical from the viewpoint of growth, in the light of an analysis of our own experience across different markets. From the successes and mistakes that we made in the past in these markets, we draw some lessons.

We also draw attention to the objective of achieving inclusion in the securities market. While economic growth has accelerated in the post-liberalisation period, a vast number of people, potential entrepreneurs, small enterprises and others remain excluded from the financial sector, which has implied a denial of opportunity for them to grow and prosper. This does not augur well for maintaining high growth or stability of the country.[1] The paper examines the concept of financial inclusion in the

---

1. The Eleventh Five-Year Plan (2007-2012) has brought inclusion to the centre of the development debate and has called for 'a growth process which yields broad-based benefits and ensures equality of opportunity for all'.

context of the securities market, the extent to which the securities market has delivered and the focus of the recent reforms.

There are two key attributes of developed financial markets: efficiency and stability. Efficiency of financial systems pertains to the role of markets in mobilising and allocating financial resources, providing liquidity and payment services and gathering information on which to base investment and saving decisions. Stability, on the other hand, is concerned with safeguarding the value of liabilities of financial institutions that serve as

Box 14.1

Linkages between Securities Markets and Economic Growth

We know from our textbooks that the financial sector on one hand provides the savers a menu of saving vehicles with differing risk and return characteristics and on the other, helps the investors find the financing they need taking into account the returns and risks on the projects they wish to undertake. The more developed a financial sector, the more efficiently it carries out these functions. By so doing, the financial sector raises the total size of investable resources in the economy and at the same time, increases the productivity of investment and thereby spurs higher economic growth.

While this is true of the entire financial sector, it is the securities markets—among all segments of the capital markets—that generates and disseminates most rapidly enormous amount of information (including firm-specific information) which get reflected in security prices. By reducing the cost of acquisition of information about investment opportunities and providing clear price signals about the prospects of companies, sectors, commodities, crops etc., securities markets help in improving resource allocation.

Securities markets also influence economic growth by providing avenues for firm financing. For growing firms, securities markets provide an avenue for raising capital at lower cost. In addition, as the securities markets develop, companies can afford to be less dependent on bank financing, which can reduce the risk of an economic slowdown due to a bank credit crunch. These markets improve not only the quantity of new investments but also past investments. It does the latter through the takeover mechanism. Theoretically, the threat of takeover provides management with an incentive to make more efficient use of the company's assets (Yartey and Charles, 2007).

stores of wealth and media of domestic and international exchange and involves questions of prudential supervision and regulation, monetary control and good governance. This paper focuses on the efficiency aspect, although there are some passing references to stability factors. Further, the paper excludes discussion on government debt market, commodities market and securitisation.

Experience and Lessons

Equity and Equity Derivatives

India's equity and equity derivative markets are widely held up as examples of success among all emerging economies. As compared to developed countries, Indian firms rely heavily on retained earnings and informal sources (such as friends and family); but relative to similarly situated developing countries, Indian equity markets are quite well developed (Armour and Lele, 2009). In 2009, India's market capitalisation to GDP ratio—an indicator of market depth—was 90 per cent. This is comparable with that of similarly situated emerging economies (Russia 70%, Brazil 74% and China 100%) and is indeed higher than some developed countries such as Germany (39%) and Japan (67%).[2] In terms of other indicators, such as turnover ratio (liquidity indicator) and number of listed companies (market size), India has also done well. Table 14.1 shows that during the last two decades, India's market capitalisation to GDP ratio

Table 14.1

Market Capitalisation as a Per cent of GDP of World Stock Markets, 1990-2008

Markets	*Market Capitalisation as a % of GDP*		
	1990	*2000*	*2008*
High income	51.6	120.6	62.9
Middle income	19.4	41.2	49.5
Low & middle income	18.8	38.7	48.9
Low income	9.8	23.6	40.5#
India	12.2	32.4	55.7

Note: #: This is data for 2007.

Source: World Bank (2010). *World Development Indicators*.

2. *S&P Global Stock Market Factbook* (2010). World Bank website.

rose from levels close to low-income countries to levels substantially higher than middle-income countries.

These achievements could be possible due to the rapid and wide-ranging reform efforts made since early 90s. These are all well known and hence, we will make only a brief mention of some reform milestones. The most important reform was the abolition of the Office of Controller of Capital Issues (CCI) and its replacement by an independent regulator, the Securities and Exchange Board of India (SEBI). SEBI was given statutory powers as a unified securities regulator in 1992, including the power to produce regulations by way of delegated legislation. In addition to the regulatory role, SEBI was assigned a developmental role.

Reforms in the securities markets that followed can be classified into three inter-related areas: governance framework, modern institutions and diversification of investor base. As regards governance framework, SEBI has effected a series of capital market reforms to ensure transparency of trading practices, speedy and safe settlement procedures, enforcement of prudential norms, full disclosure for investor protection and simplification of the initial public offering (IPO) process. Specific regulations were framed in the areas of merchant banks, disclosure requirements, takeover and insider trading. Several high powered committees set up by SEBI and Ministry of Corporate Affairs (MoCA) have contributed in a significant way to raising the corporate governance standards of our market. In the area of regulation, exchanges have played a key role as frontline regulators, apart from their role as market infrastructure providers. As a result of all these measures, a relatively more robust and dependable regulatory framework has been put in place.

Soon after the creation of SEBI, some new and independent institutions emerged, which laid the foundation for a modern and fast-growing securities market. These institutions included the National Stock Exchange (NSE) in 1992, the first clearing corporation—the National Securities Clearing Corporation Ltd. (NSCCL) in 1995, and an independent depository called the National Securities Depository Ltd. (NSDL) in 1996. The clearing corporations, who are responsible for carrying out clearing functions and guaranteeing settlement, have put together an effective risk management system and addressed the systemic risk aspects of broker defaults by acting as a central counterparty. The two depositories that are in operation now ensure faster, cleaner and cheaper settlement. The settlement time and transaction costs in India are comparable to developed financial markets in the US and Europe (Bhagwati, 2010).

The third area relates to growth and diversification of the investor base. It was only in 1992, when Foreign Institutional Investors (FIIs) were allowed to register with SEBI, that foreign investment in stock market was initiated. The number of FIIs has since grown to 1713 by March 2010 and net FII portfolio investment has risen from US $2 billion in 1995/96 to US $30 billion in 2009/10, albeit with some degree of volatility. In the early 90s, there were a few large domestic institutional investors, predominantly in the public sector. Private mutual funds have since come up, which as a group are currently mobilising much larger funds than public sector mutual funds (Ibid.). In the insurance space, many new (private) companies have also emerged as important participants. In addition to the proliferation of institutional investors, there has been an increase in the number of retail investors.

A distinctive feature of India's equity market landscape is the large presence of retail investors; currently, retail trade accounts for over 50 per cent of turnover on exchanges in equity and 55 per cent of turnover in equity derivatives. While a significant proportion of retail turnover comes from the metros, most postal districts in India are covered by multiple broker terminals.

An important side effect of internalisation of Indian capital markets and cross-listing by Indian companies abroad was a drive toward a more stringent corporate governance regime (Varotill, 2009). To successfully market their securities offering to foreign investors, Indian companies making public offerings in India were persuaded to comply with corporate governance norms that investors in the developed world (especially US and UK) were familiar with.[3] Further, Indian companies listing abroad to raise capital—mainly to establish an international reputation—were subject to full-blown corporate governance requirements applicable to listing on those exchanges. They also adhered to the norms and practices of corporate governance applicable to markets where they listed their securities. 'Consequently, those norms and practices permeated into the general

3. This was so, because, a large part of foreign investment came from these countries.

Indian corporate scenario, at least among the leading and more reputable companies.' (Varottil, 2009)

The reform path has not been entirely smooth and trouble-free. There have been some instances of wrongdoing which occurred between mid-1990s to 2002. Following the abolition of administered pricing, a number of fly-by-night companies raised funds from the market in mid-1990s and 'vanished' in the subsequent years with the investor funds. This shook investor confidence in the primary markets. This episode led to the tightening of oversight on issues and better enforcement of listing agreements.

There have been other challenges too. The FIIs have a significant impact on the market, as indicated by the strong correlation between the overall FII flows and the market movement (Figure 14.1), although no single FII dominates the market. The domestic institutions, despite their growth, have not been able to occupy centre stage in the equity market. Further, among the domestic institutions, while participation by insurance companies and mutual funds are growing, pension funds are nowhere in the picture. Traditionally, pension funds are amongst the largest institutional investors; indeed, a significant part of FII investments in India comes from pension funds. However, the domestic provident funds, which

Figure 14.1

Net FII Investments and Nifty Movements

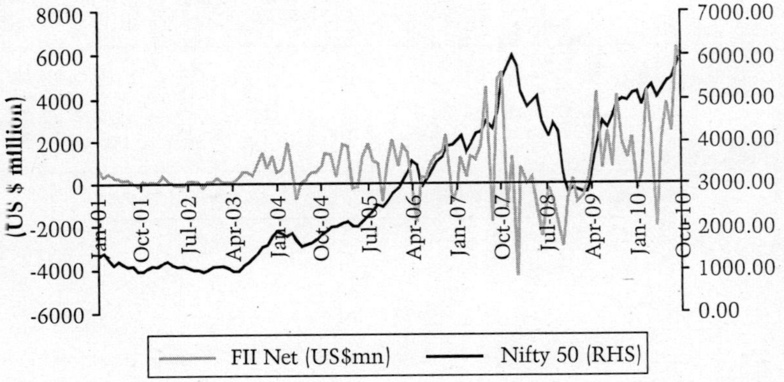

Source: Websites of SEBI, NSE.

play a dominant role in delivering retirement benefits in India, have been very reluctant to invest in the equity market.[4]

One other factor that has hurt the capital market developments in India is ownership concentration of the Indian listed companies, since the promoters of many Indian companies—including the listed companies—want their firms to be closely held. According to a recent study, the average BSE 500 Company has a promoter who owns roughly 49 per cent of the company and fewer than 9 per cent of the BSE 500 companies have promoters holding less than the critical threshold of 25 per cent (Mathew, 2007). This kind of a corporate landscape is detrimental to capital market development, because low levels of free float in the market raises the risk of stock price manipulation and increases the vulnerability of the minority shareholders to the actions of controlling shareholders.

Figure 14.2

Cash and Equity Derivatives Market Turnover at Indian Stock Exchanges

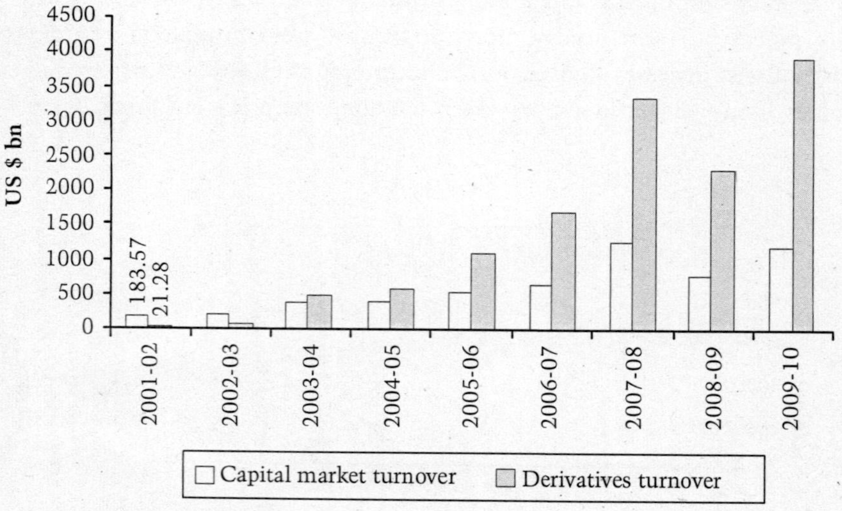

Source: SEBI.

4. Employees Provident Fund Organisation (EPFO), the predominant provident fund in India has not been investing in equity. Although there have been some equity investment under the New Pension Scheme (NPS), NPS is still in a nascent stage.

Let us now turn to equity derivative market. Since its inception in June 2000, the equity derivative market has exhibited exponential growth both in terms of volume and number of traded contracts, surpassing the equity market within a period of two years (Figure 14.2) and quickly establishing itself as a leading market in the world (see Table 14.2), a remarkable achievement for an emerging economy.

Table 14.2

Global Ranking of NSE in Equity Derivative Products (January–June 2010)

Equity Derivative Products	*Single Stock Futures*	*Single Stock Options*	*Stock Index Futures*	*Stock Index Options*
Number of contracts traded	3rd	11th	3rd	2nd
Turnover	2nd	5th	11th	5th

Source: World Federation of Exchanges (2009).

How did the market attain success in such a short period of time? Following is a discussion on how the different segments of the equity derivatives market were triggered by different factors.

The equity derivatives market has four segments (index futures, stock futures, index options and stock options). Although, all the four segments of the market (futures and options on indices and individual stocks) were introduced within a period of one and half years (June 2000 to November 2001)—they took varying periods of time to take off and developed at varying speed. Currently, the trading turnover is the highest in index options, followed by single stock futures and index futures, respectively. Single stock options still remain comparatively illiquid.

Badla, an indigeneous carry-forward system, was widely practised in India to take leveraged positions on individual stocks in the cash market. When *badla* was banned in 2001 because of its misuse, the void was quickly filled by the single stock futures market because this was seen as a cleaner, unbundled product. The experience of the market players played a key role in making the transition successful. The market at that point of time had little experience with index products. It was not surprising therefore that index futures took time to gain liquidity. Following over three years of intense and widespread training programmes by NSE for the brokers and investors, the index futures market began to gather momentum. One other reason why futures as a group developed before options is that futures, unlike options are linear contracts and are easier to understand, especially given the existing knowledge of the *badla* product.

As index futures became popular and the market gained familiarity with indices, interest in index options also began to grow. Index options however remained unattractive because of high tax burden. In 2008, when the tax base for securities transaction tax (STT) was changed from notional value of contract to premium, trading volumes immediately picked up and today index options are the most heavily traded equity derivative product. This underscores the impact that turnover taxes can have on the build-up of liquidity and usage of financial instruments. Single stock options, however, have yet to become popular; it is hoped that the market for this product would gain liquidity with the proposed move from American style options to European style options.

The discussion clearly reveals that modern market infrastructure, which had been largely established by 2000, is only a necessary condition for market development, but not a sufficient one. Other factors such as experience and education of market participants and transaction costs (such as taxes) play an important role.

Corporate Bond Market

The development of a well-functioning, deep and liquid corporate bond market is necessary for India for a number of reasons, the most important of them relates to its significance for infrastructure development. By tapping the growing pool of long-term funds available with the insurance and pension funds, as also with foreign investors, the corporate bond market can significantly benefit infrastructure investment, by better distributing the risk of financing such investment more widely across the financial system.

In the absence of a well-developed corporate bond market in India, however, rapid acceleration in infrastructure spending in recent years has been possible because of banks, whose exposure to infrastructure has grown enormously. Commercial banks are now the predominant financiers of infrastructure. Moving forward, however, banks may not be able to sustain the growth rates (in exposure to infrastructure) recorded in the past, primarily due to the fact that long duration infrastructure projects create significant maturity mismatches for banks, given the essentially short-term nature of bank deposits. Further, sectoral caps and limits on single and group borrower exposure have begun to place constraints on financing. Clearly, the need for developing the corporate bond market is being felt more strongly now than ever before.

There is no firm estimate available for the overall corporate bond market in India, but is widely believed to be in the range of 5-10 per cent of GDP—much smaller than the government debt market (about 35 per cent of GDP). The size of India's corporate bond market in relation to the size of the economy is much smaller than other emerging economies such as Korea (53 % of GDP) and Malaysia (42 %).[5] 'Even in absolute terms India's corporate bond market is miniscule in relation to its economic size. The role of various sources of corporate finance demonstrates that there is no single model for corporate finance—some economies rely more heavily on equity finance, while others on bank finance. However, few rely so little on corporate bonds as India does.' (Wells and Zibell, 2008). In recognition of this problem, the authorities have over the years set up several high powered committees to recommend measures to create a vibrant corporate bond market.[6] The most notable among them is the High Level Expert Committee on Corporate Bonds and Securitisation (also known as Patil Committee, 2005), whose recommendations have come to form the basic agenda for reforms.

A number of important initiatives have since been taken, most significantly:

- Regulatory roles relating to different segments of the corporate bond market have been clarified—SEBI has been made responsible for all primary and secondary market activities in corporate bonds issued by listed entities, and RBI for repos in corporate bonds.
- To enhance the investor base, the market lot size has been reduced from Rs. 10 lakh to Rs. 1 lakh.
- The limit of foreign institutional investors' (FIIs) investment in corporate bonds has been increased to $20 billion.

5. *Asianbondsonline.adb.org*

6. A number of recommendations have also come from institutions such as the ADB and the World Bank.

- Repo in corporate bonds has been allowed since January 2010.
- Compulsory reporting of all trades in corporate bonds to any one of the reporting platforms set up by Bombay Stock Exchange (BSE), National Stock Exchange (NSE) or the Fixed Income Money Markets and Derivatives Association (FIMMDA) has been mandated. Also, NSE and BSE have set up dedicated trading platforms for corporate bonds.
- Transactions in corporate bonds are now be cleared and settled on the clearing corporation of exchanges.
- The tax deduction at source (TDS) provision has been removed for corporate bonds that are listed and in demat mode.
- SEBI has simplified disclosure and listing requirements under SEBI (Issue and Listing of Debt Securities) Regulations 2008. Issuers with listed equity are now required to make only brief incremental disclosures. Various structural restrictions on the designing of bonds have also been done away with.

Following these reforms, activities in the primary and secondary markets have improved in recent years. The primary issuance by corporate (by way of private placement and public issue) has risen from Rs. 116,423 crore in 2007/08 to Rs. 192,657 crore in 2009/10.[7] The volume of secondary market trades in corporate bonds at NSE (including over-the-counter (OTC) trades reported to NSE) increased from Rs. 31,453 crore in 2007/08 to Rs. 156,615 crore in 2009/10.[8] Nevertheless, the size of the market in the country still remains small.

An analysis of the reform measures taken so far shows that all the recommendations of the Patil Committee relating to the exchanges and clearing corporations, have already been implemented. Among the recommendations yet to be implemented, the notable ones include: a reduced and uniform stamp duty structure in the country,[9] market making

7. Prime Database.

8. These figures exclude turnover of corporate bonds traded on capital market segment of NSE.

9. The Indian Stamp Act (1899) was amended to bring uniformity at the central level, which applies to unsecured debt. However, stamp duty is a state subject and progress has to be made at the state level. State laws are applicable for secured debt.

institutions in corporate bonds, consolidation of privately placed bonds[10] and issues relating to securitised debt.[11]

Some important lessons can be drawn from the reform efforts and the market response to those efforts.

First, the demand side issues have been largely unresolved. Typically, corporate bond markets at the initial level of development depend on demand from long-term investors such as insurance companies, and pension and provident funds. But insurance companies and pension funds are constrained by regulations that require a large portion of their funds to be invested in government securities with little flexibility for investment in corporations in the private sector, particularly the lower-rated companies.

Second, on the supply side, an important issue relates to the lack of depth in the government bond market and the absence of a yield curve for government bonds, which could serve as a benchmark for corporate bonds (World Bank, 2006). While reform efforts are in progress in this area too, it would be reasonable to say that it would take several years before we attain reasonable amount of success. This need not however slow down the continuing efforts to create a well-functioning corporate bond market.

Third, the unfinished agenda of the Patil Committee are complex, difficult and time-consuming—yet, they are critical for market development. For example, high stamp duties impact heavily the cost of debt issuance. Also, variability in stamp duties across states inhibits the development of a more broad-based market. To build consensus among states for this would require considerable efforts and perseverance. However, the recent initiatives of the Standing Committee of State Secretaries of Stamp and Registration (1999) holds some promise in this regard.

Finally, to ensure that the measures already initiated succeed, we must learn from experience. For example, following the Patil Committee recommendation, the RBI published guidelines and allowed repos in

10. The Patil Committee had recommended consolidation of the issuance process to create large floating stocks to enhance market liquidity.

11. Issues relating to securitised debt include listing of securitised debt, introduction of credit enhancement mechanism, creation of specialised debt fund for infrastructure financing.

corporate bond in 2009.[12] However, no repo contracts have actually happened since then. Market participants have cited the high mandatory haircuts, operational difficulties like lack of rollover and absence of a central clearing party as reasons why there is not much interest in the product.

Interest Rate Derivatives

Interest rates in India, which have historically been administered rates, were progressively deregulated during the 90s and by late 90s, the interest rate regime stood substantially liberalised. Further, with the business cycles becoming more pronounced over the years, interest rates have become quite volatile in the past decade. This has underscored a greater need for risk management (than ever before) for all those who are exposed to interest rate risks, particularly the institutional investors such as banks and insurance companies. These institutions are currently holding large amount of government bonds, which have exposed them to substantial amount of interest rate risk. It was expected that when given the opportunity and tools to manage these risks, these institutions would quickly take advantage of the same. This has, however, not been the experience so far.

In recent years, an OTC market in interest rate derivatives (interest rate swaps) has emerged, but has not acquired depth, because of limited participation by banks, who carry the largest interest rate risk in the system. The interest rate risk for the banks arises out of their (mandated) holding of government bonds funded by short-term liabilities. The banks however are not required to mark-to-market the securities held in the HTM (held-to-maturity) category; hence, they have not felt persuaded to use interest rate swaps to hedge their risk. Not surprisingly, the interest swaps have remained confined to just a few banks—mainly private and

---

12. Lack of repos in corporate bonds has long been considered a cause for lack of liquidity in this market segment. Without the ability to repo their stocks efficiently, it is uneconomical for bond dealers to carry corporate bonds on their books. Given a choice between trading government securities and corporate bonds, dealers would always choose the government securities because they can use the collateralised repo product—collateralised borrowing and lending obligation (CBLO) of the Clearing Corporation of India Ltd. (CCIL). Recognising this fact, Patil Committee recommended the creation of a corporate bond repo product on the lines of CBLO.

foreign banks. In a few years after the International Financial Reporting Standards (IFRS) rules are implemented, however, the HTM provision may be drastically reduced.

Interest rate futures trading in Indian exchanges began in 2003. The product did not meet much success due to the deficiencies in its design and lack of market access. All the contracts were valued using the zero coupon yield curve (ZCYC), with which the market participants were not familiar at that stage. Further, the banks—a significant group of participants in the bond market—were allowed to only hedge and not trade. Such a one-sided market was unlikely to succeed.

Interest rate futures (IRFs) have been relaunched on the NSE on August 31, 2009. The scope and design of the product have been changed from what they were in 2003.[13] The contract is based on a notional 10-year bond having a yield of 7 per cent per annum. In its present form, the contract tracks the 'cheapest-to-deliver (CTD)' government security from a basket of underlying securities, and all outstanding positions at the maturity of the contract are settled by physical delivery. After some trading in September 2009, the first month after introduction, the volume of IRF trading has fallen to negligible levels. This is in sharp contrast to the equity, and currency derivatives, whose monthly turnover has continued to grow well.

Box 14.2

Global Turnover in Interest Rate Derivatives

Interest rate futures (IRF) contracts were first traded in the United States on October 29, 1975 mainly in response to a growing market need for tools that could provide protection against sharp movements in interest rates. Since then, IRF have become fundamental risk management tools for financial markets worldwide. In terms of turnover on organised exchanges, interest rate futures and options accounted for 87 per cent of total derivatives turnover in 2009. The turnover of interest rate derivatives on exchanges reached a peak of USD 1982 trillion in 2007 and stood at USD 1451 trillion in 2009.

Source: Bank for International Settlements (2010).

13. The product design was finalised by a joint committee of RBI and SEBI.

Several factors are impeding the growth of the IRF market, significantly:

Illiquidity of the Underlying Government Securities

The illiquidity in the underlying GoI bond market is being reflected in the IRF deliverable basket of securities, which comprise only GoI securities.[14] As the CTD security is invariably an illiquid security, the IRF contracts are based on a theoretical pricing method and not on the actual traded price. This hurts the price discovery of the futures contracts. Further, the limited participation in the market for CTD securities has meant very high bid-offer spread—implying a high impact cost. Because of high impact cost and illiquidity, IRF contracts have not become popular.

Limited Contracts

Currently, there is a lack of depth in the IRF market because only one futures contract (10-year notional coupon bearing GoI security) with two expiries has been introduced for trading. In announcements made on 20 April 2010, the RBI has proposed the introduction of IRFs on five-year and two-year notional coupon bearing securities and 91-day Treasury Bills. This is a step in the right direction; to be effective, however, this initiative has to be complemented by measures to address the inter-related issues of liquidity shortage and settlement mechanism.

Physical Settlement

In India, the IRF contracts currently can only be physically settled, as in the case of developed markets. The structure of Indian GoI securities market is, however, very different from the advanced markets, because of a number of limiting factors such as severe restrictions on short selling, underdeveloped term repo market and a narrow investor base that holds GoI securities.

When the market for the underlying is illiquid, the mandatory physical settlement system deters both potential sellers and buyers from entering the market. Potential sellers recognise that procuring physically

---

14. Out of the 97 GoI securities available for trading only an average of 5 to 6 securities are actively traded and almost 50 per cent of the trading volumes are contributed by a single 10-year benchmark security.

the illiquid CTD security for delivery at settlement is difficult and that delivering a security other than the CTD would reduce their profit or increase their loss; many times, significantly. On the other hand, potential buyers are afraid that they may not be able to dispose of the illiquid security acquired at settlement.

Further, interest rate fluctuations affect each and every individual and organisation, but mandatory physical settlement restricts the use of the product to only those entities that can acquire and dispose of the GoI securities easily, such as banks, primary dealers and insurance companies. This prevents the market from being broad-based.

In view of the above, physical settlement needs to give way to cash settlement. Further, replacing the provision of basket of deliverable securities by a single on-the-run benchmark bond would facilitate efficient price discovery.

The IRF market is still in a nascent stage and may pick up momentum, if some of the insights gained from the operations of the last year are put to effective use. One important lesson from this market is that the design of the product must take into account the special features of the local market.[15] Further, the fear of failure should not deter us from developing new markets, because actual experience can give important clues on how to adapt to local conditions.

Currency Derivatives

Following India's movement from a pegged exchange rate system to a managed-floating exchange rate system in 1993, the external value of the rupee became more dependent on India's international transactions. With the gradual removal of trade barriers, beginning early 90s, India's external trade rose rapidly, raising thereby the foreign exchange obligations of Indian exporters and importers. The liberalised trade regime also forced the pricing of tradeables to be increasingly import-parity based and hence, made profitability of Indian firms more and more dependent on exchange

15. Specifically, the market feedback indicates that the 10-year product is the one to focus on since it provides the benchmark yield for the market.

rate movement. All these meant a large increase of foreign exchange risk in the economy, which underscored the need for mitigating mechanisms and currency derivatives provided the answer.

Let us first see how the currency derivative market benefits the economy. 'In the context of a flexible exchange rate, well-functioning derivatives markets help reduce financial fragility by allowing the corporate and financial sectors to better manage their exchange rate risks, ease financial surveillance, and provide useful price signals about market views on economic and financial conditions.' (Jobst, 2008) In a country like India which has flexible exchange rates and is moving towards fuller capital account convertibility, currency derivative markets are particularly important.

In India, all transactions in currency derivatives—indeed all forex transactions—have traditionally been carried out in the OTC market. In the OTC market, a transaction can be undertaken only if:

- a party has an underlying foreign exchange exposure (with the exception of banks who were authorised dealers); and
- the transaction has a bank at least on one side.

Thus, even if one engages in both export and import, one has to route both those transactions through one or more banks. In other words, all forex transactions have to be routed through a Bank. Further, in the OTC market, banks provide their forex services generally to those counterparties where they are willing to take the credit risk. This severely disadvantages the startups and the small and medium enterprises (SMEs) who either do not obtain the service, because their credit risk is perceived to be too high or secure the service by paying a large premium. Also, given the opacity of the OTC market, it is difficult for the clients to ascertain whether the price they get accurately reflects the quality of their credit risk.

Recognising the need for having an 'exchange-traded product' which allows diverse players to cover their exposure directly with each other in a transparent and efficient manner, the RBI set up a working group to examine the matter in detail. Based on their recommendations, trading in currency futures (USD-INR), under the joint supervision of SEBI and RBI, was permitted. The product was launched by NSE on August 29, 2008, followed by two other exchanges.[16]

Thus, the Indian currency derivative market currently comprises the OTC segment and the exchange-traded currency derivatives segment. The OTC market is restricted to banks and counterparties with underlying exposure, whereas the exchange-traded market is accessible by all resident Indians subject to limits defined by the regulators.

The exchange traded market has some key advantages over the OTC market, namely:

- Futures are traded on stock exchanges, which provide a platform for efficient price discovery, as the market base is much wider and orders of the best buyers are matched with those of the best sellers. This is to the advantage of all firms—big or small.
- All participants regardless of their size and credit quality can access the market at the same price.
- CCIL manages the credit risk through margining and mark-to-market mechanism and therefore brings all market participants on equal footing. This eliminates the handicap that SMEs face in the OTC market.
- This being a standardised product, there is no possibility of mis-selling which is often seen in the structured deals of the OTC market.

To take a closer look at how the market participants have responded to the availability of a new trading format, we analyse the performance of the currency futures market. The analysis shows:

- After its introduction, currency futures have grown significantly. The average daily trading volume of currency futures has risen sharply from USD 0.06 billion in September 2008 to USD 9.62 billion in October 2010 (Figure 14.3).

---

16. Subsequently, the regulators allowed futures in other currency pairs; i.e., EUR-INR, GBP-INR and JPY-INR in January 2010. Liquidity is building at a slow pace in these currency pairs as markets develop comfort in dealing in these currency combinations. The latest product introduced to this segment is USD-INR options, which was launched on October 29, 2010.

- Since September 2009, trading volumes in both the OTC and the exchange-traded segment have risen.
- There has been a strong growth in the open interest in the contract, which is a significant indicator of the depth of the market (Figure 14.4).

Figure 14.3

Average Daily Trading Volumes in Currency Futures in India

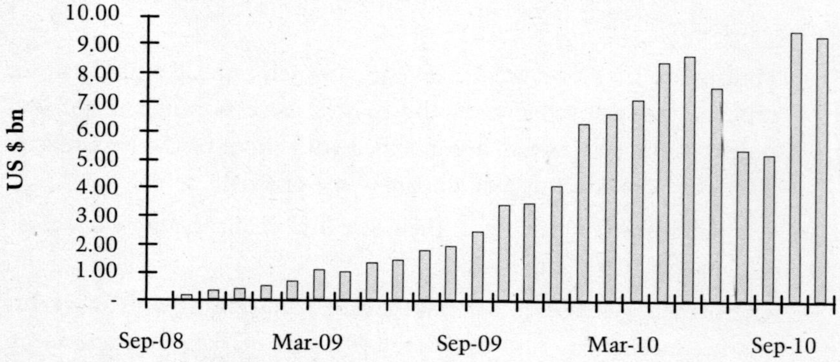

Source: Websites of NSE, SEBI, MCX-SX, USE

Figure 14.4

Open Interest in Currency Futures (In Terms of Trading Volumes)

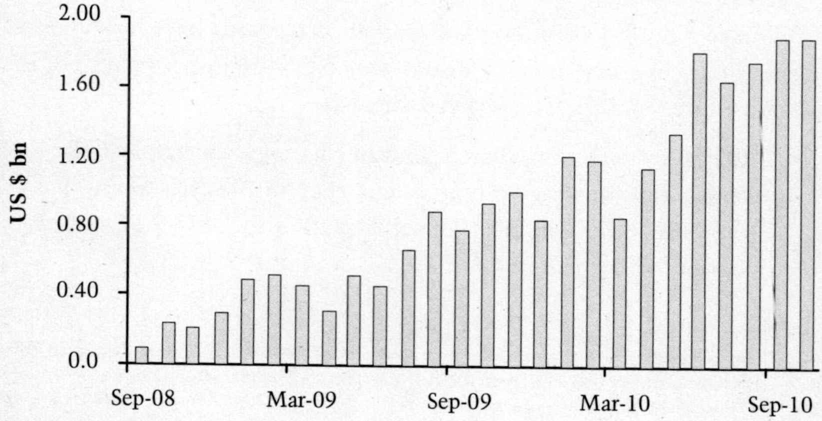

Source: Websites of NSE, MCX-SX, USE.

- However, banks and corporate users are yet to participate in a significant capacity; banks are the key institutions to bring in corporate users into this marketplace.

A review of the market performance shows that in the two years since its introduction, the currency futures has picked up substantial momentum, with a healthy trend of rising open interest. However, there has been no indication of any large-scale transition from the OTC market, although the dominant objective of creating the exchange-traded platform was to transfer the SMEs from OTC to the exchange-traded platform. Further, hedgers' presence in the exchange-traded segment has been limited, indicating that the market has delivered modestly in terms of risk management—at least so far. Stock exchanges have been consistently making efforts to create awareness amongst 'end users', particularly the small and medium corporate entities, about the usefulness of this market and such efforts have begun to yield some results of late.

While there may be some truth in the statement that the market is entering, through a process of natural progression, into a phase that would attract 'end users', there is no doubt that there are deeper issues. Principal among them is the regulation preventing delivery of foreign exchange by exchanges, which has dissuaded the corporates from easily transiting to the exchange platform. Currently, corporates participating in currency futures would have to close their positions and have to approach banks for physical delivery of foreign exchange. This entails hassles for the corporates; besides, there is no guarantee that they would get a competitive price in the spot market. Such problems do not exist in the OTC market, where banks can provide end-to-end solutions.

There is also an issue related to market access. Currently, only Resident Indians have been permitted to access the exchange markets. FIIs and non-resident Indians (NRIs) who have foreign exchange exposure through their investments in India are permitted to access the OTC market, but not the exchange-traded markets. Allowing these participants access to the exchange market will add to liquidity and open interest. This should prove beneficial to all market participants as position limits of players are linked to open interest under Indian regulation. The experience in the equities market has demonstrated that allowing access to a wider spectrum of players contributes to market growth and liquidity.

Role of Securities Market in Financial Inclusion

Of the various components of a strategy to make the growth process more inclusive, financial inclusion is a significant one.[17] The financial inclusion debate typically focuses on the delivery of financial services—including access to savings, investment, loans, insurance, payments and remittance facilities by the formal financial system—at an affordable cost to the vast sections of disadvantaged and low-income groups. This is a narrow definition of financial inclusion and focuses purely on access; the broader definition, on the other hand, includes three other attributes: opportunity (is the market providing income enhancing opportunities), capabilities (do people have the capabilities to avail the opportunities) and security (are there means to ensure protection to the participants). To achieve greater financial inclusion, it is necessary to focus on all the attributes and not just access.

Why is financial inclusion important? 'There are few, if any, instances of an economy transiting from an agrarian system to a post-industrial modern society without broad-based financial inclusion...economic opportunity is strongly intertwined with financial access. Such access is especially powerful for the poor as it provides them opportunities to build savings, make investments and avail credit' (Subbarao, 2010).

Discussion on financial inclusion has been traditionally dominated by the banking sector; for example, the percentage of poor households having credit accounts or savings accounts, number of bank branches per thousand population etc., have been typically shown as measures of financial inclusion. The role of securities market in financial inclusion debate is of relatively recent origin.

At this point, it is important to make a contextual distinction between financial inclusion in the banking sector and the securities market. The key distinction relates to risk. In the case of a bank deposit, for example, returns to savers (interest rates) can and often does remain below inflation rate, implying an erosion of real value of savings over time; but at least the principal is protected, which makes holding a bank deposit a better option

17. The other important ones being education, health care, environmental sustainability and employment opportunities.

than holding idle cash (the default option for the poor households). In the securities market, however, there is no such guarantee. An investment of Rs. 100 can be worth Rs. 70 at some point of time in the future. Can poor people earning, say, Rs. 1,000 a month afford to take such risks? Thus, while bank deposit may be a desirable product for all households, the securities market is a sensible avenue for investment only for people above a certain threshold level of income, who have the appropriate level of risk appetite.

The threshold level can however be reduced, allowing many more people to benefit from the services of the securities market, provided there are ways to mitigate the risks. The report of the Committee on Financial Sector Reforms (or Rajan Committee, 2009) has shown that, '...over the 29 years for which data are available, a passive investment in an equity index generated average nominal returns of 19 per cent per annum.' Yet equity portfolios are held by a very small number of people in India. There are currently some 1.8 crore depository accounts in the country.[18] If one includes the indirect investors, such as those subscribing to mutual funds schemes and unit-linked insurance plans (ULIPs), the total number of participants in the market would of course be higher. Potentially, however, a much larger section of the population, especially the low-income households, can benefit by making equity investment a critical element of their long-term investment plan. Equity is risky; but as we observed, a passive investment in index and over the long run can be rewarding. This has been the experience the world over.

The question then is can the low-income households afford not to dip into their savings for a very long time? The answer is 'no', unless their savings are beyond what is necessary to act as a cushion for unforeseen circumstances. For the low-income households, such surplus savings (that can be invested for a long term) are likely to be small. Will the current transaction costs make investments of such small amounts economically viable? If not, what is the way out? Efforts must continue on one hand to reduce transaction costs and on the other, to experiment with low-cost distribution models through institutions that aggregate the savings of such small magnitude to a level large enough to make intermediaries interested.

18. It is legally permissible for an individual to have more than one account. Hence, the effective number of distinctive shareholders would be fewer than this number.

The Rajan Committee report gives the example of self-help groups (SHGs) of 10 women saving Rs. 20 each and pooling it monthly to invest in a Rs. 200 per month systemic investment plan (SIP). To make this a success, mutual funds have to recognise SHGs as legitimate partners just as banks permitted SHGs to open bank accounts.

As stated earlier, there are four attributes of financial inclusion: opportunities, capabilities, access and security. Let us discuss our experience with each.

The opportunities to protect and enhance income created by the capital market have not been adequately highlighted. The liquid equity derivatives market, for example, has created opportunities for retail investors—through products such as Nifty 50 at NSE—to recoup any losses they make in their stock market investment as a result of market declines, as well as to generate income through a variety of trading strategies. Further, the exchanges are making efforts to build platforms for SMEs to raise capital quickly and at low cost.

In terms of access, NSE's online electronic trading mechanism is available to investors through some 2.1 lakh trading terminals in about 1,600 towns, more than half of which are in Tier II and Tier III towns. More recently, trading is possible through mobile phones, which can facilitate trading for several crores of people. Unlike earlier times, people in remote areas are no longer disadvantaged, given the spread of telecom. The trading system, by allowing all buyers and sellers across the country to come under the same umbrella, facilitates efficient price discovery and allows everyone equal access to this efficient price. This is unlike a loan product whose price is very different depending on whether it is obtained from a bank or a moneylender.

To enhance capabilities of people to exploit the available opportunities, financial education is critical. Financial education can be broadly defined as 'the capacity to have familiarity with and understanding of the financial market products, especially rewards and risks in order to make informed choices' (Chakrabarty, 2010b). Although no hard evidence is available, the state of financial literacy in India is believed to be very low. Efforts led by both public and private sector are under way; but are nowhere close to what is necessary, given the challenge at hand. SEBI, RBI, Ministry of Corporate Affairs (MoCA) and National Institute of Securities Markets (NISM) have played a key role in spreading financial education. Among the securities market players, the NSE has taken the lead through initiatives such as school and college level education programmes, short-duration training programmes, online certification and so on.

Finally, financial inclusion has little meaning, unless adequate attention is paid to 'security' of investors. It is possible to have a strong and healthy market if we have well-informed investors in the markets who would not fall prey to unscrupulous elements. Investor protection is one of the primary objectives of SEBI and exchanges. Toward this end, investors are informed about pitfalls in investment through face-to-face interaction, alerts through media and information on websites. As an added safety measure, the NSE for example sends out daily trade information to 250 randomly selected investors, to make the investors feel reassured that their investments are as per their instructions. Also, through regular market surveillance, exchanges have been monitoring unusual patterns in price, volumes etc., to prevent market misconduct.

What are the important lessons on financial inclusion from the securities markets? The first lesson is that the securities markets characterised by anonymous, screen-based trading on an all-India platform are inclusive by their very nature, as they facilitate people to access an efficient price on a non-discriminatory basis. Technology has played a key role in this process.

Second, intermediaries such as mutual funds and insurance companies have made it possible for a growing population to access the securities market, albeit indirectly. There is a need to strengthen these efforts rather than indiscriminately encourage direct access in the name of financial inclusion.

Third, even though people are increasingly participating through intermediaries such as mutual funds, there are still a very large number of individuals who are currently in a position to take exposure to securities market, but are not doing so. As the familiarity with the market grows and a positive perception about the security of the market gains ground, the growth in the number of individuals having direct or indirect exposure to the securities market will pick up momentum.

Fourth, despite easier access, the scope for financial inclusion in securities market is limited as compared to the banking sector, because the underlying risks and transaction costs deter households below a certain threshold to use these products. The threshold may however be reduced through innovative measures, which are beginning to happen. Innovations are necessary not only in products, but also in technology and distribution strategy.

Fifth, there are four key components of financial inclusion—opportunities, capabilities, access and security—each of which requires attention. In terms of opportunities, access, and security, the Indian securities markets have made impressive progress. In the area of building capabilities through financial literacy however India has a long way to go. To take sound decisions on investment, whether for contingency planning or wealth creation, a minimum level of literacy and understanding is required. Hence, the growth in demand for these products will have to go hand in hand with the growth of basic literacy and financial literacy.

Access for Small and Medium Enterprises

The energy and innovation of SMEs play a vital role in any country's economy and India is no exception. The reforms of 90s in India lifted many constraints that had made it difficult to start and grow new businesses. This resulted in a number of new startups, some of which went on to become large corporates. A rising part of our incremental growth has been coming from a large number of innovative and fast growing small firms and will continue to do so in the foreseeable future. Currently, there are about 2.6 crore enterprises in this sector. The sector accounts for 8 per cent of GDP and 40 per cent of manufactured exports and employs nearly 6 crore people, which is next to only to the agricultural sector. They not only provide employment to a large number of unskilled and semi-skilled people, but also support bigger industries by supplying raw materials, finished parts, components etc. (Chakrabarty, 2010a). This clearly shows that the performance of SMEs is crucial for not only economic growth, but also financial inclusion and any move to reduce their constraints is a move to further both growth and the inclusion agenda.

To grow quickly and remain internationally competitive, these firms need adequate capital at reasonable cost. Traditionally, SMEs have primarily relied on banks for bulk of their financing needs. To ensure flow of adequate bank credit to this sector, advances to this sector are treated as priority sector advances and a number of steps have been taken by the RBI from time to time. Even as the flow of bank credit has risen sharply in recent years, a need has lately been felt to improve their access to the capital markets.

Before discussing what initiatives are being taken to facilitate SMEs' access to equity capital, we will briefly describe the problems they are currently facing. Typically SMEs meet their equity capital requirement from their own resources and resources from their friends and families and to some extent from the venture capitalists (VCs). The VC community in India has grown steadily over the past decade, but VCs generally invest in projects having a threshold limit of at least a few million dollars. Most startups in India need less money than this, but more than what can be raised from their own resources and from friends and families. There are other categories of potential investors, such as 'high net worth' investors, angel investors and specialised funds, none of whom have yet to invest in SMEs on any reasonable scale.[19]

Startups are also constrained in their ability to find investors because there is no community of intermediaries to help them in the search process. The typical licenced merchant banks, like the typical VCs, do not wish to do business with companies that raise less than a few million dollars. This underscores the need to allow more intermediaries such as chartered accountant firms, who have relations with small firms, to play a role here.

Finally, the current platform has not proved to be suitable for SMEs. It may be noted that tremendous growth in trading volumes and number of investors in the equity market in the past two decades cannot obviate the need to create liquidity for small cap stocks. With top 200 stocks at NSE accounting for substantial part of all trading, several hundred small cap stocks obviously account for a small fraction of total trading volume. This has made IPOs by SMEs less attractive to the potential investors. Further, IPOs are expensive for small firms in India—estimates show that IPO costs

---

19. High net worth investors have the ability and desire to invest in SMEs, provided they can be assured of good governance. However, as minority shareholders, they cannot always protect their interest adequately *vis-à-vis* promoters.

are in the range of 8-18 per cent of the total capital being raised for small issues.[20]

Recognising these problems of early stage capital for small firms, SEBI has announced guidelines for Exchanges to create a dedicated platform for SMEs, with the following objectives:

- improve access to capital for startups and companies that need growth capital; and
- create a market where a larger community of investors can invest safely in these companies.

The framework approved by SEBI is given in Box 14.3. The initiative reflects SEBI's desire to explore the possibility of using the exchange system to fill some of the gaps that exist today in funding companies that are not yet ready for the public listed market.

Box 14.3

SEBI Framework for SME Platform

SEBI has approved a framework that consists of the following elements:

- A restricted market, where small retail investors are not encouraged to participate. This is done by setting a lower limit of Rs. 1 lakh on primary and secondary market transactions.
- Lowering entry norms by relaxing eligibility criteria prescribed under the Issue of Capital and Disclosure Regulations (ICDR).
- Higher responsibility on merchant bankers, including an obligation to do market making for three years.
- Lower periodicity of ongoing disclosure and some relaxation in what needs to be disclosed.
- Reduction in minimum number of shareholders to 50 from 1,000 and relaxations in the IPO process in order to reduce costs related to primary issue, and
- Flexibility for exchanges to choose a price discovery process that is different from the current anonymous price time priority system.

20. An analysis of IPOs between November 2006 and October 2009 shows that the cost of issue for issue size less than Rs. 100 crore ranges from 8 to18 per cent of the funds raised.

Recognised stock exchanges have responded positively to this initiative and are in the process of setting up a separate platform. Meanwhile, some concerns have been raised by some market participants. Merchant bankers, for example, who have been entrusted with the responsibility of market making for three years after the IPO, are somewhat wary. To take this responsibility, they may ask for a fee which would raise the (already high) cost for the company raising money. Similarly, merchant bankers and early stage investors are generally not interested in very small issues because of the efforts involved in managing such issues.

Even though the SME platform is work-in-progress at the time of writing this paper, there are still lessons to draw from this. The most important lesson is that even when a market is well developed, it may not serve the needs of some critical segments of the economy and special efforts are necessary to address these needs.

The second point to note is that the problems facing the SMEs in the capital markets in India are universal problems. Funding early stage risk capital has been a challenge for most countries, and there have been very few successes. Exchange platforms such as the Toronto TSX-VX and Korean KOSDAQ are exceptions. Since there is no clear evidence of what incentives, policies and regulations improve the chances of making such a platform work, policymakers will need to resort to significant experimentation and innovation in this area and encourage the market participants to do the same. The implication is that the proposed platform may or may not see early success, but it would be essential to persist with experimentation.

Summary and Conclusion

In the past two decades, significant efforts have gone into strengthening the securities market through the establishment of modern institutions, creation of a robust regulatory framework, diversification of investor base and adoption of advanced technology. This has laid the foundation for a modern and fast growing securities market and has helped the equity market, which pre-existed this modernisation process, to develop into a deep, liquid and vibrant market.

With a modern market microstructure in place, new products have been introduced over the years and attempts have been made to develop markets in these products; the SEBI and the exchanges have played a catalytic role in the market development.

The first such market to develop was the equity derivatives markets. Beginning in 2000, this market over a few years has become one of the top-ranking markets of the world. In the case of currency and interest rate derivatives, there have been attempts more recently to transit from a predominantly OTC based model to exchange traded model; but progress has been slow. In the corporate bond market too, success has been modest.

As the economy becomes more open, modern and diversified, the lopsided nature of the security market's development would constrain its ability to advance the objectives of sustaining high economic growth and achieving inclusion. For example, in the absence of a well-developed corporate bond market, a significant burden of infrastructure is being borne by the banks, which are not well-suited for this purpose because of the asset-liability mismatch. Similarly, unless the transition of the SMEs from the OTC market to the exchange traded market in currency derivatives is facilitated, SMEs, who are critical for inclusive growth, will be severely disadvantaged. It is not just SMEs, but all economic agents—banks, large firms, exporters, importers, household and so on—who are exposed to risks on account of movements in interest rates and exchange rates, need to have access to appropriate instruments and well-functioning markets to manage their risks.

Our own experience with market development provides important clues for developing quickly the hitherto underdeveloped segments of the markets. In addition to the lessons that are specific to each market, which have been discussed in the text, we highlight three key issues that we believe that are cross-cutting in nature and should underpin our future efforts to develop markets.

The first issue relates to the entry of provident and pension funds into the equity market. Pension funds are the largest institutional investors globally. Even in India, pension funds are among the biggest foreign investors. However, domestic provident funds (EPFO for example) have remained shy of the equity markets. The NPS, which allows equity investment, has yet to gain much ground. This deprives subscribers of pension funds from earning long-term returns above inflation on one hand and denies the market the benefits of further diversification of investor base.

Secondly, the role of FIIs in the Indian securities market needs to be expanded. Their role as investors is important in and of itself, but beyond that, they have helped develop the market by improving governance and the talent base of professionals such as analysts, fund managers, advisers, legal professionals and other intermediaries essential to the functioning of the markets. While the speed at and extent to which FIIs would be allowed into new markets would depend on macroeconomic conditions, a key point to note is that they represent diversity not only in terms of their geography but also their strategy and profile. Not surprisingly, we have not seen FIIs acting in unison even during periods of turbulence.

The third issue relates to the transition from the OTC market to the exchange-traded market. While OTC has a legitimate role to play in the market and must continue, an accelerated transition of at least the 'vanilla' products with the OTC market needs to be recognised as a policy objective, given the inherent advantages of the exchange-traded model in terms of risk management (through margining system) and improved disclosure.

Finally, at the policy level, it has to be recognised that while pursuing inclusion, the needs and risk appetite of the households are critical factors. In this context, the choice of appropriate investment route is important. Choosing individual stocks and determining entry and exit timing for each stock in the portfolio may not be the appropriate investment strategy for millions of households, who may have savings but not the requisite risk appetite. We need to strengthen efforts to have more and more investors to participate indirectly through mutual funds, insurance companies and pension funds. While these initiatives may take a number of years to attain a degree of success, efforts are necessary to prevent 'mis-selling' of financial products in the name of 'inclusion'. The lure of quick returns make people vulnerable to mis-selling, especially in a country such as ours where basic literacy and financial literacy are at a relatively low level. The growth in demand for the products that the security market offers will have to go hand in hand with the growth of basic literacy and financial literacy.

References

Armour, J. and Priya Lele (2009). "Law, Finance and Politics: The Case of India", *ECGI Working Paper Series in Law, Working Paper* No. 107/2008 18-20 (2008). Available at *http://ssrn.com/abstract=1116608*

Bhagwati, J. (2010). "Indian Capital Markets, 1991-2008", *India's Economy – Performance and Challenges–Essays in Honour of Montek Singh Ahluwalia*. Oxford University Press.

Bank for International Settlements (2010). *Quarterly Review* (March).

Chakrabarty, K.C. (2010a). "Bank Credit to MSMEs: Present Status and Way Forward", Address: *India Micro Small and Medium Enterprises Report*, RBI. Kochi: ISED, May 21.

———. (2010b). "Inclusive Growth for Creating an Equitable Society", in S. Kochhar (ed.), *India on the Growth Turnpike: Essays in Honour of Vijay Kelkar*. New Delhi: Academic Foundation.

Global Stock Markets Factbook (2010). Standard & Poor's.

Jobst, A. (2008). "Developing the Foreign Exchange Derivatives Market – The Case of India", *India: Selected Issues*, IMF Country Report No. 08/52.

Mathew, S.J. (2007). "Hostile Takeovers in India: New Prospects, Challenges and Regulatory Opportunities", *Columbia Business Law Review* 3.

Patil, R.H. (2005). *Report of High Level Expert Committee on Corporate Bonds and Securitization*. Ministry of Finance, Government of India.

Planning Commission (2008). Eleventh Five Year Plan (2007-2012). Government of India.

Rajan, R. (2009). "A Hundred Small Steps", *Report of the Committee on Financial Sector Reforms*. Planning Commission, Government of India.

Reserve Bank of India (2010). *Handbook of Statistics*.

SEBI *Annual Report* (2009-10) and *Monthly Bulletins*.

Subbarao, D. (2010). "Harnessing Technology to Bank the Unbanked", Remarks at the Banking Technology Excellence Awards 2009 at the IDRBT Hyderabad, RBI.

Thomas, S. and J.R. Varma (2010). "Derivatives Markets", in *Capital Markets in India*. Sage Publication, ISB Hyderabad and Nomura Institute of Capital Market Research.

Varottil, U. (2009). "A Cautionary Tale of The Transplant Effect on Indian Corporate Governance", *National Law School of India Review* 21(1).

Wells, S. and L.S. Zibell (2008). "India's Bond Market-Developments and Challenges Ahead", *WP Series on Regional Economic Integration* No. 22. Asian Development Bank.

World Bank (2006). *Developing India's Corporate Bond Market*.

———. (2010). *World Development Indicators*.

World Federation of Exchanges (2009). Annual Report.

Yartey, C.A. and Komla Adjasi Charles (2007). "Stock Market Development in Sub-Saharan Africa: Critical Issues and Challenges", *IMF Working Paper No.* WP/07/209.

The author is thankful to his colleagues Nirmal Mohanty and Vidhu Shekhar for their contribution to this paper.

15 Evolution of India's Exchange Rate Regime

Ashima Goyal

Introduction

There has been considerable evolution in India's exchange rate regime over the reform years.[1] The shift has been from a nominal fix to one-way nominal movement over the 90s to two-way with low volatility implying a tightly managed exchange rate, to greater volatility and nominal movement after the global crisis.

The paper infers the exchange rate regime and the Government's objectives from changing INR trends and volatility over the reform period, in the context of the fundamental determinants of exchange rates. Concerns to prevent appreciation given a trade deficit, large but volatile inflows, and higher Indian inflation led to reserve accumulation, a tendency for nominal depreciation, and relative constancy of the real exchange rate around the real effective exchange rate (REER) established after the double devaluation in the early 90s. A watershed was the reversal of trend nominal depreciation in 2003. Then the beginnings of two-way movement in the managed float, even while large foreign exchange reserves were accumulated. The latter helped reduce risk perceptions and outflows in the period of the global crisis. Outflows did occur although they were quickly reversed. With less intervention, probably due to a precautionary motive to conserve reserves in a time of great uncertainty, there was much more nominal and real exchange rate volatility.

As the Reserve Bank of India (RBI) Governor during the early reform years, and as a key member of committees that set the reform agenda even

1. This article draws on and updates Goyal (2004, 2010a,b).

before that, Dr. Rangarajan was one of the architects of India's exchange rate policy, as he was of many other aspects of Indian macroeconomic policy. A large part of the international praise for India's calibrated opening and relatively smooth navigation of two major international crises must go to him. The opening of the economy was a period of great learning, for Indian macroeconomists, as key macroeconomic variables began to behave differently. Scattered quotes from Rangarajan and Prasad (2008) illustrate his deep understanding of the new issues:

> With an open economy and large capital inflows, management of the exchange rate becomes an independent concern. The domestic currency can begin to appreciate (because of nominal appreciation) even with domestic price stability, if there are large capital inflows...Studies suggest that exchange rates are more volatile than can be explained by the macroeconomic fundamentals and moreover this excess volatility has in some cases inhibited international trade...Arguments in favour of a nominal appreciation of the currency are two-fold. An appreciation will help in the management of inflation and to that extent reduce the burden on policy makers to increase interest rate or tighten fiscal policy to dampen inflationary pressures. An appreciation could help choke off some of the inflows to the extent it fosters two-way rather than one-way bets in the exchange rate, and hence introduces an element of uncertainty in the market...In general, the appropriate response depends on the assessment of whether the inflows will persist. However, in actual practice, it is difficult to assess whether inflows will persist, since it depends not only on domestic fundamentals but also on global developments. The second policy option is to intervene to resist the exchange rate appreciation...Real exchange rate appreciation through inflation is less desirable than nominal exchange rate appreciation. ...Managed exchange rate system offers an attractive "middle way" between the polar choices of fixed and free floating exchange rates. The element of fixity helps avoid the volatility that might otherwise arise from cyclical and other reversible fluctuations in the current account position. And the safety valve of parity adjustments allows unsustainable disequilibria to be corrected without painful domestic deflation or inflation. Thus, instead of arguing for the exclusive use of any one of the instruments, there must be a judicious mix of all of the three instruments.

This paper tries to make precise that judicious mix, and argues that increasing sophistication of markets and policy makes it possible to achieve more objectives through exchange rate policy, but Indian policy has yet to do so. Theory suggests (Corden, 2002) exchange rate regimes can aid three policy objectives: encouraging exports and contributing to macroeconomic stabilisation; neutralising inflationary commodity shocks; deepening foreign exchange markets and reducing risk-taking. We examine the contribution of the Indian regime to each of these objectives. Depreciation allowed just before oil prices crashed in 2008 compromised the second objective. Similarly, in 2010, depreciation due to outflows after the Greek government debt scare added to already acute inflationary pressures. After the global crisis, since inflows were just sufficient to cover the current account deficit, intervention was minimal. The capital flows that drove the exchange rate aggravated inflation and acting against macrostabilisation. Inadequate commitment to two-way movement, prior to the crisis, induced firms to take large currency exposures based on expected appreciation. Some intervention and market guidance is required to achieve more objectives.

The structure of the paper presents trends in India's exchange rate; discusses the fundamental determinants of exchange rates; analyses the policy stance towards the exchange rate etc. The effect of the exchange rate on inflation and on risk-taking is also taken up. The paper concludes showing implications for exchange rate regimes with current challenges.

Trends

After the excitement of the double depreciation associated with the reforms, the next turning point in the summer of 2003 was the definitive reversal of the long trend of depreciation through the 90s. Figure 15.1 shows the consistent negative signs denoting rupee depreciation, all through the 90s. It also shows a reversal beginning in 2002, the possibility of two-way movement due to mild depreciation within sustained trend appreciation, sharp appreciation in 2007 and an even sharper depreciation in the next crisis year, followed by volatility.

Figure 15.1 gives yearly changes. But reversals can occur within a year while a one-way trend continues. Such reversals were common after 2004. Table 15.1 uses the highest and lowest daily exchange rate within a month to calculate the percentage change between the highest and the lowest exchange rate within a year, and its standard deviation.

Figure 15.1

Depreciation (-) or Appreciation (+) End December Values

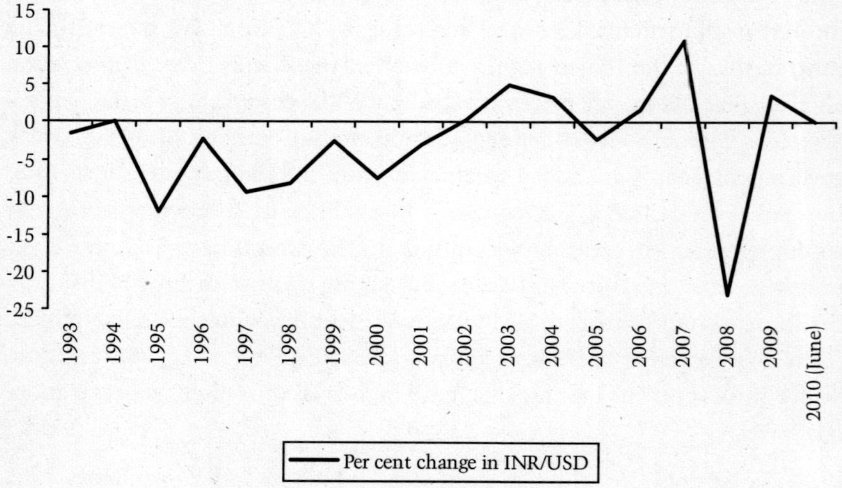

Table 15.1

Yearly Volatility of the Exchange Rate

Years	*Monthly High-Low % Change*	*Standard Deviation*
1993	0.9	0.2
1994	0.2	0.05
1995	12.2	2.7
1996	11.6	2.8
1997	11.3	2.9
1998	11.6	3.2
1999	2.8	0.9
2000	7.8	2.4
2001	4.3	1.4
2002	2.3	0.8
2003	5.3	1.7
2004	6.9	2.1
February-June 2005	1.3	0.4
2005	6.9	2.1
2006	6.6	2.1
February-March 2006	1.3	0.4
2007	12.8	3. 6
2008	26.5	7.4
2009	9.6	3.2
2010 (June)	4.9	1.5
November 2009-April 2010	1.9	0.6

Source: Calculated with data from *www.rbi.org.in*

Table 15.1 suggests that intrinsic volatility in Indian foreign exchange (FX) markets has increased from the very low levels in the fixed exchange rate regime immediately after the 90s reforms. The earlier episodes of volatility had been associated with depreciation; in 2003 for the first time volatility accompanied appreciation. But periods of high volatility tend to be associated with external shocks such as the East Asian crisis (1995-1998), the dot com bust and dollar decline in the new century, and the sub-prime and global economic crisis since 2007.

In between there were large stretches of time with low volatility. The standard deviation of the exchange rate was only 0.4 over many months in 2005 and 2006. It was just 0.6 even during the calm after the peak global crisis, and before the Greek debt crisis again led to a flight to safety on the part of foreign portfolio flows. But movements are due to shifts in foreign capital, and changes in the dollar value, not to discovery of fundamental value in domestic markets. Even so there was steady deepening of domestic FX markets, albeit from very low levels. The average daily turnover in Indian FX markets grew at the fastest rate of growth among world markets from about USD 3 billion in 2001 to USD 34 billion in 2007 (BIS, 2007).

Table 15.2

Comparing Volatilities during Two External Crises

Year	*FPI (USD bn)*	*CMR*	*Change in Reserves (- increase) (USD bn)*	*Rate of Growth (GDP)*
1994-95	3.8	15.32	-4.6	6.4
1995-96	2.8	34.83	2.9	7.3
1998-99	-0.1	10.04	-3.8	6.7
2007-08	29.4	8.33	-92.2	9.0
2008-09	-13.9	10.62	20.1	6.7

Deepening helped the economy absorb much larger movements in capital and in reserves during the global crisis compared to the East Asian crisis with continued positive growth rates (Table 15.2). The interest defense used periodically over 1996-2001 kept growth low. Growth recovered as interest rates fell after that. But a steep rise in policy rates occurred in response to inflation induced by the 2008 international peak in food and oil prices. Industrial output, which had been softening, crashed. A different combination of interest and exchange rate changes could have reduced output loss. In 2010 the interest rate defense was not used—more exchange rate flexibility was accepted. Growth loss was lower, but inflation remained high.

Until 2008 nominal changes kept the REER more or less constant. But the guiding hand behind markets seems to have become weaker in the past two years. Swings in nominal and real exchange rates have exceeded 10 per cent. If earlier the exchange rate was fixed now there seemed to be a reluctance to let reserves fall below levels achieved after peak inflows in 2007. Exchange rate policy was still not optimal.

The exchange rate affects the growing set of people with some foreign transactions. There are others whose sentiments it affects. There is scope for conflict because what benefits the one can harm the other. Each brings a different perspective to bear on what the value of the rupee should be. The exporter gains from a rupee depreciation, at the cost of the importer and the consumer. There are nationalists who want the rupee to be strong irrespective of the economic costs of overvaluation. After the global crisis developed countries are keen to export their way out of recession and want their currencies to appreciate against emerging market currencies. There is talk of currency wars. Are there objective determinants of a currency to settle these debates?

What Determines a Currency Value?

Since the nominal exchange rate is the price of money, fundamental determinants are relative money supplies, prices, output, and interest rates. More broadly they are all factors affecting the demand and supply of foreign exchange now and in the future. But research shows the random walk to outperform all fundamentals based short-term forecasts of a full float. If no systemic factors or past variables affect it, it should not be possible to predict a currency value. But market participants still make short-term forecasts based on news and on spotting trends and patterns.

Over the longer term the real equilibrium rate is determined by macroeconomic fundamentals including relative productivity and real wages. Although in the short-term market perceptions and policy can affect the exchange rate, long-term departures from equilibrium levels cannot be sustained. But uncertainty surrounds this equilibrium level, especially in a rapidly developing country. Major ways in which the FX market is not like any other limit price discovery.

First is the role of the central bank. Market players are not equal. The central bank has more information and ammunition than any other market participant. Therefore its policy with respect to the exchange rate, including intervention and communication, affects outcomes. When the economic environment is changing so there is learning communication which makes monetary policy more effective either by creating news, or by reducing noise. Conventional wisdom in central bank circles has changed from saying as little as possible to the importance and the art of managing market expectations. The empirical literature studying central bank communication has grown rapidly.[2] Since uncertainties are pervasive in emerging markets, communication should have a larger effect there. Uncertainty surrounding equilibrium values means market participants can follow each other in unstoppable one-way movements. If I believe you are going to sell the rupee I will also want to sell it before it depreciates. This is herd behaviour!

In 1997 the *Financial Times* had organised a contest designed by behavioural theorists. Contestants had to choose a whole number between 0 and 100. The winner would be the one whose entry was closest to two-thirds of the average entry. Two-thirds of this range is 20, and reasoning to get two-thirds of this would give 14; but reasoning that others would be thinking like this should lead to successively lower numbers and the rational winning entry should be 1. But the winning choice was 13, implying that the winner had to factor in that people make mistakes in reasoning, and had to have a sense of the errors that they make. In FX markets, in times of trouble, market participants are not thinking about what the correct value of the exchange rate is; but are worrying about guessing correctly what other people think it is. X needs to know not only

---

2. Blinder *et al.* (2008) offer a survey of concepts and tests. Goyal and Arora (2010) show empirically that central bank communication has a large potential in India but was not used optimally.

what Y thinks, and the mistakes he makes, but also what Y is thinking about X's thinking process.

In such situations where fundamentals are not strong, or some shocks have occurred, market participants are nervous and trying to guess what the other is going to do, credible public announcements from the central banks can help to focus expectations. The RBI used these effectively during excess market volatility after the 2004 election results, but in general chooses to say as little as possible about the exchange rate. It underutilises the communication channel. Making public announcements sometimes does not preclude secret interventions in circumstances when those might be more productive.

The central bank has a healthy respect for the market because of the sheer volume of forex transactions, and the size of resources individual transactors command. A central bank's reserves can be wiped out in minutes if it tries to defend a particular value of the exchange rate against market perceptions. So the central bank watches the market and the market watches the central bank in a guessing game. Each wants to know what the other thinks. Communication is safer if it reduces uncertainty and guides markets in the direction of fundamentals when markets tend to deviate.

In India the RBI has the added advantage over the market of the absence of full capital account convertibility. There are quantitative restrictions of various kinds on the FX exposures allowed to different kinds of transactors, which give it additional levers of control. These can be implemented with minimum rise in transaction costs, in an age of information and detailed electronic trails. Focused market-friendly controls are also gaining more acceptability after the global crisis and excessive capital movements that followed. The second advantage is the large stock of reserves it has built up, so that its market interventions command respect.

All this clout implies that the policy stance has a large impact on the Indian exchange rate. So what is the RBI's exchange rate policy?

Policy Stance

There is a gap, which has been closing, between what the RBI says and what it does. After the reforms and devaluation of the early 90s the nominal exchange rate was kept more or less fixed; but the RBI would say it was a market determined rate even as it kept buying FX to keep the Rupee from appreciating as foreign inflows began to flood in. After the volatility in the mid-90s, the story was it was intervening in order to lower volatility in the market while the level of the exchange rate was market determined. Only in 2004 did the Policy Statement declare officially that India had a managed float.

The RBI had largely sterilised domestic liquidity created through reserve accumulation by selling government bonds or raising cash reserve ratio (CRR). Its standard response to periods of exchange rate volatility, following the East Asian crisis, was to raise short-term interest rates. This prevented the smooth lowering of the domestic interest rate structure. Only after February 2001, when the bank rate was steadily brought down from 7.5 per cent, there were no disturbances in the exchange rate, and the nominal interest rates fell smoothly, did the industrial revival occur. Foreign inflows flooded in and reserves rose to more than 200 billion dollars. The monetary sterilisation scheme (MSS) was launched, with a special category of government bonds, to make continued sterilisation possible. As inflows dried up in 2008, unwinding these sterilisation balances helped accommodate increased government spending under the macroeconomic stimulus.

Indian exchange rate management earned high praise for avoiding the fallout from global crises and managing the pressures of gradually opening the economy without major trauma. But macroeconomic policy was not able to prevent volatility in growth and episodes of high inflation. For example, the industrial slowdown of the late 90s continued longer than it should have. Domestic policy prior to the global crash aggravated the contraction in 2010. Could something have been done differently?

If it is possible to avoid using the interest rate to smooth the exchange rate, the interest rate can instead be aligned to the requirements of the domestic macroeconomic cycle. In a trade-off between nominal exchange and interest rate volatility, some positive but controlled exchange rate volatility allows a smoother interest rate.

Table 15.3

Percentage Variation in Average Annual Exchange Rates (Weights Exports to 36 Countries, 1993-94=100, Appreciation +)

Year	*REER*	*NEER*
1994	3.5	-0.3
1995	-1.0	-5.9
1996	-4.9	-5.6
1997	5.2	4.0
1998	-6.1	-1.6
1999	-1.6	0.4
2000	3.4	-0
2001	0.8	-1.5
2002	-2.5	-1.9
2003	1.8	0.1
2004	0.1	0.2
2005	2.2	3.3
2006	-2.9	-3
2007	5.9 (103.2)	6.8
2008	-5.4 (97.7)	-6.6
2009 (P)	-8 (89.9)	-7.4

Note: P: provisional.
Source: *www.rbi.org.in*

The trend movement over the 90s was one-way, as policymakers corrected for India's higher inflation. The successful East Asian and Chinese growth strategy demonstrated that a competitive exchange rate was important for export growth. This ruled out sustained appreciation as a means of absorbing foreign exchange reserves through cheapening and encouraging imports. It is also the correct long-term strategy as long as the trade deficit is large, and low real wages limit real exchange rate appreciation.

The REER gives weights according to major trading partners and corrects for relative inflation. Table 15.3 shows the movements in the REER, while the nominal effective exchange rate (NEER) largely depreciated since our inflation rates were higher than those of our trading partners.

Table 15.3 shows larger fluctuations in both REER and NEER in the past few years. This need not signal a reversal of the export promotion policy. First, the appreciation was not large enough to imply an appreciation over the 1993-94 base year; second it was short term: in 2007-2008 the index reached 103.2, but this was reversed by the steep depreciation over 2008-09, only to be followed by a steep appreciation again as outflows reversed. Even so, in June 2010 the index was only 101.8; third insofar as productivity improvements were taking place in Indian industry and in exports some appreciation could occur without making exports costlier.

Export growth remained impressive in double digits despite rupee fluctuations. Even companies like Infosys and Wipro, whose exports are largely invoiced in the dollar, did well in periods of appreciation. Export growth fell steeply with the credit squeeze after the Lehman crash but recovered towards the latter half of 2009.

But just exchange rate flexibility is not enough. It has to be used effectively. Two-way movement makes it possible to achieve another objective of exchange rate policy: inflation control.

Inflation

An appreciation is an antidote to temporary commodity price shocks coming from food, oil and other intermediate inputs, for which pass through of border prices is high. An appreciation, under high inflation, is in line with the stabilisation stance of raising interest rates, but helps to reduce inflation with a lower rise in interest rates. To the extent nominal exchange rate changes reduce inflation, sharp peaks in interest rates can be avoided. A more flexible exchange rate supports a countercyclical interest rate. An appreciation reduces export demand but reduced intermediate import prices support domestic demand and supply. Also non-price factors are important for exports. So if there is a conflict, the inflation effect of the nominal exchange rate can be given precedence over its demand effect. Thus multiple policy instruments can be aligned to give markets a clear signal on the stance.

After outflows began during the global crisis, the RBI has been intervening less, letting capital flows affect the exchange rate. But the resulting changes in the exchange rate were often opposite to what was required for macro stabilisation. Figure 15.2 shows monthly changes in wholesale price index (WPI), consumer price index (CPI), and the exchange rate. In 2007 an appreciating exchange rate helped keep inflation low although oil and food prices were firming up internationally. An unprecedented 10 per cent appreciation, largely over March-May 2007, helped stabilise inflation, which had risen over 6 per cent in January 2007, to 4.5 per cent by June.

International food prices rose steeply in 2006-07 (12.5 per cent) and 2007-08 (45.28 per cent). Crude oil prices had been rising since 2002, but the rise was particularly sharp over 2007-08—from an average value of $ 67.93 per barrel in 2007 to a peak of $147 on July 11, 2008. Administered prices kept Indian commodity inflation much lower, but given the magnitude of shocks, Indian steel, food and non-administered fuel prices were raised and drove a sharp jump in WPI inflation to 7.3 per cent in March 2008. But outflows began just as cost shocks rose sharply. The exchange rate had been stable at around 40 all this time, but it depreciated to 42 in May. The government raised the prices of four administered fuel categories on June 4. Another sharp jump in the WPI index between May and June followed; annual inflation rates crossed 12 per cent. The depreciation in May contributed to the WPI peak in August. The supply shocks turned out to be temporary, as oil prices crashed in September, so avoiding depreciation could have softened inflation. Instead policy rates were raised sharply to control inflation. Industrial growth collapsed.

Despite the negative WPI due to the slump in world oil prices outflows and depreciation contributed to high CPI inflation. The exchange rate fluctuated, reached its lowest level, falling below 51 in March 2009, and began sustained appreciation after that as inflows revived with Indian growth. The appreciation countered the macroeconomic stimulus, occurring much before export growth recovered, and also before Industry began to show good growth in June 2009. It could not reduce the CPI inflation because of the effect of failed monsoons in raising food prices, which have a large weight in the CPI. CPI finally fell in February 2010, but outflows due to the Greek crisis depreciated the exchange rate and both WPI and CPI rose again.

Figure 15.2

Monthly Change in WPI, CPI, INR/USD

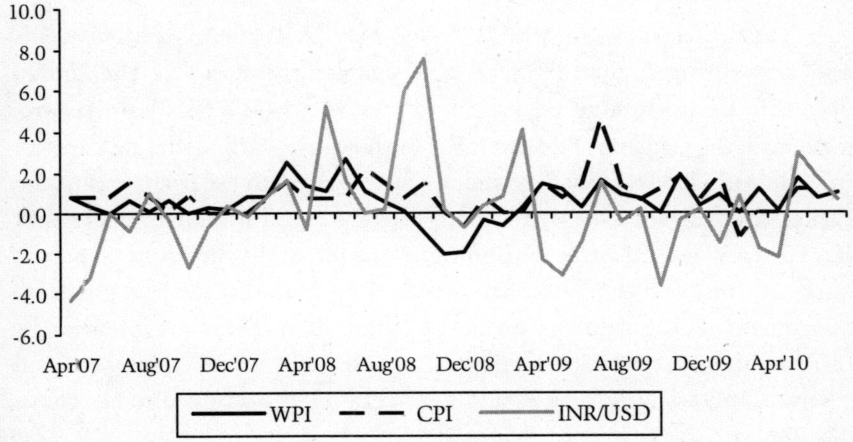

Figure 15.2 shows changes in the exchange rate are larger than in inflation, but depreciation tends to pull up inflation, while it is low in periods of appreciation. Since goods prices are sticky, large variations in the nominal exchange rate will not be passed through. Pass through is higher for commodities. But the contribution of the exchange rate to inflation is broader than just goods or commodity price pass through. Most important political bargaining over wages and prices is aborted. Border prices now affect vital intermediate goods and components of the food basket, the latter affect wages. The price of Washington apples determines that of Indian apples today. Shifting to winter daylight savings time in the US saves thousands of firms from having to change their working hours. Just so changing one exchange rate prevents thousands of nominal price changes that then become sticky and persist, requiring painful prolonged adjustment. If a nominal appreciation prevents inflation from setting in after a temporary supply shock, it prevents the real appreciation inflation results in.

A permanent supply shock, however, requires real adjustments. If real wage demands are higher than productivity inflation will continue, since only real appreciation can deliver higher real wages. But real appreciation reduces export competitiveness. This cannot be ignored when the trade deficit is large. So the only solution is to raise productivity.

The depreciations in May 2008 and May 2010 due to external events and a resulting flight to safety were against the needs of the Indian domestic cycle. It may have been perceived to be difficult to further appreciate the exchange rate given FPI outflows and large dollar demand for oil imports. The commodity shocks were feared to be permanent, and depreciation diagnosed for the rising current account deficit. There may have been a fear also of continuing outflows, and a decision to secure currency reserves for such an eventuality. But the foreign portfolio investment (FPI) outflow of about 14 billion dollars was marginal in the context of the accumulation exceeding USD 200 billion, and was soon reversed. Inflows of foreign direct investment (FDI) continued to be robust. The peak in 2010 exceeded that of 2007.

A flexible exchange rate can moderate the interest rate response. It can reduce inflation. It can also decrease the likelihood of a currency crisis. This is the third major objective two-way movement of the exchange rate can achieve.

Reducing Risk: Hedging

The RBI had been holding the exchange rate fixed and then reacting to market volatility if it occurred. Sustained one-way movement encourages market players to speculate. That is, bet on that movement and enhance it further. After 2003 the RBI allowed homeopathic doses of volatility to develop FX markets, even while continuing to prevent excess volatility.

Excessive inflows, large FX transactions and the tendency for market participants to follow each other tend to make FX markets unstable. Limited two-way movement can contribute to stability by inducing hedging and therefore reducing the number of transactors affected by a change in the nominal exchange rate. Hedging removes the effect of currency movement in any one direction on profits by creating exposure in the opposite direction. For example, to the degree an exporter is also an importer, his loss due to rupee appreciation is reduced. Apart from informal ways of hedging risk it is possible to buy cover using derivatives. Usually either importers or exporters cover their currency exposure; with two-way movement both would have an incentive to do so. During the period of steady depreciation only importers used to buy the FX they needed at a fixed price in the future. After 2003, as the rupee steadily appreciated, only exporters were hedging, for example, by buying rupees forward. Importers also rushed for cover when the rupee started depreciating in May 2004. There were reports that Infosys and Wipro would not be able to gain from the depreciation because of the forward cover they had taken. The point is precisely that with hedging they can stop worrying about the impact of the rupee on their profits, and trying to make money by placing one-way bets on rupee movements. Instead they can concentrate on what they are good at—producing better and more productive software.

Earlier policy sought to limit hedging tools to entities with direct underlying foreign exchange exposures. However, since a larger set of economic agents now had foreign exchange risk there was a shift to 'economic exposure' (the effect of exchange rates on a firm's value), to allow flexibility in managing FX risk. Gradual reforms followed comprehensive blueprints set by various government committees starting in 1995. As elsewhere, FX transactions are mostly over-the-counter (OTC) structured by banks. The most widely used derivative instruments are the forwards and foreign exchange swaps (rupee-dollar). But because of user demand for liquid and transparent exchange-traded hedging products, currency futures were started in 2008 and later extended to multiple currencies. Even so, Indian derivative trading remains a small fraction of that in other emerging markets (EMs) such as Mexico or South Korea. In futures markets intra-day trades dominate, and open interest that denotes hedging activity is low. Liquidity and robustness of volatility is far from that in the US market. Short-term instruments with maturities of less than one year dominate, and activity is concentrated among a few banks.

Even with more derivatives available, incentives from two-way movement are a prerequisite to reduce speculation. Incentives have to be created to hedge. Otherwise derivatives enable speculation by adding leverage. Just the instruments are inadequate; two-way movement gives players the correct incentives. Derivatives alone, together with the motivated advice accompanying them, actually add risk. Complex derivatives lead to poorly understood exposures. In early 2008 many companies found themselves saddled with large losses from derivative positions based on predicted movement in foreign currencies or interest rates that fell through. This was speculative betting on future rates, rather than hedging. Therefore simple instruments should be used, and exposures thoroughly understood. It is also necessary to consult experts, apart from interested parties selling the derivatives.

Moreover, the moderate two-way movement within an implicit 5 per cent band seen over 2004-2006 was not sufficient to overcome strong expectations of medium-term appreciation given India's high growth rate. In 2007, market expectations of the Rupee-USD rate had even reached Rs. 32 per dollar. Many corporates were borrowing from abroad based on such expectations, subjecting themselves to currency risk. The decline to below 50 in 2008 was a reminder of the importance of hedging. About 10 per cent variation in the nominal exchange rate increases the risks to one-way bets. But volatility above that attracts more uninformed traders, and hurts the real sector. In deep mature markets volatility seldom is so high, but in EMs the central bank has to manage volatility. Limited volatility, however, induces hedging and limits the impact of exchange rate on profits.

Exchange Rate Regime

The Indian exchange rate regime has evolved from an extreme fix to a middle position, but is not yet a full float. The academic literature has shifted away from advocating corner regimes of a full float or tight fix for merging markets towards middling regimes. Much market development is required before a full float becomes feasible. An exchange rate regime must mature and follow a well-sequenced transition path.

The crisis demonstrated that capital flows in response to external events created perverse movements in the exchange rate. So a full float with free capital movements need not suit the domestic cycle. If capital flows out during a downturn the exchange rate depreciates increasing export demand and output; as capital flows in during an upturn the exchange rate appreciation will reduce output thus contributing to stabilisation. But capital moves due to external shocks that may be totally unrelated to domestic conditions. Moreover, capital movements can be unrelated to fundamentals, sentiment-driven, and excessive.

Despite considerable development, FX markets continue to be thin. So large foreign capital movements can cause excessive exchange rate fluctuations. If a central bank does not buy/sell a currency that is not freely traded internationally, sharp spikes occur.

Export competitiveness cannot be ignored when the trade deficit is large. Letting the exchange rate be driven entirely by volatile capital flows, is dangerous. Full capital account convertibility and float at the present juncture would be fundamentally unsound.

But the exchange rate's potential to reverse their effects on inflation should be acted upon, since temporary supply shocks occur so often. In general, the exchange rate channel of monetary policy transmission has the shortest lag. Even if several policy instruments are used they can be aligned so the markets get a clear signal on the policy stance. In India convergence of CPI to WPI inflation is slow. Their differing composition implies a very different impact on each of food price and oil shocks. So engineered policy shocks to the exchange rate can aid convergence.

The past few years have given ample evidence of the impact of the interest rate on aggregate demand. The steep rise in policy rates prior to Lehman helped cause the crash in industrial output just as the steep cut post-Lehman led to an unexpectedly fast revival. Since the interest rate is effective so the exchange rate regime must support a countercyclical interest rate.

Some exchange rate flexibility deepens market and encourages hedging, but excessive change hurts the real sector. So there should be limits to exchange rate flexibility. Swings beyond a (±)5 per cent invite excessive entry of uninformed traders. But below that level, speculative one-way bets on the exchange rate rise, since the risk in such bets falls. So a 10 per cent band is the volatility level a managed float should aim at. There are other factors that have to be kept in mind. The Rupee cannot appreciate substantially unless the Renminbi does so, since China is a major trade competitor and partner. The RBI also has to control for the US factor that can influence world macroeconomic variables.

A managed float is the best alternative in current Indian conditions, not a full float.

Conclusion

Thus it can help analyse the consequences of policy choices, and suggest the course of action in the current troubled international waters. Points of RBI intervention during crisis outflows in 2008 slowed the depreciation, but it abstained from the large-scale sale of dollars that could have moderated the depreciation. Such sale was feasible given that outflows were much lower than the huge reserves. It was an opportunity to reduce costs of carrying reserves and to reverse sterilisation. In hindsight sustaining appreciation for the duration of the supply shocks would have been the correct choice since the shocks turned out to be temporary. Two-way movement should apply to reserves also—the latest level should not be seen as a threshold below, which they should not fall. Since the exchange rate channel to reduce inflation was underutilised, excessive reliance was placed on the interest rate channel, which deepened the industrial slowdown. Reducing demand is a costly and inefficient way to respond to external cost shocks.

In the post-crisis exit countries are competing to gain market shares through cheapening their currencies. But a contrarian position is currently in our interest. A country that does not join a currency war will get the cheapest imports. The cost of India's ongoing investment would fall; rising international commodity prices would be offset. The current account deficit is widening, but it is also determined by the excess of investment over savings, and should fall as firms' cash balances and government revenues recover with growth.

The nominal exchange rate has limited influence on the real exchange rate, which matters for exports. High domestic inflation appreciates the real exchange rate despite a nominal depreciation. If a nominal appreciation reduces inflation it may reduce real appreciation, and abort real appreciation if it comes from an external price shock.

A short-term nominal appreciation need not harm exporters. A large percentage of exporters are naturally hedged against an appreciating rupee since they import intermediate goods. Software exporters, who do not have this advantage, actively hedge currency risk in markets.

In the longer run, the real exchange rate must be competitive. India's 36-country real effective exchange rate has not appreciated much compared to its level in the early 90s. But if the rise in average wages exceeds that in productivity, the level of the real exchange rate consistent with low inflation may be more appreciated. Otherwise a nominal depreciation will raise imported and domestic food prices, and lower real wages. Since food is a large share of the domestic consumption basket, nominal wages will rise. This will raise prices and appreciate the real exchange rate. Only accepting the real appreciation or raising productivity could break the price-wage cycle. The issue is important given India's two-year battle with high food prices, rising average wages, and an expected rise in international food prices.

Nominal overshooting will also reduce the pull of the interest differential, which is contributing to a dangerous rise in India's short-term debt. If the exchange rate overshoots, it is expected to depreciate lowering arbitrage flows. Of course, this needs to be complemented by strategic use of controls since higher growth in EMs and continued accommodated in the West will send large inflows into India.

All instruments must be used in the middling through approach, Dr. Rangarajan recommends. Exchange rate policy can accomplish more objectives. This and use of controls, intervention, and communication can free the interest rate for the domestic cycle, even while ensuring the real exchange rate is not over- or undervalued.

References

BIS (Bank of International Settlements) (2007). "Foreign Exchange and Derivatives Market Activity in 2007", *Triennial Central Bank Survey*, December. *http://www.bis.org/publ/rpfxf07t.htm*

Blinder, A.S., M. Ehrmann, M. Fratzscher, J.D. Haan and D.-J. Jansen (2008). "Central Bank Communication and Monetary Policy: A Survey of Theory and Evidence", *Journal of Economic Literature* 46(4): 910-945.

Corden, W.M. (2002). *Too Sensational: On the Choice of Exchange Rate Regimes*. Cambridge MA: MIT Press.

Goyal, A. (2010a). "How to Manage a Rupee Float", *The Hindu Business Line*. September 9.

———. (2010b). "Dynamics of Inflation and Output", *The Hindu Business Line*. November 11.

———. (2004). "Rupee: Changing Trends", *Economic and Political Weekly* 39(23): 2335-2337, June 5.

Goyal, A. and S. Arora (2010). "The Indian Exchange Rate and Central Bank Action: A GARCH Analysis", *IGIDR WP*-2010-009. Available at *http://www.igidr.ac.in/pdf/publication/WP-2010-009.pdf*

Rangarajan, C. and A. Prasad (2008). "Capital Flows, Exchange Rate Management, Monetary Policy", *Macroeconomics and Finance in Emerging Market Economies* 1(1): 135-150.

This is a substantially revised and updated version of a paper published in the *Economic and Political Weekly* in 2004. I thank Sameer Kochhar for the invitation, Shruti Tripathi for research and Reshma Aguiar for secretarial assistance.

16 Indian Economy in the Global Meltdown

Kirit S. Parikh

Dr. Rangarajan has played a very important and critical role in the macro-economic management of the Indian economy. As Deputy Governor of Reserve Bank of India (RBI), Member Planning Commission, Member of Economic Advisory Councils of a number of Prime Ministers and as Chairman of the Economic Advisory Council of Prime Minister Dr. Manmohan Singh he has wielded great influence. The country has been fortunate to have a scholar and distinguished economist like him to help steer its economy. I am therefore delighted to write this for a festschrift that celebrates him. This paper illustrates the use of computable macro-models to analyse a complex issue and is particularly appropriate as Dr. Rangarajan has been a macro-modeller himself.

Till 1991, the Indian economy was largely inward looking, but now the Indian economy has quite integrated with the global economy. This has been quite clear in recent years. The Indian economy could not escape the impact of global meltdown. Our economic performance gets affected by the growth of the world economy. However, the extent of the impact gets determined by the counter measures we take to stimulate the economy. The impacts from the world economy is transmitted through a number of channels, fall in our exports, reduced foreign financial inflows, contagion to our domestic financial system, increased reluctance of banks to lend due to increased risk perception and fall in investment due to lower business confidence due to higher uncertainty. I examine here the projection I had made in March 2009 as to how the Indian economy would function in 2009-10 and compare it with the actual experience.

I first examined in March 2009 how the global and Indian economies had performed during 2008, and then looked at the various projections by international agencies of growth of global and Indian economies for 2009. This was followed by assessment of impact on India and finally examined alternative counter measures to stimulate the economy.

The Global Economy

In November 2008, IMF's *World Economic Outlook* (WEO) projections were as shown in Table 16.1.

Table 16.1

IMF Projections in November, 2008

Overview of the World Economic Outlook Projections (Per cent change, unless otherwise noted)

			Year over Year				*Q4 over Q4*
			March Projections		*Difference from July 2008 Projections*	*WEO*	*Estimates*
	2006	*2007*	*2008*	*2009*	*2008*	*2009*	*2007*
World output*	5.1	5.0	3.7	2.2	-0.2	-0.8	4.8
Advanced economies	3.0	2.6	1.4	-0.3	-0.2	-0.8	2.6
India	9.8	9.3	7.8	6.3	-0.1	-0.6	8.9

Source: IMF (2008). *World Economic Outlook*, October. The quarterly estimates and projections account for 90 per cent of the world purchasing power parity (PPP) weights.

The January 2009 update by IMF of *World Economic Outlook* projected lower growth of world output compared to the November 2008 forecast. While during 2008 the world output grew at 3.2 per cent, in the last quarter (Q4) of 2008 the growth rate over Q4 of 2007, was estimated to be only 1.1 per cent. The latest forecast for 2009 was -0.6 per cent and for 2010 it was 2.3 per cent. (See Table 16.2)

India's growth rate for calendar year 2008 was 7.3 per cent and in Q4 of 2007, it was 5.1 per cent. As the world economic growth rate fell by 1.8 percentage point from 2007 to 2008, India's growth rate fell from 9.3 per cent to 7.3 per cent. However, not all of it may be counted as due to global slowdown. Also the short-term impact of global slowdown may be bigger than the medium-term impact.

Table 16.2

IMF Projection in January, 2009

Overview of the World Economic Outlook Projections
(Per cent change, unless otherwise noted)

	Year over Year						Q4 over Q4
			March Projections		Difference from November 2008 WEO Projections		Estimates
	2007	2008	2009	2010	2009	2010	2008
World output*	5.1	3.2	-0.6	2.3	-2.8	-1.5	0.3
Advanced economies	2.7	0.8	-3.2	0.5	-2.9	-1.1	-1.7
India	9.3	7.3	4.5	6.0	-1.8	-0.8	4.5

Source: IMF (2009). *World Economic Outlook*, October. The quarterly estimates and projections account for 90 per cent of the world PPP weights.

Regarding IMF's projections, it may be mentioned that IMF has a history of projecting lower growth rate for India than has been actually achieved, as can be seen from the Table 16.3 given below:

Table 16.3

IMF Projections and Actual Growth Rate of India

	Growth Rate (Projected vs. Actual)	
Year	*Projected by IMF**	*Actual***
2004-05	6.4	7.5
2005-06	7.6	9.5
2006-07	8.2	9.7
2007-08	8.7	9.2
2008-09	6.3	6.7
2009-10	5.7	7.4

Source: * based on previous IMF Article IV Consultations, IMF.
** CSO's estimates, National Account Statistics, 2010.

It may be mentioned that a working paper from ADB by James *et al.*, 2008 had projected for 2009 a baseline growth rate of 6.23 per cent for India with lower growth of 5.65 per cent to 6.08 per cent under alternative assumptions of slower growth in France, Germany, Italy, Japan, Spain, UK and the USA. The World Bank had indicated that the Indian economy is expected to register a growth rate of 5.8 per cent in 2009 (Global Economic Prospects, 2009). However, projections of UN Department of Economic and Social Affairs (UNDESA) (based in part on Project LINK Model) showed that Indian economy is expected to register a growth rate of 7 per cent in 2009 (World Economic Situation and Prospects, 2009).

All these projections showed that the Indian economy was integrated with the global economy and the global meltdown will indeed affect India in a number of ways.

Exports

India's exports grew in US dollar terms at 25 per cent per year over the three years 2005-06 to 2007-08 and India's GDP grew at 9.6 per cent per year. One might conclude that an exports growth rate of around 21 per cent would facilitate a GDP growth rate of 9 per cent. World output grew at 5 per cent year over 2005, 2006 and 2007. India's exports growth rate fell to 13.6 per cent in 2008-09 from 25 per cent in the previous three years while the world output growth for 2008 was 2.8 per cent. Thus for a fall of 2.2 percentage point in world output growth, our exports fell by 11.4 percentage points. One can conclude that a reduction of one percentage point in the growth rate leads to a fall of 5.2 percentage points in the growth rate of exports.

Table 16.4

Growth Rates of India's Exports, its GDP and of World Output (Per cent)

Period	*Exports in US$*	*India's GDP*	*World Output**
2005-06	23.4	9.5	4.6
2006-07	22.6	9.7	5.2
2007-08	24.0	9.6	5.3
2008-09	13.6	6.8	2.8
2009-10	-3.6	7.4	-0.6

Note: * for calendar year.

Sources: RBI. *RBI Bulletin*, (Table No. 41, 14 January 2009 and Table No. 41, 15 February 2007).

———. (2010). *Handbook of Statistics on Indian Economy*, Table No. 127 and 196. 15 September.

IMF (2010). Data Bank (April).

If the global economic growth rate slows down to -0.6 per cent what would be the impact on India's exports? With a further fall of 0.9 per cent in 2009 compared to 2008 in world output, India's exports can further fall by another five percentage points, giving us an export growth rate of around 7 per cent in US dollars. If we assume that India's exports depend on growth rate of advance economies rather than on the growth rate of the world economy, our export growth rate in 2009 can be only 3 per cent. However, the initial impact can be larger and as exporters adjust, the growth might be higher, yet we take 3 per cent as lower bound.

Of course, growth of exports depends on not only the growth of world GDP but also on India's exchange rate as well as that of its competitors. Thus the 36-country export weighted nominal effective exchange rate (NEER) for April-November 2008 was 91.3 per cent to that of April-November 2007. The six-currency trade-based weight had not changed much over December 2008 and January 2009 compared to November 2008. Thus we can assume that without further devaluation or devaluation in step with our competitors we can maintain our export share.

Thus in March 2009 I had projected that India's export growth rate in constant dollars will be around 3 per cent in 2009-10, compared with around 21 per cent growth rate that would facilitate 9 per cent growth of GDP.

Foreign Inflows

Foreign inflows are also affected by the growth rates of India's economy and that of world output. Foreign investment inflows and direct plus portfolio were $63.76 billion in 2007-08, of which $55.65 billion came during April-December 2007. Compared to that in April-December 2008, only $13.43 billion came. In December 2008, the inflow was $1.392 billion. If we assume same monthly inflow for January to March 2009, the total inflows during 2008-09 would be around $17.5 billion. It should be noted, however, that the fall in inflows is large due to the outflow of portfolio investment. In fact the foreign direct investment during April-December 2008 at $24.69 billion was larger than the April-December 2007 inflow of $22.49 billion. I had argued in March 2009 that we can expect a turnaround in the net outflow of portfolio investment over April-December

2008 of $11.27 billion and an investment inflow of $30 to $40 billion may be expected during 2009-10.

During April-September 2007 private transfers from abroad were $17.46 billion whereas during April-September 2008 they increased to $25.76 billion. This may be an outcome of devaluation of the $/Rupee exchange rate. Since some of the Indian workers abroad are likely to lose their jobs, the inflows can go down. On the other hand as they return to India, they may bring back their accumulated savings and a one time increase may take place. During 2009-10 private transfers can be from $35 to $50 billion.

Thus I had projected that total foreign inflows, investment plus private transfers, can be around $65 to $90 billion compared to $81 billion in 2007-08 implying a fall of 20 per cent or an increase of 10 per cent.

Credit Flows

India's financial sector has not been much affected by the contagion from the global financial sector meltdown. The banks, however, have become cautious in lending as industry profits over the coming years seem more uncertain. Also the corporate sector's exposure to American Depository Receipts (ADRs) and recent acquisitions abroad has also raised uncertainty about the creditworthiness of borrowers. Thus while monetary policy has raised availability of loanable funds and reduced interest rates, credit availability may be a problem.

However, as shown in Table 16.5 outstanding credit of all scheduled banks at the end of 2006-07 was Rs. 20,08,609 crore, which increased to Rs. 24,47,646 crore by the end of 2007-08, an increase of Rs. 4,39,037 crore. The increase in credit from December 2007 to December 2008 was Rs. 5,22,554 crore. Thus credit is increasing and should not constrain investments in 2009-10.

The level of investment depends not only on the availability of credit at reasonable interest rate, but also on business confidence and expected demand growth. The National Council of Applied Economic Research (NCAER) survey showed that business confidence index in January 2009 was 24 per cent lower than in October 2008. Some fall in the growth rate of private investment during 2008-09 has to be expected. However, the Central Statistical Organisation's (CSO) advance estimates of gross fixed capital formation (GFCF), showed an increase of 8.9 per cent in 2008-09 over 2007-08 at constant prices and of 16.8 per cent in current prices. The rate of GFCF increased by 0.6 percentage point to 34.6 per cent in terms of GDP at market prices.

Table 16.5

Outstanding Credit from All Scheduled Banks (Rs. Crore)

Date: Last Friday	*Total*
March, 2007	20,08,609
December, 2007	22,04,618
March, 2008	24,47,646
December, 2008	27,27,172
March 2009	28,59,554
March, 2010	33,37,548

Source: RBI (2010). *Handbook of Statistics on Indian Economy*, Table 174, 15 September. Business Confidence and Investments.

The average growth rate of private investment in real terms was 15 per cent per year during the period 2005-06 to 2006-07. Thus there is a slowdown in growth rate of investment. However, with appropriate stimulus measures, the growth rate of private investment in 2009-10 can be expected to be higher than in 2008-09.

Projected Growth for 2009-10

The various macroeconomic models developed by different researchers in the country (Bhide and Parida, 2009; Kumar and Panda, 2009; Kar and Pradhan, 2009; Narayana and Ghosh, 2009; Sachdeva and Ghosh, 2009) have made certain projections for the economy under varying assumptions of shocks and counter measures, see Parikh (2009). These provide a basis for assessing the impact multiplier of various shocks and policy measures and can help in assessing the impact of various elements of stimulation packages. These multipliers are summarised in Table 16.6.

Table 16.6

Impact Multipliers

Shock or Policy Measures	*% Change*	*Impact on GDP (percentage point)*	
1. Private investment	1% of GDP – decrease	0.17, 0.35	- decrease
2. Public investment	1% of GDP – increase	0.35, 1.2	- increase
3. Monetary stimulus (lower interest rates, PLR etc.)	1% of GDP	0.2	- increase
4. Crude oil price (partial pass through)	US$ 20/barrel fall	0.6	- increase
5. Exports volume	10% fall	1.5	- decrease
6. Foreign inflows (including remittances)	30% decline	1.8*	- decrease
7. Government consumption	1% of GDP – increase	0.5%*, 0.8	- increase
8. Indirect tax cut (25% reduction)	2.4% of GDP	0.8%*	- increase
9. NREGs full coverage	1% of GDP – increase	0.35%*	- increase
10. Public investment in construction financed through inflows or reserve depletion	1% of GDP – increase	2.2%*	- increase

Note: * From a general equilibrium model. Thus the impacts may be overstated as in reality the adjustments to the new equilibrium may not be completed in one year.

The discussions earlier suggest that without any counter measures or stimulus, the following effects from the global scenario will affect the Indian economy. The effects are calculated in Table 16.7 from a reference (GDP) growth rate of 9 per cent.

Table 16.7

Projected Impact on India's Growth Rate in 2009-10

		% Change in Growth Rate of GDP
(a) Growth rate of exports	decrease by 18%	-2.7
(b) Foreign inflows	decrease by 20%	-1.2
(c) Crude price	falls by $20/barrel	+0.6
(d) Private investment	falls by 10 percentage points (3% of GDP)	-1.0

The net impact of these would be a reduction of 4.3 percentage point in the growth rate from 9 per cent.

I had further argued that since the impact multipliers are large and should be considered as outer bounds, the minimum growth rate that can be expected when the world GDP growth falls to -0.6 per cent and without any counter measures by the government should be 4.7 per cent.

Impact of Stimulus

The measures taken by the government by March 2009 had increased liquidity and improved credit flow, stimulated demand through increased government expenditure on various programmes and through cut in tax rates and promoted exports. The stimulus packages including the measures announced in the interim budget can be viewed as increase in public consumption (e.g. purchase of buses) and public investment (e.g. higher allocation for some plan schemes). The impact of these can be taken from lines 2 and 7 in the multiplier table (Table 16.6) as between 0.4 to 1.0. We take the lower figure to be conservative. These impacts can be summarised in Table 16.8.

Table 16.8

Impact of Stimulus Measures

(a) Monetary stimulus	1% of GDP (Rs. 50,000 crore additional liquidity)	0.2%
(b) Indirect tax cut	2.4% of GDP	0.8%
(c) NREGS safety net	Additional expenditure of 0.5% of GDP	0.2%
(d) Stimulus package expenditure	1% of GDP	0.4%

These can raise the growth rate by 1.6 percentage points to 6.3 per cent. If in addition a major effort to further increase public investment in construction can be mounted we can have a higher growth rate. An increase in construction demand by the government financed through foreign inflows or reserve depletion, gives a big boost to GDP as it increases employment. A Rs. 50,000 crore absorption i.e., 1 per cent of GDP, can raise the growth rate by upto 2.2 percentage points. Even if only half of this impact is realised, the growth rate for 2009-10 could be 7.4 per cent.

Fiscal Space

I had also discussed the question of fiscal space. If the deficit is the outcome of investment which will increase outputs in a short period and which does not create a vested interest for continued expenditure year after year, high fiscal deficit should pose no problem. For our economy which loses potential production and efficiency gains due to infrastructure constraints, investment in infrastructure is an obvious and attractive opportunity to stimulate the economy.

What Actually Happened?

The growth rate of world output for 2009 was -0.6 per cent projected by IMF in January 2009.

In dollar terms India's exports in 2009-10 over 2008-09 fell by 3.6 per cent. Thus from the desired growth rate of 21 per cent it fell by 24.6 per cent.

Foreign inflows, portfolio and FDI, in 2009-10 were projected in March 2009 to be $65-$90 billion dollars. The actual inflows in 2009-10, see Table 16.9, were $116 billion which were larger than $114 billion in 2007-08. It is difficult to assess how much foreign inflows are required to give a growth rate of 9 per cent. We take a range of a shortfall of 5 per cent to 10 per cent.

Table 16.9

Foreign Inflows into India (US $ Billion)

Period	*FDI*	*Portfolio*	*Remittances etc.*	*Total*
2007-08	34,729	27,271	41,707	103,707
2008-09	34,991	-13,853	44,566	65,704
2009-10	31,682	21,138	52,055	116,112

Source: RBI (2010). *Handbook of Statistics on Indian Economy*, Table 200; 15 September.

The gross fixed capital formation (GFCF) grew at 15 per cent in 2007-2008 when GDP grew at 9.2 per cent, at 4 per cent in 2008-09 and at 7 per cent in 2009-10. We do not have estimates of private investment for 2009-2010. However the ratio of private to total GFCF has been more or less around 0.75. Assuming this ratio, private GFCF would have grown at 7 per cent in 2009-10. Since private investment would have increased due to the stimulus measures, one can argue that private investment was short by some 10 per cent compared to 15 per cent to 16 per cent needed for 9 per cent growth rate.

The crude price for Indian basket was $83.6 per barrel in 2008-09 and fell to $59.8 per barrel in 2009-10, a fall of $13.8 against $20 that I had anticipated.

Thus corresponding to items in Table 16.8, we see that growth rate of exports fell by 24.6 percentage points, foreign inflows were 12 per cent more, crude price fell by $13.8 per barrel and private investments fell by 10 percentage points.

Following the logic of Tables 16.7 and 16.8, the net impact on the growth rate of GDP should have been around 3.7 percentage point reduction from 9 per cent. This is a bit smaller reduction but comparable to 4.3 per cent assessed in Table 16.8. I had also assessed that with the stimulus package growth rate could be as high as 7.4 per cent. This is what actually happened. This also shows that the multipliers shown in Table 16.6 worked out from simulations of different models gave reasonable results.

What does this tell us about how well is Indian economy integrated with the global economy? We have seen that our growth rate is affected by growth of exports, rate of foreign inflows and crude price. The impact of these factors which is quite substantial in turn depends on the growth rate of world output. Around four percentage point reduction in our growth rate can be ascribed to global slowdown. Domestic policies, however, recovered some of this loss. Thus while we benefit from integration with the world economy, the world economy does fully drive India's economy. Domestic policies have an important role to play.

References

Bhide, Shashank and Purna Chandra Parida (2009). "Impact of External Economic Environment: An Assessment Using a Macroeconomic Model", in Kirit S. Parikh (ed.), *Macro-Modelling for the Eleventh Five Year Plan of India*. New Delhi: Academic Foundation.

Kumar, Ganesh A. and Manoj Panda (2009). "Global Economic Shocks and Indian Policy Response: An Analysis Using a CGE Model", in Kirit S. Parikh (ed.), *Macro-Modelling for the Eleventh Five Year Plan of India*. New Delhi: Academic Foundation.

Kar, Sabyasachi and Basant Kumar Pradhan (2009). "Shocks, Meltdowns, Policy Responses and Feasibility of High Growth in the Indian Economy: A Macroeconometric Approach", in Kirit S. Parikh (ed.), *Macro-Modelling for the Eleventh Five Year Plan of India*. New Delhi: Academic Foundation.

James, William, D. Park, S. Jha, J. Jongwanich, A. Terada-Hagiwara and L. Sumulong (2008). "The US Financial Crisis, Global Financial Turmoil, and Developing Asia: Is the Era of High Growth at an End?", *ADB Economics Working Paper Series* No. 139. December

Narayana, N.S.S. and Probal P. Ghosh (2009). "Macroeconomic Simulations based on VEC Models", in Kirit S. Parikh (ed.), *Macro-Modelling for the Eleventh Five Year Plan of India*. New Delhi: Academic Foundation.

Parikh, Kirit S. (ed.) (2009). *Macro-Modelling for the Eleventh Five Year Plan of India*. Planning Commission. New Delhi: Academic Foundation.

Sachdeva, S. Arvinder and Probal P. Ghosh (2009). "A Macro Consistency planning Model", in Kirit S. Parikh (ed.), *Macro-Modelling for the Eleventh Five Year Plan of India*. New Delhi: Academic Foundation.

Index

E

F